POWER IN THE PARTY

Also by Graeme Gill

PEASANTS AND REVOLUTION IN THE RUSSIAN REVOLUTION

STALINISM

THE COLLAPSE OF THE SINGLE-PARTY SYSTEM: The Disintegration of the Communist Party of the Soviet Union

THE ORIGINS OF THE STALINIST POLITICAL SYSTEM

THE POLITICS OF TRANSITION: Shaping a Post-Soviet Future (*with Stephen White and Darrel Slider*)

THE RULES OF THE COMMUNIST PARTY OF THE SOVIET UNION

TWENTIETH-CENTURY RUSSIA: The Search for Power and Authority

Power in the Party

The Organization of Power and Central–Republican Relations in the CPSU

Graeme Gill
Professor
Department of Government
University of Sydney
Australia

and

Roderic Pitty
Lecturer
Department of Government
University of Sydney
Australia

First published in Great Britain 1997 by
MACMILLAN PRESS LTD
Houndmills, Basingstoke, Hampshire RG21 6XS and London
Companies and representatives throughout the world

A catalogue record for this book is available from the British Library.

ISBN 0-333-66656-9

First published in the United States of America 1997 by
ST. MARTIN'S PRESS, INC.,
Scholarly and Reference Division,
175 Fifth Avenue, New York, N.Y. 10010

ISBN 0-312-16550-1

Library of Congress Cataloging-in-Publication Data
Gill, Graeme J.
Power in the party : the organization of power and central
–republican relations in the CPSU / Graeme Gill and Roderic Pitty.
p.   cm.
Includes bibliographical references and index.
ISBN 0-312-16550-1 (cloth)
1. Kommunisticheskaiā partiiā Sovetskogo Soiūza.   2. Regionalism–
–Soviet Union.   3. Regionalism—Russia (Federation)   4. Federal
government—Soviet Union.   5. Federal government—Russia
(Federation)   6. Soviet Union—Politics and government.   7. Russia
(Federation)—Politics and government—1991–   I. Title.
JN6598.K7G5237   1996
324.247'075—dc20   96-34345
                                                                  CIP

© Graeme Gill and Roderic Pitty 1997

All rights reserved. No reproduction, copy or transmission of this publication may be made without written permission.

No paragraph of this publication may be reproduced, copied or transmitted save with written permission or in accordance with the provisions of the Copyright, Designs and Patents Act 1988, or under the terms of any licence permitting limited copying issued by the Copyright Licensing Agency, 90 Tottenham Court Road, London W1P 9HE.

Any person who does any unauthorised act in relation to this publication may be liable to criminal prosecution and civil claims for damages.

The authors have asserted their rights to be identified as the authors of this work in accordance with the Copyright, Designs and Patents Act 1988.

This book is printed on paper suitable for recycling and made from fully managed and sustained forest sources.

10 9   8   7   6   5   4   3   2   1
06 05 04 03 02 01 00 99 98 97

Printed and bound in Great Britain by Antony Rowe Ltd, Chippenham, Wiltshire

Contents

Preface	vi
Glossary and Abbreviations	viii
1. What Sort of Organisation was the Communist Party?	1
2. Campaigning for Reform	23
3. Variants of Republican Autonomy	45
4. Radicalism During the 1980s	72
5. Why this Pattern?	101
6. The Pattern of Power	149
Conclusion: The Weakness of Infrastructural Power	174
Notes	184
Select Bibliography	211
Index	217

Preface

Work on this book began in the months leading up to the March 1989 election to the Congress of People's Deputies, an event which many saw as presaging the Communist Party's loss of control over Soviet society. It was completed in the week following the election to the State Duma in December 1995, an election which many at this time believe signals the return of the Communist Party to a more prominent place in the Russian political system. One thing which links these two events is what they seem to suggest about the informal structure of power at the heart of the party. The first election seemed to suggest that that structure had been significantly weakened. The second may indicate that, although weaker than it was before 1985, that structure has been sufficiently strong, particularly outside the major cities, to sustain the party through the assaults mounted on it in the wake of the August 1991 coup and the dispersal of the parliament in autumn 1993. During the six and a half years between these elections there were major changes in the personnel, formal organisation and professed ideology of the party in Russia, but the pragmatic core of the *modus operandi* of the party, reliance on personal networks to handle an uncertain environment, remained. This informal structure of power was always of fundamental importance in the Soviet Union, but it has rarely been adequately understood. It is the aim of this book to examine that structure.

This work was generously supported by the Australian Research Council, and without the funds provided by that body, it would not have been completed. Some of the ideas in this book have been tried out on colleagues too numerous to mention, and although those ideas did not always receive a positive response, we appreciate the time and effort people put into discussing them. We have been greatly assisted by librarians in Sydney, Moscow and Washington, and particularly those in the Australian National Library in Canberra, and we offer them our thanks. Finally, the Department of Government and Public Administration at the University of Sydney has housed us both and given us various sorts of support without which this project would have faltered. Finally our most important debt is to our respective families, without whose support and love we could not have continued.

Glossary and Abbreviations

administrirovanie	a preoccupation with administrative details above all else
aktiv	section of the public taking on leadership and/or organisational roles in the conduct of political activity
BCP	Belorussian Communist Party
CC	Central Committee
CPSC	Committee for Party-State Control
CPSU	Communist Party of the Soviet Union
CPT	Communist Party of Tajikistan
CPU	Communist Party of Ukraine
CPUz	Communist Party of Uzbekistan
glasnost'	openness; one of the elements of Gorbachev's reform policies
gorispolkom	executive committee of a city soviet
gorkom	city party committee
ideinost'	strong moral commitment to and belief in the official ideology, Marxism-Leninism
ispolkom	executive committee of a soviet
KCP	Kazakh Communist Party
kolkhoz	collective farm
komsomol	Young Communist League – Soviet youth organisation
KP	*Kazakhstanskaia Pravda*
krai	territory
kraikom	territory party committee
KT	*Kommunist Tajikistana*
nomenklatura	official personnel system; also used to refer to people in privileged or responsible positions
obkom	provincial party committee
oblast	province
oblispolkom	provincial executive committee of the soviet
otdel	department

Glossary and Abbreviations

perestroika	restructuring; one of the elements of Gorbachev's reform policies; sometimes used to refer to his entire policy of reform
podmena	substitutionism; usually party organs taking over the functions of other bodies
pokazuka	a situation in which things are arranged purely for show
PPO	primary party organisation
PU	*Pravda Ukrainy*
PV	*Pravda Vostoka*
raiispolkom	executive committee of a raion soviet
raikom	district party committee
RSFSR	Russian Soviet Federated Socialist Republic
SB	*Sovetskaia Belorussia*
sovkhoz	state farm
sovnarkhoz	regional economic council
vozhd'	leader; similar connotations to the German führer
vozhdism	leader dominance

1 What Sort of Organisation was the Communist Party?

Throughout its life, the study of Soviet affairs has been marked by a curious dualism. On the one hand, students have emphasised the importance of a single political institution, the Communist Party of the Soviet Union (CPSU). It was the all-encompassing nature of this organisation, with its tentacles in every factory, farm, school and residential area in the country, which was the central point of many of the major theoretical frameworks constructed to explain Soviet affairs, including the mono-organisational society and totalitarianism. It was the party and the power it wielded which was believed to set the Soviet system apart from its contemporaries, to make it unique among political systems. The fact that this system was exported following the war reinforced the apparent significance of the communist party-centred system by suggesting that this was not a chance occurrence resulting from Russia's unique historical heritage. It was a system which could operate in other historical and cultural contexts and was not therefore a one-off, chance development. Moreover the erosion of the monopoly of political power by a single organisation has widely been seen as central to the collapse of communism in both the Soviet Union and the countries of Eastern Europe.

On the other hand, the study of Soviet affairs has been marked by a tendency to define the main periods of Soviet development in terms of the identity of the leaders. The main building blocks of such studies have been the so-called Lenin period, the Stalin period, the Khrushchev period, the Brezhnev period and, following the Andropov–Chernenko interregnum, the Gorbachev period. Such an approach has not been universal, with many studies emanating from inside the Soviet Union in particular seeking to play down the personal factor, nor has it been unique to the study of Soviet affairs. However, it has been a prominent approach in Western studies of the Soviet period. Although it is little more than a shorthand means of referring to a series of complex periods of Soviet history, its use to define the most relevant periodisation has been a major factor structuring our understanding of the Soviet experience. This focus upon the role of the leader has also featured prominently in explanations of the Soviet collapse. Whilst Gorbachev's policies have been evaluated in widely different terms throughout both the West and the former Soviet Union, the significance of the changes he introduced is undisputed.

This dualistic approach to Soviet affairs is not surprising. It reflects the fact that both the organisational structure that was the party and the individual leaders at all levels of the political hierarchy played significant continuing roles in the shaping of Soviet politics. One issue that this raises is the relationship between institution and individual, between party and leader. This issue has been a major focus of concern for those interested in Soviet affairs for some time. It has been approached principally in terms of trying to establish the degree to which an individual party leader had escaped the control of party-imposed constraints, interpreted chiefly in terms of collective leadership. The terms in which this usually was discussed were those of elite relations, the ability of an individual leader to build up his support within leading organs and thereby liberate himself from the imperatives of factional competition and opposition. Its focus was thus primarily intra-elite conflict and the implications this had for the personal power of individual leaders.[1]

This sort of *realpolitik* elite approach is a valid mode of political analysis. It emphasises the important role played by individuals and the way in which politics is shaped by individual actions and preferences. It focuses upon the immediate machinations and manoeuvring of political life and, by presenting it in terms of human hopes, aspirations and desires, makes it easily understandable to the ordinary populace. But this sort of focus on personalities can downplay the institutional factors which constitute the context within which political actors play their parts. The relationship between personalities and institutional factors should not be seen only in terms of competition; while in general terms it may be true that the stronger the individual leader, the weaker the institutional constraints, this is not the only sort of relationship between these two factors which is of interest. A crucial dimension of this relationship is the way in which the two sides shape one another. The institutional contours and norms which characterised the party were in part shaped by the experience of personalised power manifested in the activities of successive leaders. Similarly, the forms of personal power were moulded by the institutional contexts within which they were found. It is this relationship between institutional development and personal power which is of interest here. And this can be approached by looking at the nature of organisation in general.

THE NATURE OF ORGANISATION: FROM PRE-MODERN TO MODERN?

One of the most enduring themes of intellectual investigation has been the study of the rise of the modern state. This has not always been conceptualised strictly in these terms; the state-making formulation attained wide currency only with the prominence gained by state theory in the late 1970s and 1980s. But even when earlier writers like Moore and McNeill[2] were discussing questions like the origins of democracy and dictatorship and 'the rise of the West', they were looking at the circumstances of the emergence of the modern state form. Those seeking to analyse the emergence of the modern state rather than simply recount the course of historical development[3] have focused upon a range of different types of factors as indicating the growth of a modern state form. Among these have been the differentiation of state organisation from other types of organised structures in the society, specialisation of function, and the integration of the performance of state functions into a single overall structure. Implicit in such considerations is the development of a specific machinery of government and administration, characterised by routinised procedures and impersonal norms and a move away from a model resting on personalised power. The shift to the modern state is marked by the application of supposedly neutral bureaucratic rules and norms to particular cases rather than those cases being handled on the basis of the personal idiosyncrasies of the functionaries concerned or, ultimately, of the monarch.

The shift to impersonal norms involves a change in the nature of power being exercised. Although he does not discuss it in personal power/impersonal power terms, Michael Mann has identified two different sorts of power:[4]

1. Despotic power: 'the range of actions which the (state) elite is empowered to undertake without routine, institutionalized negotiation with civil society groups'. It is power over civil society.
2. Infrastructural power: 'the capacity of the state actually to penetrate civil society, and to implement logistically political decisions throughout the realm'. It is the power to penetrate and coordinate the activities of civil society.

While in practice it is not always easy to distinguish which of these two types of power may be being exercised in any particular instance, they are in principle clearly distinguishable. Infrastructural power is routinised and institutionalised, exercised through established channels which do not have continually to be re-established in order to carry out desired functions. Despotic power lacks this regularised character, is more dependent upon 'extraordinary' measures, and represents the state's lack of established and accepted instruments for the realisation of its will, at least in the areas in which despotic power is being exercised. Despotic power tends to be episodic and short-term in its use, infrastructural power more regularised and continuing.

At base, this distinction is about capacity and how the state is able to achieve its aims. In cases of despotic power, the state exercises power in order to achieve certain goals without the prior agreement of other major actors in society. State action may thus be seen as arbitrary, even capricious, and may violate any established understandings about the form and nature of the relationship between state and society. In contrast, infrastructural power is characterised by the state seeking to establish stable patterns of interaction and relationship with civil society and its major actors. Through a process of cooperation and coordination, the state extends its capacity to act in a regularised fashion throughout civil society. By enlisting the cooperation of agents in society and institutionalising this into a stable and recurring pattern, the state is able to extend its reach both vertically into society and horizontally across society's various sectors, and thereby strengthen the power it can wield and improve its capacity to achieve its goals. Thus whereas the notion of despotic power assumes the state acts alone and may override objections from within society, infrastructural power assumes that the state collaborates with society (or elements of it) in a consistent pattern and by so doing achieves more than could be achieved using despotic means.[5]

This characterisation explains why Mann argues that there has been a long-term historical tendency for the growth of infrastructural power at the expense of despotic power. As the logistics of control have become more sophisticated, with the growth of national bureaucracies, the development of transport and communications facilities, and increasing levels of national economic integration, state power has become more routinised and exercised through the newly developing bureaucratic hierarchies. The basis of power and authority has thus shifted away from personal factors in the direction of the dominance of bureaucratic norms and procedures. The classic illustration of this is the shift in notions of legitimation from divine right to the procedural norms of democracy. The personalist element has been subordinated to the institutional. This has also meant that state power has become both more all-encompassing and more wide-ranging. With the greater technical facilities at its disposal, the modern state is able to exercise control in areas (both geographical and functional) of which its earlier counterpart could only dream; infrastructural power can be projected across significant distances, despotic power cannot. Furthermore, the modern state's reliance on impersonal norms rather than personal idiosyncrasy has given a greater sense of predictability to its actions.[6]

The expansion of infrastructural power has not meant the elimination of despotic power. Both types of power can, and in most political systems do, coexist. There may be some sectors of life even in the most modern society where the state lacks regularised channels of access but feels it must intervene. This sort of situation often occurs when a crisis which cannot be handled through established procedures confronts the state. But even in non-crisis situations, there may be circumstances where the state lacks the regularised procedures and tools to cope and must therefore resort to methods which are not sanctioned by current practice or cannot be introduced through regular channels. This means that a modern state is characterised not by the presence only of infrastructural power and the complete absence of despotic power, but by a balance between the two in which the normal functioning of the state is overwhelmingly conducted through infrastructural forms. Movement from the pre-modern to the modern state form therefore involves an expansion of infrastructural power and a contraction of despotic power.[7]

The notions of infrastructural and despotic power have been used in discussions of the state and the extension of central control over the territory, people and organisations within the territorially prescribed region over which the state claims sovereignty. But the utility of the infrastructural–despotic distinction need not be restricted to entities defined in territorial terms. The essence of the distinction is the regularisation of power through the development of an effective mechanism through which that power can be projected. In this sense the distinction could also be used to discuss the disposition of power within a single, non-state organisational structure. In applying the distinction to an organisation, the predisposition must be that the primary form of power will become infrastructural; any modern organisation implies some degree of regularity and routinisation. But in no organisation is all activity contained within the bounds prescribed by organisational norms and rules. There are always areas of activity which are only loosely structured by such norms and in which, if the centre is to exercise power, it must have resort to despotic means. On the state analogy, the more dominant infrastructural power is, the more modern the organisation is likely to be considered.

ORGANISATIONAL POWER

If the transition from the pre-modern to the modern state is represented by the shift from the personalised rule of the monarch to the impersonal rule of the bureaucratic state machine, the same transition in an institution is marked by the dominance of organisational norms and principles over personal will. This process is often seen in terms of institutionalisation, but it is important not to confuse infrastructural power with the process of institutionalisation. The two often go together, but they are not the same. Institutionalisation is that process whereby repeated patterns of action become entrenched in lore and thereby accepted as the normal or usual way of doing things; it is the regularisation of behaviour through adherence to binding norms.[8] Patterns of behaviour acquire a sense of normative authority, principles which *should* be obeyed, even if there are no explicit sanctions attached to disobedience. If those principles are part of the means whereby the state penetrates into and cooperates with society, they will contribute to infrastructural power. If they only regulate state functions at the central or national level and do not structure relations between state and society, and state activities are institutionalised only at the centre, they will not contribute to infrastructural power. Infrastructural power is unlikely without institutionalisation, but institutionalisation could occur without infrastructural power.

Institutionalisation can take place on two bases:

1. Personalist basis. Procedures of operating and patterns of action can emerge which serve power that rests on a personalist basis. The most extreme form of this is the personal dictator who is unrestrained by rules or conventions but who has at his disposal organisational weapons to implement his will. These organisations exist at his pleasure and gain legitimacy only through association with him, and although he is able at any time to violate the procedures and routines that are established, the relationship between leader and organisation will in part be structured by those procedures and routines; the highly stylised patterns of the court of the absolute monarchy would be an example of this. A more moderate form of this is the patrimonial system, but here too all notion of authority is personalistic, emanating from the leader.
2. Organisational basis. Procedures of operating and patterns of action emanating from the needs of the organisational structure itself become embedded in the political culture. What is important is the continued functioning of the organisational structure, and the patterns of behaviour which emerge are functional to that end.

In principle, institutionalisation on both bases could produce infrastructural power, but by its nature a personalist system is

Table 1.1. Types of power and institutionalisation

	Organisational institutional'n	Personalist institutional'n
Infrastructural power	high	low
Despotic power	low	high

more likely to be associated with despotic power than with infrastructural power. The relationship could be sketched as in Table 1.1.

However, the longer personalist power survives, the greater the tendency to institutionalisation. As it becomes institutionalised, personalist power comes under increasing pressure to shift onto an organisational basis.[9] As organisations originally designed to serve the personal ruler become consolidated, they generate their own organisational rules and norms designed to facilitate their internal functioning. Tension is thereby created between the imperatives of an organisation responding to the ruler's will and structuring its own activities in an organised fashion. This tension between procedures based on organisational imperatives and those resting on personalist demands may be most clearly seen in the position of the supreme leader, but it is a potent force in the structuring of behaviour throughout the whole organisation.

THE STALINIST PARTY

The personality-based party has been an institution of frequent comment in the scholarly literature.[10] Not so common has been acceptance of the Stalinist system, and within it the Stalinist party, as an example of a patrimonial political system.[11] But this is precisely what the Stalinist system was. At the national, or all-union, level, Stalin was the supreme arbiter, and although his power initially rested in part upon his position as General Secretary and the opportunities that provided, by the late 1930s his power could no longer be defined in institutional terms. The chief basis of authority in the system had become the cult of Stalin, which sought to rest that authority in the personal qualities of the leader. This became the most extreme form of personalised power possible, whereby the authority of all parts of the system was seen to stem from the leader himself. Moreover, the power that Stalin exercised after 1938 was unrestrained by any party conventions, norms or principles. In this sense, he was an untrammelled dictator.

This personal principle operated not only at the national level; it was suffused throughout the party as a whole. At most levels of the system, and particularly within the party, cliques dominated by the local leader were the normal means of structuring power. Referred to in the party literature as 'family groups', these were usually coalitions of local notables (often the heads of the major institutional structures in the region – party, soviet, trade union, security apparatus, factories, collective farms) usually centred around the local party secretary. The main currency of politics was personal influence and contacts, not official position. These family groups were often linked vertically through chains of patrons and clients, culminating in a leader at the national level.[12] The support of such structures was crucial for Stalin's rise to political dominance. But the important factor about both the family groups and their links with higher authorities was that they rested upon a personalist basis; it was the personal connections which were primary, the institutional positions secondary.

The power exercised by the family groups at lower levels was a function in part of the deficiencies of the institutional means whereby the centre sought to control the localities. While the centre was able to intervene at will in the affairs of the party at lower levels, it was unable to exercise continuing close control over what happened in the regions far from Moscow. The poor state of communications and the underdeveloped nature of the party's internal machinery meant that control could only be episodic; regularised mechanisms of control were underdeveloped. In other words, the level of infrastructural power in the party was quite low, with the centre often having to rely on despotic methods to achieve its ends; the despatch of functionaries to local areas, activisation of control and security structures, the mounting of public campaigns, and ultimately use of the purge were all instances of this. It was the episodic nature of central control which created the room for lower-level leaders to enjoy autonomy from central control and which invested the personal links of the patron–client chains with increased potency.

The personalised basis of power in the party was not unchallenged during the Stalin period. At the centre, there was a developing organisational machinery concentrated in the Central Committee (CC) Secretariat designed to administer party affairs on a regularised basis. It sought to generate the links between different levels of the party which would enable the centre to exercise continuing organisational control over all aspects of party activities. There were frequent re-organisations at the centre in an attempt to develop a system which could effectively structure this work. Many of the main organs of the party did continue to meet (although not the CC and congress after 1939), but on an irregular basis. At the lower levels too, there was pressure for party organs to become more regularised in their functioning. Although the power of local secretaries may have been personalised, the mere presence of organised structures of party bodies generated pressures for a higher level of institutionalisation based on organisational norms; simply by meeting and trying to conduct party work in an organised fashion, party organs generated pressures for institutionalisation on an organisational basis.

This tension between personalised and organisational pressures was never resolved during the Stalin period. The continued functioning of the party's organisational structure meant that there was always a source for the generation of pressures for organisational institutionalisation. Short of abolishing the party, Stalin could not eliminate those pressures. But similarly, the party structure could not eliminate the continuing personalist element. In part this was because of the personal dominance of Stalin himself. His position of dominance enabled him to ignore party norms, with the result that they could never generate the sort of normative authority that was essential if they were to restrict personalised power. Furthermore, Stalin was able to use extra-party instruments, chiefly the security apparatus, to discipline the party, keep it off balance, and reinforce his personal power. Thus although there was tension between organisational and personalist pressures, these could not be resolved while the chief repository of personalist power remained unchallenged.

The question is: what happened after Stalin died? With the

main focus of personalised power gone, were the pressures for organisational institutionalisation able to overcome those sustaining personalised power? Or was the latter so firmly embedded in the system and its culture, that it was able to withstand organisationally based pressures? Was infrastructural power able substantially to displace despotic power through the generation of organisationally based mechanisms for governing intra-party affairs?

THE STRENGTHENING OF INFRASTRUCTURAL POWER?

The functioning of an organisational structure will generate pressures for the consolidation of institutionalisation on an organisational basis. The sort of regularity of procedure that is necessary for a complex organisation to function effectively produces its own norms and principles which combine to create a regulative milieu which should limit and constrain the arbitrariness of those operating within its bounds. For the post-Stalin party, the first step was to establish the essential regularity of functioning of party institutions. This was attempted through the continuing public emphasis throughout both the Khrushchev and Brezhnev periods upon the need for party bodies to meet on a regular basis, a requirement that central party bodies substantially met, to fulfil their functions and to carry out the tasks assigned to them. But there was also an attempt to regularise the party's functioning by strengthening the organisational infrastructure. The party's Rules, which constituted the basic law of the party, underwent a series of changes during this period; new versions were introduced in 1961, 1986 and 1990, while amendments were made in 1956, 1966 and 1971.[13] Throughout the post-Stalin period various changes were made in the structure of the party (the most significant were the bifurcation of the party apparatus in 1962 and its reunification two years later) and the formal responsibilities of its constituent parts. The stream of communications from central party organs to those at lower levels was significant, a development greatly aided by the improvement in the Soviet communications network during this period. The expansion of the telephone system, and the spreading of the electronic and printed communications media, greatly facilitated contacts between the centre and lower party levels. In addition, the machinery at the centre of the party's organisation in Moscow seems to have expanded and become better organised in the decades following Stalin's death. All of this seemed to place the party's internal functioning on a more regular and stable basis, and all were designed in part with an eye to strengthening vertical linkages and higher-level supervision through the development of regularised procedures.[14] Thus the general strategy of organisational institutionalisation was aimed at strengthening the centre through the development of infrastructural power.

The regularisation of the party's internal machinery in this way was by itself likely to be insufficient to establish effective infrastructural power in the party. Formal procedures have little meaning unless officials feel bound always to abide by them in their actions. The achievement of this required a change in the culture of party life, a change which would not be easy to bring about given some of the imperatives emanating from the structure of incentives built into the politico-economic environment. Throughout its life prior to the death of Stalin, the Soviet political structure was characterised by an overwhelming emphasis upon the achievement of set goals and tasks. For political functionaries at middle and lower levels of the political structure, their primary task was to satisfy the demands coming from above in the form of plan targets and leadership demands. The system was goal-oriented, or teleological, in its emphasis and mode of legitimation.[15] The achievement of set goals was considered a much higher priority than the following of established procedures; if procedures and norms had to be violated in order to satisfy the demands, that was an acceptable price to pay. This sort of priority ran counter to the attempt to build up infrastructural power by strengthening organisational norms and it encouraged the continued salience of family groups. Lower-level functionaries were in an ambiguous and potentially vulnerable position: usually they could not fulfil their goals without violating organisational norms, but by violating such norms they rendered themselves potentially subject to criticism and attack from above for disobeying party rules. The fostering of family groups was a common method of attempting to meet such ambiguity. The family group was one means of facilitating the achievement of demands from above, because such groups combined people whose personal relations should have enabled them to work cooperatively to achieve a common goal as well as maximising the commonality of interest that each individual had in successful joint performance. Furthermore, if necessary the family group could also offer some prospect of covering up from higher-standing authorities any failures in performance on the part of local officials; the generation of official documents reporting in glowing terms about the region's successes, allied to the closing off of independent avenues of information to the centre, could hamper the centre's ability to see clearly what was really happening in the region. The family group was thus an informal network which could both get the work done and offer some protection to its members.

If infrastructural power was to be consolidated, the power and position of these Stalin-era family groups had to be undermined. In the absence of a willingness to change the incentive structure within the politico-economic milieu, and thereby to place greater rewards upon observance of formal procedures than achievement of plan targets, some other means of changing the behaviour of lower-level officials had to be found. The method adopted was a rhetorical emphasis upon observance of party norms and regulations supported by criticism of poor performance and threats (sometimes carried out) of punishment, but without any change in the incentive structure underlying the patterns of activity characteristic of the Stalin era. This rhetoric of party discipline was accompanied by a steady increase in the number of administrative commanders, particularly during the Brezhnev years, together with a decrease in the reliability of this administrative apparatus. In response to the growing complexity of administration in the post-Stalin era, the stress on official discipline affirmed existing techniques of command while expanding the number of subordinates who could be held responsible for administrative failures. At a time when the bureaucratisation of Soviet society had resulted in 'a gradual withering away of the political centre (or top), which in turn created an uncontrolled, limitless and completely absurd dominion of officials', demands for party discipline constituted symbolic 'rituals of dominion', only spuriously addressing problems of administration.[16] In this situation, raikom leaders retained 'in many cases almost limitless power', while primary party organisations remained 'quite often directly dependent not only on raikoms, but also on [enterprise] administrations'.[17] Despotic power had become entrenched on a personalised basis.

A major means of projecting the need for greater observance of party norms was through emphasis upon party discipline. While this was reflected at the all-union level in the exchange of party cards undertaken between 1972 and 1975, institutionally it was based in the activity of the control apparatus and represented by the expulsion from the party of members deemed to have committed misdemeanours. It was also evident in the continuing criticism of performance on the part of lower-level functionaries by higher-standing officials. While such criticism ebbed and flowed, as discussed in the following chapters, it remained a continuing feature of party life throughout the post-Stalin period. A crucial part was played in this by the party press.

Party newspapers had always played an important part in the history of the party. While the party was an underground revolutionary organisation in tsarist times, the press had been the main channel of communication between the leadership and party workers scattered throughout the Russian Empire. Following the seizure of power, in the absence of an effective communications network reaching all parts of the country, the party press remained a crucial link in the web of intra-party communications. It constituted an important complement to the regular communication between centre and localities conducted through the despatch of internal party documents and instructions by courier, post, telegraph or telephone. The party press did not carry the confidential sort of material that was sent through these channels, but it was the vehicle for instructions from the centre, reports from the localities, outlines of party positions and discussions of particular questions. It was a major vehicle for the discussion of questions related to intra-party life.

Unlike the other vehicles of communication noted above, the party press was a public channel of communication. Whatever was published in its pages could be read by anyone, and this clearly affected both what appeared and the perceived purpose of the press more generally. Material published in the press was meant to have broad and general application. Criticisms like that of, for example, Tbilisi gorkom in 1972 were designed to generate rules about the performance of party organs in general, not to be applied only to the particular organ in question. Reports of deficiencies, criticisms of shortcomings, laudatory words about performance, and discussions of particular difficulties or specific situations were all designed to have broad provenance throughout the party. Reports in the press thus had something of a campaign element about them; they contained the messages and cues which party members at all levels were expected to pick up and act upon. They were thus meant to provide guidance not only for party officials, but for the rank-and-file members as well.

Historically one advantage of the press as a vehicle of communication in the eyes of central leaders was that it was a means of circumventing the control that family groups potentially could exercise over the regions they dominated. One of the keys to family group power had been control over communications. By dominating the main institutions in the region (party, state organs, soviets, trade unions, security apparatus, and productive enterprises), the family group could control most of the main channels of communication into and out of the region, including the local press. This meant that they had a significant level of control over popular access to information, including that emanating from central sources. If the local party first secretary chose to keep secret the contents of central communications sent to him, he was largely able to do so. As a result, central criticism of local affairs made through internal party channels could be kept relatively secret unless central authorities sought to make it public or local family group control slipped such that a local dissident was able to air the issue. If central leaders wished to ensure that the message they sought to convey to lower levels did not remain secret, the best means of achieving this was by publishing it in the party press. By virtue of the wide circulation of central party press organs, and particularly *Pravda*, attempts by family groups to prevent central criticism from becoming public could be circumvented.

The central press was thus a major vehicle through which party campaigns could be launched and conducted. The central authorities could use the press to lay the groundwork for a campaign by giving publicity to a particular sort of deficiency in party life, then announcing a series of measures designed to remedy the identified defects. Party members often would be encouraged to play an active part in combating these defects, while regular reports could appear in the press both chronicling the course of the campaign and highlighting instances of activity that were to be either held up as positive examples or condemned. Local party officials would be expected to play a full and leading part in this process, but so too would party members who did not hold responsible party office. The press could thus be used by the central authorities not only to place pressure upon leading party officials from above, but also to mobilise pressure from below. This sort of strategy was well-established in party life as a means of getting around the control exercised by local family groups.[18]

The press was thus meant in part as a vehicle for projecting central views throughout the party structure. It was the one way the central leadership could be sure of reaching most party members without regional filtering and thereby of getting its message through to the rank-and-file. A crucial element in the centre's approach to the lower levels of the party was the desire to ensure that central policy was carried out, allied to a suspicion that local leaders were often less than wholehearted in their efforts to satisfy central demands. As a result, the press was generally characterised by continuing criticism of lower-level performance. This sort of criticism, which varied in its intensity at different times of Soviet history, was part of the staple fare of media coverage of party affairs. Disappointing performance was publicised, criticised and made an example from which all were meant to learn; good performance was praised and presented as an exemplar. Occasionally criticism became much more vigorous, usually with significant consequences for the continued tenure in office of lower-level leaders. One such period was the early to mid-1930s. Two others are discussed later in this book. But the important point to recognise here is that criticism was not unusual. It was a common, continuing feature, usually tending to take standardised, formulaic patterns and to be relatively unthreatening to lower-level leaders as a corporate group, but sometimes becoming more vigorous and portending a more direct threat to the positions of lower-level leaders.

What Sort of Organisation was the Communist Party? 17

When criticism was expressed in its more standard, less threatening form, it focused on problems of lower-level party functioning that could be attributed to bureaucratic malfunction, personal mistakes, or general slackness rather than to abuses or crimes. The sorts of criticisms which were common in this regard were:

- podmena, or substitutionism, with party organs effectively supplanting economic organs in the making or implementation of decisions;
- poor checking on the implementation of decisions;
- the absence of effective appropriate leadership by higher-standing organs over lower, with the former having little knowledge about the real situation in the latter;
- excessive domination of lower-standing organs by higher ones, allowing the former little autonomy or initiative;
- deficiencies in the conduct of party meetings, such as irregular meetings, domination by the executive, little rank-and-file involvement, ignoring the views from below;
- lack of criticism and self-criticism;
- weakness of the collective principle in leadership, usually reflected in the excessive dominance of one or a few people and the failure regularly to involve the rank-and-file in party matters;
- weakness of intra-party democracy;
- insufficient attention to questions of party entry, usually enabling people to enter the party who should not have been admitted;
- neglecting Leninist norms in cadre policy, with cadres selected and promoted on the basis of considerations other than their professional and businesslike qualities.

This list of charges relates to problems which were essentially seen as being of a housekeeping nature, adjusting and rectifying the regular functioning of the institutional structure. They were problems which could arise in any major institutional structure, and their presence was acknowledged during all periods of the life of the party.

Occasionally there were also a number of more serious charges that occurred in party criticism. These were not matters of institutional housekeeping or of weaknesses in the bureaucratic regime, but reflected personal abuses and sometimes even crimes by party leaders. This sort of criticism included charges relating to:

- familyness, nepotism, rule by a small clique, protectionism, mutual guarantees, toadyism and localism;
- fraud, deception, cover-up, showiness and exaggeration of success;
- the appointment of people on the basis of kinship, friendship, personal acquaintance, personal devotion, or common region of origin;
- abuse of position, corruption;
- suppression of criticism and self-criticism;
- infringement of party and state discipline;
- bribery, waste, embezzlement, the plundering of socialist property, and toleration of all of these.[19]

These were explicit charges about the way in which individual party leaders were abusing their positions of responsibility and trust, often for personal financial gain. Party criticism was most acute and vigorous and most threatening for lower-level leaders when charges of this kind dominated. When the currency of criticism was the regular sort of charges noted in the preceding paragraph, criticism was more standardised and formulaic and constituted less of a threat to lower-level party leaders. The answer to this more moderate criticism was the rectification of procedures; the answer to the more vigorous sorts of criticism noted in this paragraph was removal of the offenders.

The import of the more standardised charges was in part contingent upon the presence or absence of the more vigorous criticisms. When the more standardised charges dominated party criticism, there was much less threat to party leaders than when those relating to abuses constituted the main currency. When the tone of criticism was being set by the more vigorous charges, the relatively benign nature of the standardised charges could take on a different countenance. Deficiencies normally interpreted as resulting from problems with institutional functioning could now be seen as evidence of unsatisfactory behaviour by party leaders, with the result that the charges against individuals were immediately compounded. Thus the crucial factor in determining how serious the criticism being made was for incumbent party leaders was the presence or absence of the more serious type of charges noted above. If they were present, they could transform the nature of the more benign charges and thereby involve them in a major, threatening campaign of intra-party criticism.

THE RESPONSE OF LOCAL LEADERS

The use of the central press as an instrument of the central authorities raises the issue of the role of the local press and, more particularly in the case of this work, of the republican press. Formally and to a significant extent in practice, the press at the local/republican level was under the control of the party authorities at that level; the leading republican newspaper was usually the organ of the republican CC, sometimes in conjunction with the Council of Ministers, and a similar situation applied at oblast, krai and lower levels. Where family group control existed, it therefore extended to the press; even where it did not, the shape of discussion in the press was profoundly affected by the local party first secretary, whose words were a major element structuring discussion at this level. But what appeared in the press was not solely a function of the wishes of the local elite. Newspapers below the all-union level had as one of their major functions reprinting the most important decisions, announcements and discussions appearing in the central press. They were an intrinsic part of the Soviet information network, and as such were seen as important vehicles for conveying central messages. Even when the central press was critical of performance in a particular area, it was normal for the press from that area to reprint those criticisms.

The local/republican press was not purely a vehicle for central criticism of local performance. It could also be an important arena within which local figures responded to such criticism. Local leaders could respond to central messages and cues in a number of ways:

1. ignore the charges in the hope that the centre would not pursue them and they would expire without having any effect;
2. reject the charges as having no application to their par-

ticular area; this was of course far easier to do if the charges were being levelled against a party organisation elsewhere but were nevertheless designed for general application;
3. accept the validity of the charges; the form in which this would be done and the consequences depended in part on local power configurations.

Ultimately, which of these responses local figures made depended upon local circumstances, and in particular the degree to which the local elite was secure and unchallenged in its position and its relationship with the centre. But even if the third type of response was adopted, the language that was used, and thereby the form of the response, was a matter of choice for local figures. In many cases, the terminology and formulations used by the centre were simply picked up and repeated by local speakers, and used for their own ends. On other occasions, the terminology used could differ quite substantially; harsh condemnations from the centre could be toned down to make their implications and impact less severe, or vice versa. This too could be a function of the local power disposition, but it could also reflect the relationship between local and central leaderships.

This means that both the timing and the nature of reports in the press reflect fundamentally political considerations. But the fact that political considerations play such an important part in the form that such reports in the press take does not mean that the content and implications of those reports are purely political artifices. While criticism of graft and corruption superficially presents a very different picture from that projected by criticism of mistakes made by a leadership out of touch with the people, the essence of the type of local power structure implicit in both approaches may be the same. The implication of this is that local power elites are able to act with substantial independence from the structural constraints imposed by the party and its norms. In such a situation, the level of organisational institutionalisation is low and the capacity for the exercise of infrastructural power by the centre is weak.

The pattern of central attempts to strengthen infrastructural power thus comprised a combination of threats to lower-level officials, attempts to strengthen the routine functioning of party organs, and the mounting of comment and criticism through the press. As later analysis will show, this pattern was applied neither vigorously nor consistently, with obvious implications for its success.

THE STRUCTURE OF THE BOOK

The aim of this book is to analyse the course and nature of criticism of party leaderships below the all-union level as it unrolled in the republican press in an attempt to explain the patterns of that criticism and what it tells us about the nature of power in the party. The main focus will be upon five republics: Uzbekistan, Tajikistan, Kazakhstan, Ukraine and Belorussia. These five republics have been chosen to provide a broad cross-section of republics and party organisations. They show the range of local responses to central criticisms, and we believe that the other nine republics (excluding Russia which did not have its own party organisation until 1990) would present merely variations on these themes; a superficial reading of the press in some of these other republics reinforces this view.

The republics chosen represent a variety of social and industrial structures, cultural backgrounds, settlement patterns, party histories and experience of anti-corruption campaigns. During the period studied, Uzbekistan and Tajikistan remained largely rural with a growth in the educated local elites there deriving from central concern to maintain stability rather than from economic causes.[20] A similar growth of the local elite occurred in Kazakhstan during the late 1960s and 1970s after the massive influx of Russians in the early Khrushchev years associated with the policies of agricultural expansion. In the more industrialised republics of Ukraine and Belorussia, the local elites were more firmly established and, particularly in Ukraine, more closely integrated with Russia. At the end of the Brezhnev period, Ukraine accounted for over 11 per cent of the full-time party apparatus membership of the CPSU Central Committee, Kazakhstan for nearly 7 per cent, Uzbekistan and Belorussia for about 3 per cent, and Tajikistan 1 per cent, the same as the other nine republics (excluding Russia).[21] Thus, as well as representing a variety of social and cultural situations, the five republics studied here comprise the four most important non-Russian republics of the USSR plus Tajikistan, the most distant republic from Moscow which provides a Central Asian comparison with Uzbekistan. In Chapters 2, 3 and 4 the experiences of criticism in these republics are simply outlined. Chapter 5 seeks to explain the different patterns in terms of politics at both the all-union and republican levels. Chapter 6 analyses the structure of power at the local level. The Conclusion relates this material back to the argument about institutionalisation and infrastructural power outlined in this chapter.

2 Campaigning for Reform

As Chapter 1 argued, a key element in the party press was criticism of lower-level party leaders and their performance of the functions assigned to them. Throughout most of the Soviet period such criticism was not threatening to party leaders because of its routinised nature. Certainly individuals criticised specifically could experience setbacks to their careers, but as a corporate group party leaders were generally not threatened by this discourse. This could change if the discourse changed, with the criticism being jolted out of its routinised forms and escalated to new levels in a sustained fashion. If maintained over time, this could herald a central campaign against lower-level leaders as a group with potentially serious consequences for them, as in the early to mid-1930s.[1] In the post-Stalin period, such campaigns occurred on two major occasions, under Khrushchev and under Gorbachev, although the latter was actually set in motion by Andropov.

The fact that campaigns occurred under these leaders should not be a surprise. The basic problem the Soviet structure had faced from the outset was ensuring that those at the lower-levels of that structure abided by and implemented the decisions taken at the centre. The party, and the Soviet structure more generally, was an enormous hierarchical machine with its head, the national leadership, meant to be the main source of guidance and initiative for all. This put a premium on the effectiveness of the channels linking the different levels of the structure. Unfortunately for the centre, it could never rely wholly upon those channels; at the best of times information flow could be somewhat uncertain, and it was always vulnerable to interference by leaders at lower levels seeking to filter the information that reached the centre. Under Stalin from the mid-1930s, the centre sought in part to overcome these problems through terror, with the threat of arbitrary force designed to counter lower-level subversion of the communication process. There is no evidence that this strategy worked, but when Stalin died and the threat of terror was removed with the arrest of Beria and reassertion of party control over the security apparatus in 1953, the central leadership found itself wholly reliant upon the existing channels without the back-up of any meaningful mechanisms of persuasion other than rhetoric, the possibility of organisational restructuring, and personnel change. For activist party leaders like Khrushchev and Gorbachev, who were trying to achieve major political change, in their standard format such mechanisms were unlikely to be sufficient. Increased pressure had to be brought to bear on lower-level leaders to increase their responsiveness to the centre. Within this context the pattern of criticism appearing in the republican press is interesting. This chapter will outline the pattern in the Khrushchev period. The following chapters will do the same for the Brezhnev and Gorbachev periods. In Chapter 5 those patterns will be explained.

UZBEKISTAN

In Uzbekistan, the death of Stalin was followed by significant, if short-lived, vigorous criticism of abuses in the conduct of personnel policy. Important here was disclosure of the strength of familyness in party organisations in Uzbekistan, with local party officials criticised for cultivating toadyism and for transferring objectionable people elsewhere; Samarkand obkom was accused of allowing those who had committed crimes to remain in leading posts. There had been cases of people being appointed to positions on the basis of personal devotion, personal acquaintance, friendship, kinship and common region of origin. This produced toadyism, servility and a lack of criticism.[2] Showiness, the embroidering of all reports about work performed by the 'flush of success',[3] was a common result. Criticism of this sort of situation was accompanied by complaints about the lack of adequate oversight or supervision of lower-standing party bodies by those at higher levels. There were charges of inadequate guidance from above, of leadership by telephone, and a lack of knowledge about the real situation on the ground.[4] Most obkoms in Uzbekistan were said to be isolated from raikoms, giving only telephone leadership without monitoring the implementation of party decisions.[5] This reflected a lack of organisational direction from the republican party apparatus: only 42 out of 301 decisions received by one obkom in 1954 concerned party work.[6] Linked with this was also criticism about the way in which in some party organisations months passed without official party meetings being called and, when one was convened, many communists did not take part. Proceedings were dominated by the leadership, decisions were taken perfunctorily, and there was no criticism from below of the performance of leading figures.[7] Personal rather than collegial decision-making and a failure to report back to the rank-and-file was characteristic of some party organisations.[8]

Over the following five years, the Uzbek press continued to criticise deficiencies in lower-level leadership, but this rarely referred to familyness or groupism as a source of these problems.[9] There were complaints about the lack of criticism from below, even in one instance the 'suppression of criticism',[10] of unsatisfactory leadership from above and of the poor organisation of meetings. Excessive concern with administrative details rather than the giving of specific policy assistance was also a common concern. The problem of poor personnel selection continued, and is reflected in the repeated calls by the Communist Party of Uzbekistan (CPUz) first secretary Mukhitdinov for increased party discipline and the personal responsibility of officials. However, before his promotion to the central leadership at the end of 1957 it was claimed that local intrigues and groupism had been overcome.[11]

Concern about inadequate party supervision of production continued from 1959, but was now reinforced by increasing attention to failures in personnel work and by a much harsher tone in the discussion of those deficiencies. In Uzbekistan S.K. Kamalov lasted only 14 months as first secretary, before being replaced in March 1959 by Rashidov, who identified himself with Khrushchev's proposals for the speedy mechanisation of agriculture.[12] A major criticism campaign was now launched in the republic. The first and second secretaries of Tashkent obkom were soon sacked, and Rashidov expressed strong criticism of localism and fraud in speeches in July and September 1959.[13] Throughout 1960 and 1961 this sort of criticism reached new heights. Local party officials were accused of engaging in localism, nepotism and deception. Some responded to criticism only in words rather than deeds, some suppressed criticism, and some were involved in 'crude infringements of socialist legality'. Familyness, nepotism, groupism and careerism were all identified as occurring in some party organisations, while an absence of effective leadership by higher-standing organs was also criticised. There was declared to be a clear need for stricter observance of party and state discipline.[14] Serious personnel mistakes were reported in February 1961 in Fergana, Tashkent, Bukhara and Surkhandar'ia obkoms, with obkom officials criticised for tolerating deception and eyewash. In some areas there was a tolerant attitude to abuses and there was deception of higher-standing organs by lower bodies.[15] A report in early March 1961 noted the importance of political education and said that deception of party and state, eyewash, localism and false reporting are usually associated with unimaginative people, secluded in a narrow circle of egoistic interests, careerists, philistines and narrow-minded people.[16] Similar problems were reported in Karakalpak obkom, Chirchik gorkom and Tashkent oblast: the appointment of toadies, the covering up of poor performance, the selection of cadres on the basis of familyness, kinship, personal devotion or common region of origin, servility, mutual cover-ups, and the plundering of public property were noted.[17] At the XVI CPUz Congress in September 1961 Rashidov said that deception was widespread, and he criticised the reliance on a narrow circle of people, the movement of cadres from place to place, reliance on people who lacked political or professional qualities, deception and false reporting, abuses and infringements of leadership collectivity. Yet he also claimed party leadership had improved, with more regular reports to the Bureau and Secretariat from leading party and other organs.[18]

Personnel mistakes received somewhat less attention during 1962, and generally the discussion of them was less vigorous than it had been in the two preceding years. Nevertheless, criticism of failures in Tashkent and Bukhara obkoms did refer to low levels of demandingness which enabled abuses by economic leaders, deception and the covering up of poor performance, while localism and deception were said to result from a lack of criticism.[19] At the December plenum Rashidov reiterated the message from the November CC CPSU plenum that improvement in party, state and public control was an important weapon in the struggle against abuses, deception, false reporting, localism, bribery, waste and the misappropriation of state wealth.[20] In February 1963 there was further criticism[21] of infringements of intra-party democracy, a friendly approach to the selection of cadres and the suppression of criticism and self-criticism. This was the soil in a number of areas where administrirovanie, toadyism and the mutual cover-up of mistakes flourished. General personnel problems were highlighted again in mid-1963 by CC CPUz second secretary Karlov. He reiterated the need for party organs to be more involved in the leadership of production, while affirming the need for recent sackings and complaining that Samarkand obkom was still tolerating deception and fraud.[22] Yet at the same time Rashidov claimed some success had been achieved in personnel work through sacking windbags, eyewashers, careerists and those involved in local cliques.[23] Such failings were still criticised in June 1964, but with less intensity.[24] Clearly Uzbekistan was characterised by a major campaign of criticism with strongly worded charges of abuse of office in the republican press between 1959 and 1962–63, with a considerable slackening off of this during 1963–64.

TAJIKISTAN

In Tajikistan the initial post-Stalin period, as in Uzbekistan, saw some criticism of aspects of intra-party life. The standard of leadership from above was unsatisfactory; the CC otdel for party organs used telephone calls instead of direct work supervising lower organs.[25] Also poor was the state of leadership collectivism and criticism and self-criticism.[26] Many party committees were accused of conducting meetings irregularly, ignoring the views and criticisms from below, trying to suppress criticism, thereby denying collectivity in leadership, while in some areas cadre work was said to be characterised by the appointment and promotion of people on the basis of common region of origin and friendship.[27] Poor leadership, including leadership by telephone, the absence of concrete party guidance, the isolation of leading organs from those below them and problems with the conduct of party meetings continued to be criticised in the mid-1950s,[28] but usually not with reference to the sort of abuses that were to become evident in the early 1960s.

Instructors had been introduced into the party to increase

local party control over production, but they were barely involved in production in late 1958, despite an editorial early that year criticising raikom secretaries for not ensuring that instructors focused on the most important matters of party organisation on the ground.[29] The republican first secretary Ul'dzhabaev painted a largely favourable picture of the restructuring of raikoms at the XII Communist Party of Tajikistan (CPT) Congress in January 1959, but six months later he acknowledged the existence of fraud, nepotism and other abuses including expulsion of critics from the party.[30] In the latter case he complained about individual leaders who forgot about their duty, abused the faith of the party and people, put their personal interests above those of the state, crudely infringed party and state discipline and sought personal profit and enrichment through bribery and the siphoning off of resources. He said that there were cases of the selection of cadres on the basis of common region of origin and personal devotion which led to corruption and a lack of demandingness. There had been a liberal attitude to abuse of position and neglect of party duty and he called for criticism and self-criticism in order to combat complacency, parasitism, deception and the suppression of criticism.

Such lack of party discipline was also highlighted in August 1959, when the putting of personal interest above state interests was again criticised, as was eyewash, false reporting, deception and localism; party organs were particularly enjoined to struggle against localism.[31] This sort of language was then downplayed, with Ul'dzhabaev's address to the CC CPSU plenum in January 1961 claiming improved party work had led to economic successes.[32] Following Khrushchev's criticism of deception at this plenum, some raikom leaders in Kirovabad and Leninskii districts were sacked for this failing, while some party leaders were also accused of discussing issues only within a narrow circle of people.[33] This was followed in April by the sacking of Ul'dzhabaev and the Council of Ministers head Dodkhudoev, who were accused of directly deceiving the party and state about production in agriculture, especially of cotton, claiming plan fulfilment in 17 regions in 1960 when the real figure was four. The existence of personnel mistakes, including the promotion of rogues, rascals and plunderers of state property on the basis of their place of birth or kinship with or personal devotion to superiors, which gave birth to familyness and mutual guarantees, was noted. This was the main reason given for the superficial and unqualified nature of raikom economic leadership. It was claimed that workers who had compromised themselves had been put into responsible positions, with their personal devotion to Ul'dzhabaev protecting them and allowing them to move from one leading post to another. All speakers at this plenum attacked the criminal role of Ul'dzhabaev and Dodkhudoev.[34] The new CC CPT first secretary Rasulov, who had been dropped in August 1960 as a secretary and Bureau member, continued criticism of personnel mistakes during 1961 while consolidating his position by replacing the leaders of Leninabad obkom and Stalinabad gorkom before the XIV CPT Congress in September.[35] At that congress there was further criticism[36] of the lack of responsibility shown by some leaders, of the abuses, eyewash, deception and fraudulent reporting, and of the selection of cadres on the basis of common region of origin, kinship and personal devotion. Showiness, paper-creation, toadyism and servility were also criticised.

In 1962 the tone of criticism was moderated, and personnel mistakes were highlighted only occasionally, as in July 1963 when the first secretary of Gorno-Badakhshan obkom, Dzhavov, was sacked for nepotism and fraud.[37] Old methods of party leadership were still used in Dushanbe (Stalinabad) gorkom despite the personnel changes two years before, but Rasulov did not seem very concerned by this at the XV CPT Congress in late 1963.[38] Throughout the 1962–64 period, there was little attention given to deficiencies in party functioning or personnel work. Thus, as in Uzbekistan, the tone of criticism in Tajikistan was most severe in the period 1959–61, especially following the 1961 sacking of the republican party and state leaders for criminal deception of the centre.

KAZAKHSTAN

The initial post-Stalin criticism of leadership was more severe than it was to become later in the 1950s in Kazakhstan, but at a lower level than in Uzbekistan. There was initial criticism of higher organs being isolated from those they were meant to be leading, of irregular and poorly conducted party meetings, and of failed officials either being retained or given another responsible position.[39] The Kazakh first secretary Shaiakhmetov, replaced by Ponomarenko in early 1954 because of his opposition to the Virgin Lands Scheme, was accused in *Pravda* and the local press of having broken 'the principle of collective leadership' by selecting officials on the basis of their family, friendship and place of origin.[40] He was demoted to first secretary of South Kazakhstan obkom, then sacked from that post with his deputy Tarasenko in June 1955, after two Alma Ata obkom bosses had been sacked along with the first secretaries of Semipalatinsk obkom and Alma Ata gorkom.[41] Shaiakhmetov had 'essentially disorganised the work of the obkom Bureau and Secretariat'. He attended only 17 out of the 41 Bureau sessions and five out of the 16 Secretariat sessions held in 1954.[42]

Poor leadership from above remained a concern during 1954–55. Obkoms were not involved in the restructuring of raikoms, made decisions without knowing the local situation, sent raikoms too many paper directives, and left positions vacant for months before promoting officials who had failed in their previous work.[43] An editorial at the end of 1955 observed that a number of obkoms, especially Alma Ata, lacked specific knowledge of the agricultural situation and showed 'a desire to hide faults and create the appearance of well-being'.[44] Such weak leadership continued throughout 1956.[45] Furthermore, one obkom secretary was charged with promoting untrained and unsuccessful officials because of friendship or family connections.[46] A number of obkoms were accused of showing 'a desire to hide faults and create the appearance of well-being'[47] while exercising only 'general' or 'paper' leadership; in Pavlodar a first secretary was sacked for 'gross infringements of collegiality', protectionism, and failure to convene sessions and to consult.[48] But these were exceptions to the general press treatment throughout the rest of the 1950s, most of which either did not discuss party personnel work or treated it in a mild fashion.

Throughout 1959 personnel matters constituted the main theme of political meetings, but this was mostly discussed in mild terms. In January 1959 Beliaev said that it was 'necessary to get rid of useless officials incapable of coping with the given tasks and to promote reliable, literate, cultured leaders who are able to organise things well'. Having singled out South Kazakhstan, Kustanai and North Kazakhstan obkoms for specific criticism, he reported to the IX Kazakh Communist Party (KCP) Congress later that same month that obkoms were poorly aware of the quality of their personnel, retaining officials who 'already for a long time have been unsuited to leading posts'. While the leaders of Kzyl-Orda obkom were sacked in August for ignoring maize production, South Kazakhstan obkom leader Yusupov was promoted to become CC KCP secretary and Bureau member in October. After Beliaev admitted the failure of raikom restructuring at the CC CPSU plenum in December 1959, he was replaced at the following CC KCP plenum in January 1960 by the Council of Ministers chairman Kunaev, with Brezhnev in attendance.[49]

The tone of criticism became much more vigorous in 1960, although different emphases were evident under Kunaev and Yusupov, the successive party leaders during the early 1960s. In February a raikom secretary complained about how obkom leaders gave little practical assistance, became confused when away from a telephone and indulged in paper-chasing.[50] In his report to the X KCP Congress in March 1960 Kunaev expressed concern about the excessive turnover of officials in some provinces, noting that Zhurin, now boss of North Kazakhstan obkom, was criticised at the December CC CPSU plenum (together with Kokchetav and Kustanai obkoms) for conducting 'mass replacement and unjustified transfers of officials from one place to another'. He criticised personnel policy in some areas where fabrication, fraud, parochialism and substitutionism had not been controlled and where effective criticism had not occurred. Kunaev said 548 party officials on the CC KCP nomenklatura had been sacked since the previous congress 14 months before. While observing that 'the harmful practice has taken root of officials who have committed faults and mistakes not being told openly about this', he warned against sacking poor officials hastily because experienced replacements were scarce.[51] Ironically, this warning was confirmed by the eventual result of Kunaev's sacking of the Semipalatinsk obkom first secretary M.A. Suzhikov (who had been a CC KCP secretary until June 1954) in September 1960. Suzhikov, who was accused of 'bossing and roughness' as well as swamping lower party organs with a 'paper wave', was replaced by S.D. Daulenov, who was soon promoted to be Council of Ministers chairman but sacked in disgrace in late 1962 for drunkenly abusing local officials. This 'clear mistake' in promoting Daulenov was acknowledged by Kunaev as the fault which caused his own replacement by Yusupov in December 1962.[52]

During 1961 there was strong criticism of officials who, as Kunaev put it in February, 'take the criminal path of defrauding the party and state in an organised way'; the following month a speaker at a conference in the Virgin Lands referred to 'leaders who strive to create the appearance of well-being and take the criminal path of defrauding the state'.[53] But Khrushchev's advice about 'the need to replace weak leaders with experienced and stronger ones', in order to eliminate the problem of the excessive turnover of local officials such as sovkhoz directors, was not effective, despite his visits to Kazakhstan in March and June.[54] There were still references at this time to falsification and fraud in economic production and to the party organisations' failure to combat this.[55] At the XI KCP Congress in September 1961 Yusupov argued that the only way to stop the excessive turnover of local officials was to replace some of their superiors. Discussing the new CPSU Rules, he said: 'In a whole number of party organisations leading party officials have been allowed to stay in one and the same job for far too long. Particular leaders, viewing themselves as irreplacable, consider that anything goes for them, so they create foul conditions of nepotism, lack of principle and jobs for the boys, and in some cases engage in non-party conduct.' He complained that it was still the case that 'unreliable and incapable people are often promoted to responsible posts'. He warned that the new provisions of the Rules regarding the continual renewal of the composition of leading organs provided the necessary means for ensuring the correct combination of old and new cadres, and for excluding 'the possibility of an excessive concentration of power in the hands of particular officials and prevent them from escaping from the collective's control'.[56] Kunaev responded by acknowledging personnel stagnation as a general problem in his speech to the congress: 'People who have failed at one place are transferred to another no less important place, then to a second and a third and so on. In short, a narrow circle of "nomenklatura officials" operates, without noting that they have become tired of life, have lost creative spirit, and that new, fresh forces have arisen who are capable of keeping in step with the great tasks of our time.' He then pointed out that 33 gorkom and raikom secretaries had been sacked already during 1961, implying that there was no need for a radical change to personnel policy. Significantly, the congress resolutions ignored Yusupov's call for replacing old leaders in a number of party organisations. Other speakers ignored the issue of the excessive concentration of power, and Kunaev's closing speech was a routine call for greater responsibility.[57]

Throughout 1962 there was little discussion of personnel problems until the IV CC KCP plenum in December 1962 which replaced Kunaev by Yusupov. The resolutions of this meeting affirmed the seriousness of personnel mistakes, stating that:

> In the republican party organisation there are cases of gross infringements of Leninist principles of selecting and placing personnel, with those promoted to leading work not always being deeply and thoroughly assessed for their political and professional qualities, and leading posts going in a number of cases to weak, incapable and at times shady people. The pernicious practice of exactly the same officials being shifted around from one post to another, despite some of them having lost a feeling for what is new and being tired of life, has not been eliminated.

It was said that party leaders 'often tolerate cases of the non-fulfilment of party, government and their own decisions, plus infringements of party and state discipline, falsification of results, toadying, nepotism and shirking responsibility'. This endorsement of Yusupov's perspective followed stern criticism of Kazakhstan by Khrushchev at the November CC CPSU plenum.[58] The former head of the CC KCP party organs department, S.M. Novikov, was sacked as first secretary of Kokchetav rural obkom for protecting failed officials on the eve of the V CC KCP plenum in March 1963 which focused on personnel work.[59] The discussion at this plenum concerned general personnel problems, not the bifurcation of the party apparatus, which in Kazakhstan affected only Karaganda, Alma Ata and East Kazakhstan.[60]

The personnel problems identified in December were again

raised in March 1963. Yusupov observed that personnel work had been discussed on only one occasion each by four obkoms during the previous five years, and the republican CC had not extensively discussed personnel problems since 1951, 12 years before. Mistaken appointments to leading posts had occurred because only 'a narrow circle' of Bureau members considered candidates for these positions. Yusupov called for serious reform of the current practice of appointing officials, though not for any systemic change. 'All of this takes place because we often move within a closed circle of the so-called "nomenklatura", transferring the same people from one place to another, not studying as we should their political and professional qualities and organisational capacities, and not seeing the main thing – the new fresh forces who have grown up and deserve promotion.' He stressed that: 'It is necessary to stop the useless practice of only a narrow circle of people being concerned with selecting and promoting personnel, which often leads to mistakes.' He reiterated the need for some turnover of senior officials to control the practice of local leaders being moved 'from one place to another without any justification', for which the KCP had been criticised by the CC CPSU 'more than once'. Since personnel mistakes had continued in several oblasts despite such criticism, Yusupov said it was now time to demand responsibility from all obkom leaders. He criticised former Tselino kraikom boss Sokolov for showiness, saying he 'decided many important questions unilaterally and often incorrectly, conducted himself improperly and even allowed boozing directly in his office'. Yusupov said pilfering had continued in Pavlodar obkom, and complained that unqualified people had been accepted into the republican apparatus. He suggested tougher times for many officials by stressing that: 'We should put a stop to the pernicious practice of leaders who have failed at one post being reassigned to another post of the same or greater responsibility only by virtue of the fact that at some time they happened to get into the nomenklatura'.[61]

Most obkom leaders supported Yusupov at this plenum, which called for greater consultation from republican authorities. Semipalatinsk obkom first secretary Karpenko said the CC KCP apparatus favoured officials from Alma Ata rather than the regions, and rarely consulted oblast organs on personnel matters. He also objected to the special privileges (a flat in Alma Ata plus salary) given by Kunaev to the 'inert' former Council of Ministers chairman Daulenov after his sacking; in his attitude to Daulenov, Kunaev was said to have been motivated by 'personal favouritism' rather than party principles. Aktiubinsk rural obkom boss Bekturganov also criticised favouritism toward Alma Ata officials, and said 'some officials have occupied leading posts for decades while displaying bad features and committing abuses'. South Kazakhstan leader Niiazbekov, who was promoted to head the reunified Alma Ata obkom after Yusupov's fall in December 1964, said the CC Bureau had 'lacked a serious approach to selecting and promoting personnel to leading posts', but he warned against the practice of sacking officials when they make mistakes, instead of helping them to learn from their failures. Nekliudov, boss of East Kazakhstan obkom, agreed, saying that the republican CC Bureau (including Yusupov) had not reprimanded officials for improper conduct and 'spared their vanity', with the result that the officials had to be sacked after intervention from the CC CPSU. This occurred particularly with Sokolov in the Virgin Lands, and Yusupov acknowledged in his concluding speech that Sokolov's degeneration might have been avoided. The plenum resolutions supported Yusupov's call for greater personnel discipline, saying that nepotism and the protection of failed officials had 'quite artificially created a pernicious circle of "nomenklatury", the so-called irreplacable officials'.[62]

Yusupov's campaign for personnel reform did not yield positive results during 1963 and 1964. Old problems showing inadequate party supervision (such as telephone leadership, pilfering, alcoholism, paper-chasing and timidity in telling officials of their mistakes) continued, along with 'old, declarative methods of running the economy' in which 'many decisions adopted by party committees dissolve into thin air since there is no control over their implementation'.[63] Personnel mistakes remained 'obvious' in South Kazakhstan, while bossing, irregular meetings and podmena were common.[64] At the VII CC KCP plenum in November 1963 Yusupov said local party leadership was still 'unsatisfactory', with continued cases where 'weak officials who have failed at work are transferred from one place to another while good people go unnoticed'.[65] Problems remained in the Virgin Lands, where the new boss in Tselinograd, Demidenko, was criticised by the kraikom first secretary Kolomiets for being 'firmly in the grip of old, long outdated methods of leadership which have been condemned by the party'. Demidenko was also rebuked for 'trying to resolve everything himself', the same charge that had been made against former kraikom boss Sokolov. Kolomiets suggested the problem was not personal by acknowledging that 'we sometimes send directives to obkoms and party committees which could easily be done without'.[66] The new system of party-state control committees, Khrushchev's attempt to use public discontent to discipline incompetent officials, was ineffective. CC KCP second secretary Solomentsev declared in July 1964 that not one party-state control committee had seriously investigated the pilfering of resources, which remained widespread in Karaganda and South Kazakhstan.[67] Podmena was strongly criticised by Yusupov in his last major speech as republican leader in late July 1964. He claimed that bifurcation had 'enabled party work to be more closely connected with production', but blamed obkoms and kraikoms 'for the fact that party committees are extremely slowly getting rid of old methods of work', since these oblast organs themselves 'often mix up the functions of party committees and production administrations, forcing party committees onto the path of substituting for economic organs, petty tutelage and bossing'.[68] It is clear that, however threatening some of Yusupov's language may have been to those 'nomenklatura units' he viewed as worthy of dismissal, he was unable to significantly address the basic problem of inadequate party supervision of economic life.

Thus Kazakhstan experienced a significant increase in the level of criticism of personnel problems in 1960–61, with a resurgence of more severe criticism under Yusupov in 1963. The criticism in 1963 reflected Yusupov's attempt to expose the faults of his predecessor and rival Kunaev, who remained influential as chairman of the republican Council of Ministers. Indeed, even in 1961 it had been Yusupov who had given the harsher tone to the criticism of party failings at that time. However, he did not get much support from obkom leaders in Kazakhstan before replacing Kunaev, and the extensive review of personnel work which he demanded soon after becoming republican leader was not realised. The severity of the campaign in Kazakhstan as reflected in the sorts of charges made in 1960–61 did not match that of Uzbekistan where charges relating to familyness and nepotism were much more prominent. The vigorous criticism of personnel faults during 1963 was peculiar to Kazakhstan but it was not sustained.

UKRAINE

The criticism of personnel matters in Ukraine in the period immediately after Stalin's death was much more restrained than it was in Uzbekistan. Party officials were accused of inadequately conducting the verification of the fulfilment of decisions and there was a reference to officials being no longer able to 'break the law',[69] but the principal source of complaint throughout the 1950s was the nature of leadership from above. This was said to be purely declarative, uninformed by real knowledge about the situation on the ground and often conducted through waves of paper and the issuing of directives.[70] Obkoms produced too many paper resolutions, creating 'an appearance of energetic activity, but nothing in the form of results'.[71] Communist Party of Ukraine (CPU) first secretary Kirichenko complained in March 1954 about obkoms that had 'an aggregate approach' to leadership which ignored specific conditions and led to podmena; nearly two years later he noted that the situation had not improved.[72] In November 1956, three years after the restructuring of rural raikoms was meant to bring them closer to production, an editorial in Ukraine lamented that: 'One still meets secretaries and other raikom officials who are mad clerks and administrators with a disdain for organisational work in the masses. Such leaders suggest that working and talking with people and studying their needs and concerns is a duty only for lower party officials and agitators.'[73]

Complaints about poor leadership from above in Ukraine were more restrained in the two years after the defeat of the anti-party group than in the years immediately following Stalin's death. In 1959 and 1960 such complaints became stronger, together with concerns about localism and also isolated cases of deception and fraud. At the XX CPU Congress in January 1959 first secretary Podgornyi endorsed Khrushchev's view that leaders without initiative should be removed.[74] Yet leaders of troubled obkoms were not accused of bad intentions. Following the Stalino obkom plenum in March, it was reported that: 'It is clear to everyone that the leaders of the oblast have a great wish to correct faults. But from wish to implementation there is still, as they say, an enormous distance.'[75] Khrushchev, speaking in Ukraine in May 1959, claimed that differences in agricultural productivity were determined by personnel work. He said 'it follows that if the leaders are not up to it, if they have reached their "ceiling" and cannot give more, then others must be boldly promoted'. He said the CC CPSU would 'very closely' supervise party work 'and will demand a great deal from personnel'[76] When the CC CPU discussed personnel problems at its October plenum, serious faults remained. Failed officials were being recycled, new people were selected 'from a narrow circle of those known to the given leader', and party committees did not encourage a reserve of those suitable for promotion. There were cases of the infringing of collegiality, and of podmena and petty tutelage over economic and soviet organs.[77] The resolutions criticised obkoms and raikoms for a simplistic attitude to economic leadership, for tolerating dishonesty in the food industry, and for allowing some leading officials to abuse their positions and deceive the state; report-padding and parochialism should be stamped out.[78] Khrushchev visited Ukraine again in December 1959, and soon after the leaders of Stalino obkom were criticised anew for not supporting ordinary communists who complained about officials abusing their positions.[79] Despite this, Podgornyi's report to the XXI CPU Congress in February 1960 barely addressed personnel issues.[80]

The lack of an effective hierarchy of party leadership in Ukraine meant that the production obligations undertaken by local officials were 'rarely checked'.[81] An article on agriculture in late 1960 reported 'no few cases of obkom officials being satisfied with apparently good economic reports and not paying serious attention to the fact that some raikom leaders are bossing and substituting themselves for the soviet apparatus and for specialists, and do not listen to the voices of communists'.[82] At a CC CPU plenum in January 1961 Podgornyi singled out fraudulent officials in Kiev oblast and said measures taken to stamp out anti-state and anti-party activity were inadequate. He said many raikom and obkom leaders were complacent, and stressed that 'party organisations must instil in personnel a spirit of honesty and correctness before the party and people, and a great responsibility for their work'.[83] When Khrushchev reaffirmed the need for material incentives at this plenum, he warned that fraudulent officials must not be pardoned.[84] The plenum resolutions condemned a liberal attitude towards 'infringers of party and state discipline, towards careerists trying, by fooling the party and state through fraud, report-padding and other abuses, to create an appearance of well-being and hide their inactivity or inability to fulfil obligations they have accepted'.[85] This warning was followed within weeks by the sacking of obkom first secretaries in Odessa and L'vov, where bureaucratic methods of supervision predominated.[86] The oblispolkom chairman in Chernigov was sacked, and the obkom boss and deputy head of the Kiev sovnarkhoz were both reprimanded for permitting 'the illegal construction of a stadium'.[87] Podgornyi told the XXII CPU Congress in autumn 1961 that the deputy chairman of the L'vov sovnarkhoz had been sacked for retaining too much production and supplying important materials to other sovnarkozy without approval.[88] Administrative pressure in Ukraine was most intrusive in 1961. Khrushchev ended the year rebuking local leaders who 'take decisions like generals give out orders' and calling for 'a ruthless struggle against babblers and idle noise' in order to overcome 'bureaucratism'.[89] These injunctions had little effect. Three months later Podgornyi noted that some raikoms 'often adopt a conciliatory attitude toward those officials who have failed at work, conducting themselves improperly and appropriating public wealth'.[90] In August 1962 he called for improved personnel work, complaining that 'crudeness, bureaucratism, careerism, bossing, the abuse of official positions, the breaking of Soviet laws and the gulf between words and deeds ... brings harm to party work and undermines the party's authority'.[91] The lack of substantial organisational change in Ukraine was acknowledged in July by Khrushchev, who, when opening a hydro-electric power station on the Dnepr, said that 'though Stalin is long dead and the party has exposed what was negative under Stalin, in the matter of supplying electricity to kolkhozy and sovkhozy the situation has changed little' since Stalin's rejection of rural services as worthless.[92]

The bifurcation of the party apparatus was introduced by

Podgornyi at the December 1962 CC CPU plenum as a way of overcoming the problems of a campaignist style of leadership by enabling party officials to concentrate on one specific branch of the economy. He claimed that the growth of party membership by 800 000 in Ukraine since 1953 and the doubling of party specialists since 1957 meant conditions were ripe for bifurcation. Replacing gorkoms by industrial obkoms was meant to 'get rid of an excessive link and bring leadership closer to the raikoms and PPOs [primary party organisations]'.[93] This was an admission of the failure of previous attempts at administrative reform under Khrushchev, which were all directed towards increasing party control from above. Podgornyi attacked in a routine way those leaders 'who have lost a feeling for what is new, who lead superficially, who poorly use existing reserves and opportunities for production, and who assess the results of their work uncritically'. Saying that party bifurcation was 'directed at eliminating declarativeness', he affirmed the basic need for 'a single centre of control, which could simultaneously realise control over party and state lines in the centre and on the ground'. Part of the problem was the alliance between sovnarkhozy and local party organs who were still often pushing for the construction of new projects without considering the state's interests.[94] Bifurcation did not improve party supervision, despite a declaration from Podgornyi in March 1963 that it was already a success. He admitted that bureaucratic methods prevailed, and stressed the need to 'decisively get rid of incompetent leaders' instead of transferring them 'from one post to another'.[95] In his last speech as CPU leader before moving to Moscow, Podgornyi acknowledged that party officials still resorted to 'administrative methods' in practice, just meeting targets instead of trying to increase the party's political influence.[96] His successor Shelest began by noting personnel work was inadequate. A year later he again affirmed that 'Party organisations from top to bottom must take continual control of all questions concerned with the acceleration of technical progress.'[97]

In Ukraine in the Khrushchev period the rhetoric of reform changed even less frequently than the republican leaders, with the strongest criticism occurring during 1961 in the middle of Podgornyi's period as republican boss. While Khrushchev visited Ukraine more often than he visited other republics, there was even less evidence of a criticism campaign in Ukraine than in Kazakhstan. The bifurcation of the party apparatus received more attention in Ukraine than in the less populous and much less industrialised republics discussed above, but it failed substantially to increase the organisational influence of party officials on the ground.

BELORUSSIA

Criticism of personnel work in the mid-1950s was more severe in Belorussia than in Ukraine. Formalism and showiness were criticised, with some party organs accused of making a lot of noise about sending personnel to the countryside, but in practice doing very little in this regard; sometimes when people were despatched, they were unqualified for the positions they were to fill.[98] Some party organisations made decisions about personnel among a small group of people, while Vitebsk obkom was accused of selecting personnel 'not according to professional or business considerations, but on the basis of friendship, personal devotion and acquaintance, reassigning failed officials from one place to another with detrimental effects on the job at hand'.[99] There was said to be poor leadership from above, conducted with little knowledge of what was happening on the ground, exercised by telephone, paper waves and numerous demands for reports; declarative rather than practical leadership was common.[100] The need for 'continual not episodic' checking of lower party organs was said to be pressing where leadership of raikoms by obkoms in 1954 was only declarative, exercised 'largely by telephone and by way of frequent summonses of local officials to the oblast centre'.[101] In late 1955 obkom party supervision was still being reduced to 'general directive instructions, extensive correspondence and "cannings" on the telephone'.[102] Obkom secretaries claimed in January 1956 at the XXII Belorussian Communist Party (BCP) Congress that their behaviour was a response to demands for numerous reports from the republican leadership, who they described as cut off from lower-level party committees.[103]

The problem of poor linkages between obkoms and raikoms and PPOs was discussed regularly during the second half of the 1950s. There was much criticism of bureaucratism and inadequate party supervision in 1958 and 1959. The practice of obkoms ignoring abuses and failings in raikoms, which was strongly criticised in 1954, continued five years later. The first secretary of Voronovo raikom in Grodno oblast said in 1959 that:

> we have received almost no answers to requests and suggestions sent to the obkom. The protocols of raikom plena and bureau sessions which we send to the obkom are analysed only from a grammatical viewpoint. Actual conclusions are never drawn. There has been talk for many years in the obkom about the lagging of some districts, including Voronovo, but no help is given to us to overcome this.[104]

This complaint occurred three years after the first secretary of Grodno obkom said that 'there has not been one case when any CC secretary has called a meeting of raikom secretaries in the oblast and shown an interest in how they work, how they solve this or that problem, what obstructs them and what they need'.[105] This organisational inertia in the oblast party apparatus reflected poor supervision from the republican level. At the XXIII BCP Congress in January 1959 Mazurov said the republican CC apparatus lacked initiative, often ignored incompetent leaders, inadequately supervised soviet and economic organisations and failed to verify the implementation of decisions. In an understatement he also said 'elements of showiness and vagueness have not been removed from the work of obkoms'.[106] This 'general and undifferentiated approach to guiding districts' remained entrenched two years later, according to the first secretary of Mogilev obkom.[107] It was claimed at the XXV BCP Congress in September 1961 that the republican CC apparatus was more in contact with lower party organs than before, but reports of bureaucratism continued. The first secretary of Gomel' obkom, D. Filiminov, stated in March 1963 that 'many party committees have still not renounced showy methods of work and paper-chasing. At their sessions they discuss several important problems and note steps to eliminate this or that fault, but they lack the persistence and patience needed to put these measures into practice.'[108] The persistence of such poor leadership suggests a systemic failing in party control even in Belorussia, where cases of officials abusing their authority featured much less regularly in the press than in Central Asia or Kazakhstan.

The persistence of personnel mistakes remained an issue from 1958 onwards, with talk of the need to demand more from leading officials and to get rid of those who did not measure up,[109] but from 1959 the tone in which this was discussed had more threatening elements. Cover-ups, lawlessness and deception were criticised in mid-1959, while in February 1960 Mazurov called for honesty in 'the decisive struggle with different kinds of embezzlement', adding: 'unfortunately we have had to sack some party leaders who became philistines'.[110] During 1961 there were continuing reports of falsification, deception, fraud and illegality.[111] It was also stressed that officials should be promoted only according to their proven qualities for the post, not due to their position or acquaintances.[112] In early 1962 Mazurov warned again:

> There is no greater mistake in work with personnel than to connive with passive drunkards and people greedy for social wealth. We must once and for all do away with the myth about 'irreplaceability'. Life shows that if a person fails in one leading post, then he will work no better at another; and if he disregards criticism from communists and especially from party organs, then work cannot be expected from him.[113]

This message was ignored, since a year later Mazurov ordered: 'agricultural obkoms must change from gossiping about personnel to replacing those who cannot cope with work or who conduct themselves disrespectfully'.[114] In 1964 the problem of poor personnel work remained: it was observed that 'often a person who has failed in one place will be moved to similar leading work in another place, being considered as an "experienced" and "irreplaceable" official'.[115] In 1963–64 the more threatening tone of the earlier two years was less in evidence.

Thus in Belorussia there was more severe criticism of officials during the Khrushchev period than in Ukraine, but the vigorous approach to personnel problems characteristic of the campaign periods in Central Asia was not in evidence. For the most part discussion of party life saw the problems as mistakes rather than crimes, with their discussion taking place in a routinised, relatively unthreatening fashion. There was certainly stronger language used at times in the 1959–62 period, in the middle of Mazurov's tenure as republican leader, but this did not amount to a campaign.

THE KHRUSHCHEV PATTERN

The pattern of criticism in the republican press during the Khrushchev period is broadly standard with significant republican variations. In the first five years of the post-Stalin period, discussion of the questions of local leadership reflected the standard Soviet pattern, with problems overwhelmingly attributed to incompetence, slackness or bureaucratic malfunctioning rather than conscious malfeasance by individuals. This pattern was essentially sustained throughout the remainder of the Khrushchev period in Ukraine and Belorussia, although in both there may have been feint echoes of something more serious respectively in 1961 and 1959–62. In Uzbekistan a vigorous campaign of criticism emerged in 1959 and was sustained through until the end of 1961 and early 1962. The level of criticism was higher and the object of criticism was systematic criminal activity by party officials as opposed to simple bureaucratic bungling or isolated cases of fraud. In Tajikistan there were echoes of such a campaign in 1959, but it was not really until 1961 that it gained major prominence, with the same sort of features as in Uzbekistan. In Kazakhstan, while there was no campaign along the Central Asian lines, there was an increase in levels of criticism over the 1961–64 period, and while this remained much weaker than in Uzbekistan or Tajikistan, it was greater than in either Ukraine or Belorussia. The continuation of such criticism in Kazakhstan throughout 1963 reflected rivalry between first secretary Yusupov and his predecessor Kunaev, who remained powerful in the Kazakh government. The peaks of criticism in Ukraine and Belorussia occurred in the middle of consolidated periods of rule by Podgornyi and Mazurov respectively, while the much more threatening criticism in Uzbekistan and Tajikistan occurred when new republican leaders (Rashidov and Rasulov respectively) were beginning to establish their networks of power.

3 Variants of Republican Autonomy

A major change in the operation of the CPSU between the ousting of Khrushchev and the ascension of Gorbachev was the growth in the autonomy of republican party leaderships with a decline in effective control from the centre. There were a number of related reasons for this change. First, the policy of retaining senior personnel except when they had committed very serious abuses (the 'stability of cadres' policy) allowed republican leaders much greater room for manoeuvre than under Khrushchev. Most changes to republican party leaderships under Brezhnev occurred because incumbents died rather than because of failures in party supervision or corruption, the main exception being the leadership changes in the Caucasus between 1969 and 1974. Second, the longevity of tenure of most republican leaderships increased the extent to which these politicians relied on their informal networks of patronage rather than on the nominally superior authority of the central party apparatus in Moscow. Republican leaders like Kunaev, Rashidov and Shcherbitsky depended on Brezhnev for their positions in the top leadership. Brezhnev in turn depended on their ability to keep their fiefdoms in order. The interventionism of the centre in the late Khrushchev period was replaced by a form of mutual complacency about socioeconomic problems, symbolised by the ritual awarding by central officials of banners of achievement to republican party officials. Third, when these economic problems became increasingly serious in the late 1970s the dominant Brezhnev faction in the top leadership lacked the willingness, if not the capacity, to intervene in most republican party affairs. The reflection of this policy can be seen clearly in the patterns of criticism in the republican press during this period. For most of this period and throughout much of the country, the levels of criticism were lower and the tone less vigorous than it had been during the period discussed in Chapter 2. Although there were some instances of vigorous criticism, including in the Caucasus, Tambov (February 1975) and Turkmenistan (June

1979), generally criticism was restrained and directed at mistakes, confusion and bureaucratic poor performance rather than abuses, crimes and misdemeanours.

UZBEKISTAN

The early months following the ouster of Khrushchev saw some references to serious charges in Uzbekistan. In November Rashidov called on party cadres to struggle against bureaucratism, showiness and shortcomings, while the following month, in a discussion of the deficiencies of the bifurcation of the party apparatus, it was said that while there were many good cadres in Tashkent oblast, there had also been cases of infringement of party and state discipline, eyewash, deception, boastfulness, careerism and the ignoring of public and state interests.[1] In January 1965 a discussion of party conferences called upon them to overcome problems of paper-creation, a surfeit of sessions, blind faith in directives, administrirovanie and petty tutelage over economic organs, showiness, ballyhoo and bragging.[2] Such concerns were not expressed in the following months when discussion of the party was limited and there was no serious criticism. In his report to the XVII CPUz Congress in March 1966 Rashidov claimed that cadre questions had always been resolved collegially and that the republican CC regularly reviewed the activities of obkoms. The Congress resolutions proclaimed an improvement in cadre work while noting that bossing, petty tutelage, podmena, showiness and ballyhoo still remained.[3]

Throughout 1966 and 1967 there was a focus on improving the work of PPOs in Uzbekistan in order to raise economic performance. Rashidov said PPOs had been strengthened by the reunification of local party committees. He claimed this move had abolished showiness and bragging, but acknowledged that regularisation was lacking in the work of many party organisations, with documents out of order and tolerance of various personal abuses. The party decision following this speech criticised the way in which party meetings were never lively fora for the discussion of questions of intra-party life and how a liberal attitude often was taken towards communists who had infringed; there was only a weak struggle against both collective leadership and the individual responsibility of officials.[12] But beside this sort of criticism, there was also at this time a more vigorous line of complaint and criticism in the press. A general discussion of party meetings (which referred specifically to the CC CPSU decision on Yaroslavl – see Chapter 5) criticised the involvement in them of only a narrow circle of communists, with issues not properly discussed, meetings characterised by criticism from above rather than below, and in some cases leaders reacted adversely to any criticism; in one case a meeting was said to be 'too organised', with no attempt to bring a deficient party leader to account.[13] In 1971 the level and vigour of criticism picked up. Among criticism of a lack of practical activity by party bodies, it was charged that there had been a liberal attitude toward deficiencies.[14] At the XVIII Congress in March, there were complaints about passivity and complacency, a liberal attitude toward those who infringed party rules and failed to carry out their responsibilities, abuse of the faith placed in responsible people and deception.[15] Three months later passivity and complacency, a liberal attitude toward those who infringed discipline and abused their positions, declarative leadership and formalism, and subjectivism in personnel questions were all criticised within a report saying that there had been improvement in party performance.[16] Poor entry procedures, in particular the failure to closely scrutinize all potential members, was also criticised at this time.[17] In early 1972 a discussion of the role of cadres in the economy[18] noted that party committees had to rebuff any lack of principle, lack of responsibility and abuse of position for profitable ends. It was also said that not only those who committed abuses but those who had recommended them for high office should be called to account, while national narrow-mindedness, localism and careerism must be combated. Later that year the Tashkent gorkom was blamed for some leaders abusing their positions in the distribution of housing, and allowing false reporting and deception, extravagance and infringement of laws and discipline.[19] The last major case of this sort of vigorous criticism at this time occurred in March 1973[20] when a raikom first secretary was accused, among other things, of failing to act against cases of infringement of rules and financial discipline, eyewash and deception. He was also accused of choosing cadres on the basis of friendly relations and personal such anti-social phenomena as drunkenness, hooliganism, self-seeking, careerism, toadyism and inadmissible personal conduct.[4] Obkoms, gorkoms and raikoms were criticised in November 1966 for taking little interest in the work of PPOs and for overriding them.[5] Despite specific criticism of Surkhandar'ia obkom in July 1967 for, among other things, passivity and an absence of criticism and self-criticism among its members, there was little general improvement by early 1968, when irregular meetings and weak supervision of adopted decisions remained common problems in the republic.[6] In January and February 1968 the tone of criticism became harsher, with the sacking of the Andizhan obkom leadership; the former obkom leadership was accused of giving poor economic leadership and, in personnel matters, of infringing the principles of collegiality, of judging people 'not according to their political and professional qualities, but according to their personal attitudes to leaders of the obkom', and of allowing careerists and those who had plundered state and kolkhoz property into positions of economic leadership.[7] Other obkoms were told not to protect dishonourable and compromised officials (in one case people who had been involved in embezzlement and plunder) or they would face a similar fate.[8] This criticism coincided with Brezhnev's qualification of the 'trust in cadres' principle (see Chapter 5), but it was not sustained. Criticism reverted to the standard line of inadequate leadership, collecting too many reports and providing too little assistance to lower party organs. In Samarkand obkom during 1970 there was a lot of criticism and self-criticism but then no action; whilst questions of intra-party life were rarely discussed at party meetings, this failing was not regarded as serious enough to require changing the obkom leadership.[9]

In the early 1970s, the discussion of party life retained a strong tone of criticism of poor operating procedures, particularly in economic leadership. Rashidov's attention at party congresses and meetings was principally on economic performance.[10] The failure of PPOs to increase supervision in the economy through careful cadre work was largely explained as a result of inadequate attention from obkoms, gorkoms and raikoms.[11] The need to improve cadre work in order to make supervision in the economy more than episodic was stressed by Rashidov in early 1972, when he again professed to believe in sympathies rather than professional and political qualities, of defending people convicted of abuse of official position, illegal activity and immoral conduct, of surrounding himself with fawners and toadies who would fulfil any wish, and of using his position for personal profitable ends. Reflective of the decline in vigour of the criticism is the initial report on the success of the exchange of party cards in December 1973[21] in which inertia, passivity and complacency seem to have been the most serious faults mentioned.

From the latter part of 1972 there was also a focus on the inadequacy of the leadership exercised by higher-standing party bodies over those at lower levels. In the republic more than 30 gorkoms and raikoms heard no reports from PPOs during 1972, while a report on party conferences in early 1974 criticised raikom leaders for using old methods of bossing instead of becoming familiar with economic matters.[22] This, along with complaints about the absence of criticism and self-criticism, continued to be the main problem discussed routinely in republican party meetings in Uzbekistan throughout the rest of the Brezhnev period. The very positive interpretation of the exchange of party documents in 1975 set the scene for further stability, with old problems discussed occasionally in subsequent years in a purely ritual way.[23] The XIX Congress in February 1976 projected a generally positive view of the state of intra-party life, but some problems were noted: infringement of party principles in the selection and distribution of cadres, abuse of official position and poor work, infringements of discipline, norms and morals, a liberal attitude to infringements, and poor criticism and self-criticism were all mentioned.[24] But this was unusual; throughout most of the rest of the 1970s the press did not focus upon abuses in party life.

In the last three years of the Brezhnev period, although the tone of comment remained overwhelmingly the standard type of criticism of party operations, there was some mention of more serious problems. Eulogistic self-reporting and deception,[25] and embezzlement[26] were reported, but there was no republic-wide campaign as these problems were said to be under control.[27] In his last CPUz Congress report in February 1981, Rashidov still claimed that party work was improving. He described complacency, weak supervision of party organs and irresponsible leaders as being isolated problems.[28] This message was reflected in an editorial after Brezhnev's visit to Uzbekistan in autumn 1982, which claimed most party leaders possessed not only 'competence' but 'personal modesty'.[29] A previous editorial had noted again that party committees devoted insufficient attention to hearing reports of PPOs.[30] This old problem was discussed at a CC CPUz plenum in April 1982, at which local party officials were told to establish an atmosphere of real comradeliness, high demandingness and implacability towards shortcomings,[31] while the following month there was criticism of a paper style of leadership and emphasis on the need to struggle against all negative phenomena – abuse of official position, embezzlement of socialist property, eyewash, bribery, drunkenness, and a liberal attitude toward those who infringe the norms of communist morals.[32] This was clearly only ritual advice, since the actual conduct of the republican party leadership set a very different example. Serious criticism of the failures of party organs to both improve economic leadership and ensure discipline only occurred in Uzbekistan after Rashidov died.

In Uzbekistan the prevailing tenor of discussion of party life during the Brezhnev period was not characterised by a vigorous criticism of abuses. Rather it focused upon the sort of standard criticisms of party functioning: the weakness of higher-level leadership, poor economic leadership, bureaucratic slip-ups and malfunctioning, and the weakness of criticism. The problem was generally seen as not being abuse of position but bureaucratic deficiencies. There were pale echoes of the more vigorous attack upon abuses at the end of the 1960s and in the early 1970s and towards the end of the period, but these were very pale compared with the more vigorous episodes under Khrushchev and what was to come in the 1980s.

TAJIKISTAN

A very similar situation existed in Tajikistan during the Brezhnev period. Problems with cadre work were exposed in Dushanbe gorkom in late 1964, including the selection of cadres on the basis of factors other than their professional and political qualities, and the election of party secretaries who could not cope with the work, infringed the norms of party life, compromised themselves and allowed abuses.³³ This tone of criticism was not maintained; throughout late 1964–65 discussion of party life tended to concentrate on the inadequacy of leadership from above and the deficient organisation of party meetings. At the XII plenum in January 1966 there was a hint of more serious problems; reference was made to the removal of cadres who had permitted mistakes, complacency, the promotion of cadres on the basis of common region of origin, kinship and personal devotion, the movement of failed workers from one place to another, a liberal attitude to dishonest workers, infringements of party and state discipline, and ballyhoo.³⁴ But again, such criticism was not maintained, with discussion over the following years rarely raising any suspicion about abuses in party life.

Despite warnings from Rasulov during 1966 against complacency in cadre work, the situation had not improved by early 1969 when a CC CPSU resolution on Tajikistan sharply complained that cadre work was still deficient in many organisations, including the Tajik CC; it also noted that in some parts of the republic party organisations had failed to make a principled evaluation of the deception and false reporting undertaken by enterprise managers.³⁵ The need for a cleansing of the republican party from degenerates and fraudsters was stressed at a plenum in March 1970.³⁶ The plenum also criticised the conduct of party meetings, the taking of a liberal attitude to the plunder of socialist property, showiness, conceit, complacency, localism, the infringement of Leninist principles on the selection and distribution of cadres, and the suppression of criticism. Yet less than a year later Rasulov declared that the republican CC (strongly criticised by the centre in 1969) had largely controlled the situation, though some abuse of official position, squandering of socialist property, fraudulent behaviour, localism, nepotism and poor supervision of PPOs remained.³⁷ Vigorous criticism was not sustained; despite a reference to protectionism, abuse of position and a liberal attitude towards infringements in February 1976,³⁸ discussion throughout the remainder of the 1970s remained couched in terms of standard bureaucratic failings rather than abuses.

At the start of the 1980s raikoms were still being criticised for the fault of not focusing enough on selecting economic personnel.[39] There were some harsher comments at the end of 1980 and early 1981, with references to promotion on the basis of localism, friendship, kinship and comradely protection, abuse of position, infringement of discipline, eyewash and false reporting, and suppression of criticism, but these were combined with continuing claims that party work was improving.[40] The overall picture was one of the party operating effectively with only some minor problems rather than major abuses.

As in Uzbekistan, the dominant message throughout the Brezhnev period was one of trusting cadres and effective party operation. Harsh comments about abuse of position and inadequate supervision by party officials in Tajikistan were rare. At no time did such comments in Tajikistan begin to develop into a republic-wide campaign against compromised officials, not even after the CPSU resolution on Tajikistan in early 1969, which was very critical of poor cadre work. In comparison with Uzbekistan, there was less sustained exposure in the Tajik party press of particular party committees in which abuses were occurring. Indeed, there was less discussion of party affairs generally. This does not mean problems of party supervision in Tajikistan were less serious than in Uzbekistan; the ritualistic nature of official criticism and self-criticism under Rasulov was even clearer than under Rashidov.

KAZAKHSTAN

When Kunaev returned to dominance in Kazakhstan within two months of Brezhnev's elevation to lead the central party, he claimed that reunifying the party apparatus would mean a heightened role for raikoms in managing economic affairs.[41] At the next KCP Congress in early 1966 Kunaev expressed his 'great trust in local personnel', and said that the sacking of officials is 'an extreme measure which must be applied only in those cases when all other means of influence have been exhausted'.[42] This sort of attitude is reflected in the fact that discussion of party life throughout the entire Brezhnev period was characterised by a tone which rarely raised concerns about abuses or major problems, instead concentrating on problems of bureaucratic procedure or mistakes in policy implementation. An editorial in July 1966 criticised the repeated 'transferring of failed officials from one responsible post to another'.[43] Reforming unified party committees did not resolve any of the basic problems of poor linkages between different levels of the apparatus. Second secretary Titov said some PPOs were not even told of raikom decisions concerning them. The decisions remained on paper while raikoms intervened only irregularly through podmena, and also conducted personnel selection on a narrow and unprofessional basis.[44] This problem of very poor party supervision continued to be discussed in 1967, when it was noted that about three-quarters of all gorkoms and raikoms in Alma Ata and Karaganda oblasts failed to call regular plena. At the same time Titov also noted that some party committees spent too much time discussing issues instead of giving practical leadership, while in some cases failed officials were protected at the expense of promoting younger capable people.[45] After Brezhnev's qualification of 'trust in cadres' in 1968 (see Chapter 5), Kunaev called for a struggle against nationalism and parochialism,[46] and briefly made a strong criticism of the way untrained officials were often selected by 'a narrow circle of figures in the "nomenklatura"'. He said younger personnel were not promoted partly because 'in places there has formed a narrow circle of so-called "irreplaceable" officials, who are shifted around from one post to another, thereby blocking the way for an influx of fresh forces'.[47] This tone of criticism did not continue into the 1970s, when formulations about cadre work became routine statements of the need for trust plus responsibility. Reports of almost all obkom plena said faults existed only in 'isolated party organisations'.[48] Serious faults in personnel work in Alma Ata and Karaganda were noted again in early 1974, but there was no CC KCP plenum devoted to this problem as there had been in 1967.[49]

During the second half of the 1970s, Kunaev focused on the practice of reducing plan targets, which 'allows particular leaders to shirk their responsibility and sometimes even become heroes with no effort at all'.[50] But he also criticised other aspects of party life. In March 1975 he called for no leniency toward those who filled their pockets from state funds and the following month he called for obkoms to give more attention to rural raikoms, and criticised Karaganda obkom for being satisfied with paper leadership in the economy.⁵¹ According to second secretary Mesiats, many PPOs still did not hold regular meetings or exercise restraint over 'officials who put personal self-glorification above social interests'.⁵² At the XIV Congress of the KCP in early 1976 Kunaev criticised those party leaders who had 'lost touch with life' and who continued podmena, but claimed that 'trust and respect for personnel, combined with high performance, has become firmly entrenched in our party'.⁵³ This endorsement of the basic principle of cadre stability limited the significance of Kunaev's occasional calls for greater responsibility from officials. In April 1976 he complained that 'under the pretext of a respectful attitude to officials, particular party committees tolerate leaders who cannot cope with their duties and abuse their official positions', but he described this as an 'extreme' phenomenon which could be readily eliminated.⁵⁴ Fraud in the construction industry supervised by Alma Ata gorkom was disclosed in August 1976. Yet Kunaev's criticism six months later was quite general, merely calling for an end to 'any signs of irresponsibility, window-dressing and showiness'.⁵⁵ There was no sustained campaign criticising corrupt leaders.

In July 1978 Kunaev referred to the protection of failed officials as a problem in agriculture because of the irresponsibility of obkom leaders. He also criticised raikoms for the old fault of not restructuring their work in order to cope with the need to increase production.⁵⁶ This problem went back to the earliest years of Khrushchev's rule, but Kunaev regarded it as routine. In November 1978 Kunaev used his speech about Brezhnev's achievements to refer to 'personnel mistakes' in Kazakhstan back in 1954 which Brezhnev had been sent to fix. Of that time Kunaev said: 'The mistakes showed that some leaders, having lost a feeling of responsibility, selected officials not according to their professional qualities but according to a principle of personal devotion'.⁵⁷ This was not really a direct warning to corrupt party leaders. The point was rather that a quarter of a century before Moscow had the authority to intervene in Kazakhstan, especially in order to control the independence of nationalist leaders, whereas now Kunaev clearly enjoyed the support of Brezhnev's faction which allowed him to do as he pleased. The message to party officials in Kazakhstan was that Kunaev determined who was responsible and who was not. Hence all aspirants for leading party positions, including Nursultan Nazarbaev who had recently become an obkom secretary in Karaganda, had to demonstrate their personal devotion to the republican boss.[58] At a Karaganda obkom party conference in December 1978 it was reported that 38 nomenklatura officials of the obkom had been sacked for not coping with their work or for having compromised themselves.[59] This volume of turnover within the oblast elite suggested that irresponsibility was more than just a marginal phenomenon, but it evoked no sustained republican-level comment.

The extent to which structures of party supervision in the economy had deteriorated in Kazakhstan during Brezhnev's era of stability became increasingly evident in reports in the early 1980s. The situation was particularly bad in Semipalatinsk, where in one raikom 198 out of 280 nomenklatura officials had been replaced in the previous two and a half years as a result of the fact that the first secretary 'often resolves personnel questions in a drunken state'.[60] At the IV CC KCP plenum held a year after this report, Kunaev observed that 'often different kinds of symposia conclude with extensive drinking at the state's expense'.[61] Poor leadership of PPOs continued in Karaganda and Semipalatinsk, and in Kustanai where the old fault existed of raikom instructors spending too much of their time 'compiling all sorts of papers and talking on the phone'.[62] Poor links between different levels of the party hierarchy and poor verification of decisions remained basic problems.[63] In one case a raikom took more than three months to send resolutions to PPOs. Other raikoms often just duplicated the decisions of obkoms instead of implementing them. Many raikoms were still getting involved in too many particular economic matters rather than setting basic priorities and concentrating on improving cadre work. One raikom in Alma Ata oblast had considered no less than 716 questions at 24 Bureau sessions during 1981.[64] At the same time Kunaev criticised 'isolated leaders who loudly call for the careful use of resources while themselves taking from the state pocket as if it were their own'.[65]

The course of party criticism in Kazakhstan was mild throughout the entire Brezhnev period, with some vigour in the criticism of obstacles to personnel renewal occurring only briefly at the end of the 1960s. Rarely was there mention of major abuses, or even major problems, and even when these were noted, they did not receive sustained republican-level discussion, criticism or even comment. Where there were difficulties, these were overwhelmingly viewed as bureaucratic malfunctioning or isolated mistakes, even at the end of the Brezhnev period when reporting of particular abuses began to increase.

UKRAINE

Generally during the 1960s, the criticism of party functioning in Ukraine was mild with little hint of major abuses. There was criticism of raikoms,[66] gorkoms and obkoms for adopting general resolutions which were difficult to check. Shelest also complained about continuing faults in admissions, the promotion of discredited officials, and the practice of 'reassigning people endlessly from one place to another and handing out a multitude of party reprimands'.[67] Having pointed out at the CPU Congress in March 1966 that hasty promotions of discredited officials at the expense of capable young organisers had occurred in Odessa, L'vov, Kherson and Volynsk oblasts, he warned in December that 'cases of a rude, tactless attitude from particular leading officials to subordinates' must not be tolerated.[68] The resolution of the March 1968 CC CPU plenum accused some party committees of 'dressing up reality, hiding faults and errors in work, not disclosing their real causes and not always giving them a correct political evaluation'.[69] Such warnings to officials, including over a conciliatory attitude towards waste and inactivity, continued in Ukraine into the early 1970s.[70]

In March 1971 Shelest said that abuses of authority still existed in Zhitomir because the obkom had 'often shown a liberal attitude toward officials who have infringed the norms of party life and acted irresponsibly toward fulfilling party decisions'. Untried people were being hastily promoted to leading positions, and party supervision of the economy was still reduced to 'a multitude of sessions and meetings' at the expense of organisational work.[71] Shelest's continued use of administrative threats in the manner of Khrushchev was evident at the CC CPU plenum in June 1971. There he said that, while the 'stability of personnel' was an 'important prerequisite for successful work', officials who failed in their job should not only be censured but even sacked. He criticised local party organisations for tolerating poor discipline, podmena, failure to fulfil party requirements and infringements of party and state discipline, and called for the misdemeanours of local party leaders to be regularly discussed in PPOs.[72] In March 1972 this policy of continually pressurising officials was reiterated, with party committees ordered not to permit 'the retention in some posts of officials who are incapable of ensuring the successful fulfilment of new, more complex tasks'.[73] Shortly after, in May 1972, Shelest was replaced by Shcherbitsky.[74]

The tone of more vigorous criticism that had begun under Shelest was continued under his successor Shcherbitsky, although as under the former leader, this was not more important than the criticism of bureaucratic mismanagement evident earlier. Initially some dismissals occurred, as with a Poltava obkom secretary who was sacked in January 1973 for permitting economic managers to reduce production targets, often with the connivance of local party officials.[75] By April 1973 the recommended response to those officials who abused their positions amounted only to strict reprimands, and attention was focused on the need to make sure leading officials gained experience of production.[76] In September Shcherbitsky declared that raikoms were performing better, though 'the force of inertia and habit' was evident in unnecessary paperwork common in many party committees.[77] There was criticism at the Dnepropetrovsk obkom plenum in October 1973 of 'manifestations of a liberal attitude toward those who infringe party and state discipline'.[78] In January 1974 declarative leadership and the lack of an exacting approach were criticised, with Shcherbitsky declaring 'life itself demands that we decisively get rid of bureaucrats, toadies, those who are indifferent and who take what is not theirs', but he pointed out that this should not lead to whining or a lack of respect for personnel.[79] Within a month the emphasis on stability became a much greater priority than discipline. Clearly responding to Khrushchev's personnel policy of administrative pressure, under which he had been demoted (in June 1963 he had been shifted from chairmanship of the Council of Ministers back to his former position as Dnepropetrovsk obkom first secretary), Shcherbitsky declared in February 1974 that sacked leaders could now 'return in their time' to some posts once they acknowledged their failings, because 'it is not right to deprive all these people of prospects for their whole life'. He stressed that collective leadership was essential in order to avoid 'nervousness' on the part of officials, and observed that: 'The absence of a planned, well thought-out system in personnel work leads to the situation that many responsible official positions in party committees remain vacant for months.'[80] The problem of 'corruption and protectionism' in Kiev gorkom, Crimea obkom and the Ministry of Internal Affairs was noted a few months later, but this did not change the new focus on stability.[81] With more 'respect' for leading personnel, economic failings were seen not as abuses of authority but as poor leadership.

The problem of complacency in economic leadership remained an issue in the mid-1970s. Donetsk obkom was criticised in early 1975 for tolerating infringers of discipline and formal methods of party supervision.[82] Kiev gorkom was criticised for the old problem of poor leadership of PPOs, with Shcherbitsky observing that: 'responsible officials from the departments of a number of party committees, especially their instructors, work largely in their offices "on instructions", instead of instructing on the ground'.[83] In a May 1975 report on the exchange of party documents, it was noted that PPO secretaries acting with integrity 'have not received reliable support from particular raikoms and gorkoms'. Continuing personnel mistakes were attributed to the fact that PPO views were ignored. The 'great harm' that cliques and subjectivism caused in cadre work was noted, as was the presence of paper-shuffling, declarative leadership and complacency, and the continuing weak influence of PPOs in economic ministries was lamented.[84] At this time Shcherbitsky said officials who breached party discipline were not needed. He criticised the Kiev gorkom boss Botvin for complacency.[85] Over six months later Shcherbitsky again criticised Botvin for 'an unprincipled attitude toward figures who had committed serious faults in work and even compromised themselves'. Kiev gorkom was now subordinated directly to the CC CPU rather than the obkom, but poor party supervision had still enabled leading officials to engage in 'report-padding, pilfering, protectionism and other abuses'.[86] Weak coordination between obkoms, gorkoms and raikoms was prevalent, especially in Kharkov where the obkom demanded too many reports about purely technical tasks and demands for better party work were mistakenly identified 'only with measures of force and punishment'.[87] Shcherbitsky attacked his predecessor Shelest at the XXV CPU Congress in February 1976, saying that the former leader had by 1972 'lost any link with the republic's party organisation . . . and lost the moral right' to remain in the Ukrainian leadership. Obkom leaders were very laudatory about Shcherbitsky, who criticised economic managers but not party leaders.[88] When serious personnel mistakes were noted in Kiev and Odessa obkoms in mid-1977, the problem was said to be that some local party committees were 'often changing officials, and doing this hastily'. It was emphasised that 'high demands toward personnel must be combined with a clear and respectful attitude toward them, to their needs and requests'.[89] Shcherbitsky said all party committees must become 'organs of political leadership' and 'develop collegiality in their activity', but new methods for achieving these declared goals were not discussed.[90]

In the last five years of the Brezhnev period economic problems continued to be the focus of press discussion in Ukraine, but the tone of criticism became less complacent. Shcherbitsky warned officials in July 1978 that 'one cannot live by old honours' and specified several lagging obkoms.[91] In December he called on obkoms to 'make serious demands on those who fail to ensure that planned objects are operating on time'. He now qualified the basic need for 'a respectful regard for people and protecting the authority of leading personnel' by saying: 'it is necessary to conduct the most decisive struggle against those who by their actions degrade the high standing of a party member, who permit or tolerate cases of waste, abuse the trust placed in them and treat the duties of a citizen of the USSR with scorn'.[92] In April 1979 it was disclosed that some party committees tolerated 'all kinds of infringements and abuses' in the retail sector.[93] The old problem of instructors not assisting PPOs because they preferred to live in oblast capitals instead of where they should work remained. Shcherbitsky continued his more critical assessment of personnel mistakes, saying:

> some raikoms and gorkoms, and even certain obkoms, do not always have a good knowledge of personnel, do not

prepare reserves of personnel, work within a limited circle of people, and at times even reassign from one post to another officials who cannot cope with things. Sometimes there is an attempt to justify such an approach with ideas of a careful, attentive regard for personnel. In truth this is nothing but liberalism and connivance, which cause great harm.[94]

This tone was reinforced by Shcherbitsky's statement in October 1979 that the CC CPU had recently responded to abuses in some cities by 'expelling certain leaders from the party as well as sacking them'.[95] In December 1979 Shcherbitsky called on oblast party leaders to increase discipline. He said officials involved in falsification, deception, fraud, waste, parochialism, self-servingness and other infringements of state discipline should be expelled and even face trial, but he also said leaders whose fault was merely not adapting to new tasks need only be promptly reassigned to other posts.[96]

In the early 1980s the problem of economic fraud remained a theme in Ukraine.[97] To stress the size of the problem, Shcherbitsky singled out protectionism in Cherkassy obkom (run by the former CC CPU second secretary Lutak) where 'some officials previously called to account for different infringements have even been elected to leading party and soviet organs'.[98] The need for criticism and self-criticism to combat complacency, bureaucratism and eyewash, and the threat of 'strict measures, right up to sacking and expulsion from the party', were reiterated at the XXVI CPU Congress in February 1981, though Shcherbitsky subsequently claimed Brezhnev had 'positively evaluated the personnel work of party organisations' in Ukraine on a visit in mid-1981. But he also said in the same speech that protectionism would not be tolerated.[99] As well as highlighting the old problems of podmena and the lack of systematic links between different levels of the party apparatus, Shcherbitsky now said that 'a leading post is not given once and for all. The trust of the party must be earned by deeds every day and every hour.'[100] Local leaders in Kirovograd were criticised for seeing 'the trust shown to them as a right to be free from any social control and criticism' and for their conceited and arrogant belief that 'a high "chair" by itself ensures them authority and respect'.[101] In early 1982 Shcherbitsky observed that the faults in party committees were caused 'in the end' by poor personnel. He criticised several raikoms for podmena and for their failure to exercise their right of control over the administration of particular enterprises. Party supervision of PPOs was poor, and general meetings of party members were no longer occurring in some large organisations because of weak leadership from obkoms.[102] In Donetsk gorkom attempts by some raikoms 'to retain a spurious "stability" of personnel' were criticised, as was the failure of party committees to control economic administrators. It was noted that 'at three of the five gorkom plena held during 1981 there was not one critical remark addressed to the secretaries, bureau members or gorkom departments'.[103]

In Ukraine the general tone of discussion was mainly of the standard type, emphasising personnel and bureaucratic mistakes rather than abuses or crimes, although during the early 1970s and from 1979 to 1981, there were echoes of more serious charges. The stronger criticism in the early 1970s reflected a continuation under Shelest of Khrushchev's basic personnel policy of administrative pressure, but this was toned down considerably by Shcherbitsky for most of the 1970s. The resurgence of more serious charges of deception and fraud at the end of the decade was a response to increasing problems of economic maladministration in industrialised Ukraine, but this did not develop into anything approaching a fully fledged republican campaign against abuses.

BELORUSSIA

In the initial year of the Brezhnev period, the language of criticism was harsher than it was to become for much of the rest of the decade and harked back to that typical in the republic in the early 1960s. The covering up of mistakes by local party organisations was said to be associated with bossiness and commandism, with 'a wave of paper, instructions and directives, which distracts personnel from practical work'.[104] In places decision-making was concentrated in a narrow circle of leaders, with some officials abnormally promoting themselves as 'simultaneously members of the PPO bureau, members of the raikom or gorkom, members of the obkom, and deputies to the regional and city soviet etc.'.[105] This style of leadership led to abuses of power and poor supervision. A speaker at the Minsk obkom party aktiv meeting in October 1965 said: 'It is necessary to conduct an unceasing struggle with manifestations of bureaucratism, fraud, plundering of popular wealth committed by figures abusing their official positions and committing immoral offences.'[106] The problem of bossing and commandism remained despite the unification of the oblast party apparatus in late 1964. A year later a speaker at a district party conference said: 'In the district there still occur cavalier attacks on this or that lagging farm, paper-chasing and discussion of leaders at the bureau without previously studying things deeply and helping eliminate faults.'[107] Criticism of podmena continued throughout the latter half of the 1960s. This problem was linked with personnel mistakes, with the retention of many middle-level officials 'lacking initiative, who do not strive to increase their knowledge, who display coarseness and self-importance, and sometimes even have dirty hands'.[108] Many raikoms and obkoms were not giving satisfactory guidance to PPOs, but instead were trying to run everything themselves with raikom officials visiting PPOs only to prepare reports.[109] While rejecting the belief that 'the most important thing in life is to take decisions', the Mogilev obkom had 'still not succeeded in fundamentally improving the activity of party committees' which remained limited by red tape, paper-chasing and poor verification of the implementation of decisions.[110] Similar problems existed in Brest, while in Grodno and Minsk irregular meetings and infringements of collective leadership occurred.[111] Masherov in his speech to the XXVI BCP Congress in March 1966 called for an end to unnecessary regimentation of PPOs and for a 'decisive struggle against manifestations of provincialism and a narrowly bureaucratic approach to things'.[112] There was criticism in the congress resolution of party committees for infringements of Leninist principles of personnel selection and for having 'slackened demands that leading personnel fulfil party directives and observe party and state discipline'.[113]

Criticisms of local party leaders in Belorussia for complacency and forgetting the need for common discipline for both leaders and rank-and-file continued during the late 1960s.[114] In early 1968 Masherov complained that CC decisions were not being carried out because 'leading officials exaggerate existing successes, and in essence rest on their laurels'.[115] Party directives were implemented only 'superficially, unprofessionally and at times formally', and the demand for a decisive struggle against infringers of discipline had been ignored.[116] Higher party organs were criticised for failing to guide PPOs.[117] In late 1969 the CC BCP noted that: 'In particular PPOs the conditions for making high demands on leading communists have not been created, and liberalism is shown toward party members who infringe discipline'.[118] Poor links between the different levels of the party apparatus and the practice of raikoms adopting too many resolutions were basic causes of the slack discipline in PPOs. The problem of implementation was shown in February 1971 with the example of Brest obkom:

> Last year the obkom received 247 resolutions from higher party organs, demanding study and organising implementation, and itself adopted 208 resolutions. Naturally, with so many resolutions it is very difficult to organise their implementation. Indeed, many resolutions could have been avoided, and the problems raised in them resolved in the appropriate ministries, republican authorities and oblast organisations. . . . A great quantity of resolutions leads to the party apparatus wasting much time on their preparation and sometimes simply never being occupied with organising and controlling verification. Can a raikom, say, adopting 70–80 resolutions per year on important problems, ensure that they are put into life. Analysis shows that this is difficult to do.[119]

Masherov said at the XXVII BCP Congress that the CC Bureau and party apparatus in Minsk were partly responsible for the poor party supervision of raikoms and PPOs. He called for an end to petty tutelage and podmena in economic leadership, and said no leniency should be shown toward party officials who committed abuses, citing the December 1969 CC CPSU slogan of 'a combination of discipline with the broad initiative of officials'.[120] This was a variation on the combination of discipline with elite stability which was espoused by republican party leaders in the early 1970s in Central Asia, Kazakhstan, and to a lesser extent in Ukraine.

Pressure on local party officials for more regular and

responsible administrative work was maintained in Belorussia during the first half of the 1970s. In July 1971 Masherov called on party bureaux to inform plena periodically about their activities. He demanded more attention to cadre work, complaining that 'we often meet cases when particular party members conduct themselves improperly, ignore the opinion of the collective, and infringe the norms of our morals, yet party organisations do not show the necessary concern for principle and punishment'. He also observed that: 'Often the selection of personnel is reduced to a mechanical filling of vacant posts. As a result unreliable people are sometimes found in responsible posts.'[121] The following month he hinted at the need for forms of control similar to those used by Khrushchev, implicitly recognising the failure of party mechanisms to achieve this end: 'Separation from the electors and weak control from party committees and ispolkoms leads particular soviet officials and even leaders to lose modesty and commit abuses of their official positions.'[122] In Mogilev it was noted in 1972 that: 'As a consequence of insufficient knowledge of personnel and of hastiness, incompetent people are often advanced to leading work, which in turn leads to a frequent turnover of leading personnel.'[123] In Gomel', where the oblast elite had been changed following criticism of agricultural failures in *Pravda* in late 1969,[124] the faults remained while the new leaders waited for instructions from above about almost everything.[125] In early 1974 agricultural problems in Gomel' were attributed to the failure of party committees to restructure their work to eliminate formalism, showiness, complacency and fraud.[126] This had been acknowledged as a broader problem at the CC BCP plenum in December 1973, when it was noted that: 'The apparat as before is excessively occupied with collecting and compiling different kinds of reports and assessments, and spends an unjustifiably large time on sessions and meetings.' Party committees were again told to 'fundamentally restructure their personnel work', considering not just political loyalty and professional competence but also the ability of officials to meet new demands to improve economic efficiency.[127] A September 1974 discussion of a CC CPSU decision on the selection and education of ideological cadres in Belorussia, noted that although work in the BCP was being conducted 'largely in a correct fashion', there were still 'serious faults', principally in the neglect of practical activity.[128] At the end of the year there were references to the over-regulation of meetings whereby only official speakers with prepared texts were able to speak, and to the need for higher bodies to 'strictly question officials who infringe party and state discipline and abuse their official positions'.[129] In March 1975 the report about the exchange of party documents in Belorussia was critical of gorkoms, raikoms and PPOs for not using this exchange to strengthen discipline, which was needed to stop 'the incorrect conduct of particular communists, especially leading personnel'. The 'extraordinary belief in the force of paper' held by local party leaders was again criticised, and officials who suppressed criticism were warned that they might be dismissed.[130]

The criticism of officials in Belorussia in the early 1970s seems to have been more sustained than it was in the other republics, and this was maintained for the remainder of the Brezhnev period. In July 1975 Masherov called for an end to euphemisms in personnel work:

> The completely impermissible practice in some of our obkoms, gorkoms and raikoms of resorting to different convenient formulae when sacking officials who have compromised themselves and not justified trust, like they have been sacked according to a statement they have given or in connection with a transfer to other work, deserves sharp criticism and condemnation. Acting thus, party committees as it were knowingly whitewash unsuitable officials, thereby bringing harm to the task of correctly educating personnel in a spirit of great watchfulness, unwillingness to compromise and utmost honesty.... Meanwhile we have not got rid of leaders, even of a high rank, who recommend and insistently affirm figures with whom they are friendly to very important posts.

Masherov criticised duplicitous officials, those with 'two faces', and 'luminaries... who consider that nobody can work better, see further and run an economy more cleverly than them'. He observed that the promotion of new creative leaders 'gives the "luminaries by service" a feeling of unhealthy jealousy and envy', with the result that some of them 'resort to different kinds of contrivances, padding and abuses' in an attempt to get even.[131] In September 1975 it was reported that Minsk obkom plena often left faults 'in the dark', while gorkoms and raikoms 'at times permit a liberal attitude and a lack of principle regarding leaders who infringe party and state discipline'.[132] At the Minsk oblast party conference in December it was noted that, while the obkom regularly considered personnel matters, there were still serious failings. It still happens that 'casual people lacking initiative are given leading posts', and officials who misuse their positions or fail to meet targets are often treated leniently. 'Some party committees have still not overcome the pernicious practice of reassigning from place to place officials who have failed, and permit a great turnover of personnel, above all kolkhoz chairmen and sovkhoz directors.'[133] Failures of personnel work remained in Vitebsk, where plena discussions were superficial and there was inadequate organisational work on the ground.[134]

In his speech to the XXVIII BCP Congress in February 1976, Masherov said the role of obkoms, gorkoms and raikoms in ensuring economic efficiency had grown, but some gorkoms and raikoms had not overcome the old faults of bureaucratism and self-praise. He said some officials, including a raikom first secretary, had been sacked for abusing their positions, and complained that some party committees listened to reports from the same organisations on the same problems several times.[135] The focus on economic efficiency was maintained in a resolution in March 1976 on deficiencies in the spring sowing which observed that: 'Obkoms and raikoms display liberalism in relation to careless officials who permit with impunity many cases of economic waste that are almost criminal.'[136] From mid-1976 criticism began to be concentrated increasingly on obkoms such as Vitebsk and Brest run by the anti-Masherov group of Brezhnev clients, whereas improvements including a regular procedure for verifying implementation were noted in other obkoms such as Gomel'.[137] In July 1976 Vitebsk obkom was criticised for not specifying officials responsible for faults, and for allowing a high turnover of personnel and substantial embezzlement. The CC BCP resolution stated that: 'It is necessary decisively to sack leaders who have lost the capacity critically to evaluate their work, have lost the trust of communists, have lost touch with the masses and incorrectly react to criticism, perceiving justified remarks addressed to them as undermining their authority, and who place personal self-love above social interests.'¹³⁸ There were serious personnel mistakes in Kobrin raikom, where in 'the past year and a half every fourth official in the raikom's nomenklatura has been replaced'; the raikom was also alleged to have been drowning in paperwork.¹³⁹ In March 1977 Masherov responded to oblast resistance to his demands: 'Some simply whine and whimper, others speak about super difficulties, calling into question the reality of the proposed demands, and consequently conduct themselves with some passivity. A third lot simply quibble, not wanting to take on added responsibility and to work at the maximum possible intensity.' Masherov listed several local party leaders 'sacked for abusing official positions and other infringements of the norms of party life' since the XXVIII BCP Congress in the previous year. Referring to party committees who turned a blind eye to immorality, he said 'such a "protective approach" is often motivated by false concepts and understandings about supporting the authority of a leader'. While unintended mistakes could be forgiven, Masherov stressed he would not tolerate 'those who deliberately distort the real results of work, consciously cover up faults, and knowingly send to higher party and state organs false information and inflated reports in which the situation is presented not as it actually is on the ground'.¹⁴⁰ Two months later Brest obkom was criticised for not condemning serious offences in a raikom¹⁴¹ and in October there was criticism of bureaucratism, abuse of official position and the falsification of results.¹⁴² In November 1977 it was reported that despite improvements in Mozyr' raikom, there were still 'cases when party organisations show tolerance and liberalism toward communists who infringe party discipline and commit offences'.¹⁴³ In July 1978 Masherov criticised the 'tolerant attitude of some party committees' showing 'boundless liberalism' towards 'politically immature people' involved in bribery and fraud, and to leaders who failed to draw serious conclusions from prior criticism.¹⁴⁴

During his last two years in power before dying in a car crash in October 1980, Masherov began to draw broader conclusions in response to the failure of his basic policy of administrative pressure to produce results. In December 1978 he said some gorkoms and raikoms were still conducting personnel work 'episodically, often lack principle and are shortsighted' Verification was often 'purely formal', with investigators being 'satisfied with mere reports, prepared by those they investigate, and these admittedly safe documents are passed off as the material of investigations'. This formalism could have been overcome if party organs had used their right of control over administrations instead of tolerating chronic faults in economic leadership, like falsification and fraud. Formal cadre work had facilitated abuses of authority, which must be ended through sacking, expelling and bringing to trial those who defraud the state and their protectors.[145] In June 1979 Masherov highlighted the 'special danger' presented by 'the still not eliminated cases of fabrication and fraud, when attempts are made to cover up an inability to organise things with the help of all kinds of cheating, machinations and trickery. . . . Such figures, as a rule, attract into their anti-state actions a great number of officials and literally corrupt them.'[146] He said these faults should not be tolerated, but should be rooted out. In November Masherov commented with regard to economic failures that:

> In short, whatever aspect of economic life we look at, everything rests on the level of management and the quality of administration. A radical restructuring of work is needed in all branches, and at all levels a fundamental, decisive breaking-up of outdated methods of running things is necessary. Here we cannot get by with partial solutions, half-measures and patching or darning old holes in traditionally established practice.[147]

Masherov continued to criticise the failure to act against fraud and falsification and the practice of 'the same censured or failed officials travelling from one armchair to another, replacing each other'.[148] In May 1980 he said 'we have not fully succeeded in turning public opinion against such immoral phenomena as waste, inefficiency, fraud, bureaucratism, a callous attitude to people and business for the benefit of personal interests'. He attacked leaders who 'still try to live at society's expense and acquire for themselves cheap authority and an inflated popularity', a description which clearly could be read as applying beyond Belorussia. Falsification and fraud in the economic sphere and toleration of them remained key problems.[149] At the last two CC BCP plena he attended in mid-1980, Masherov called again for an end to formalism in economic leadership and cadre work, declaring: 'it is completely obvious that showiness, clamouring and abstract pronouncements do not bring success'.[150]

The criticism expressed at the oblast party conferences in Belorussia three months after Kiselev became BCP leader was comparatively restrained, referring to bureaucratism and poor verification but not the abuses of authority that Masherov had highlighted.[151] At the XXIX BCP Congress in early 1981 Kiselev said many obkoms, gorkoms and raikoms committed serious personnel mistakes but he did not follow Masherov in describing the consequences of this as intolerably evil.[152] The congress resolution was forthright. It criticised poor personnel work, the toleration of faults, inefficiency, falsification, bureaucratism, paper-chasing and misuse (not abuse) of official positions. But by this time such criticism was standard, even in Ukraine. The conservative BCP second secretary Brovikov referred critically in September 1981 to the way in which many party committees 'not only do not demand a lot from personnel, but commit liberalism and intrigue with them. It is very bad that particular party and soviet officials arrange their relations with managers on an unprofessional basis, take part with them in different drinking contests, putting themselves in a false, ambiguous position.'[153] Kiselev even criticised some party committees for operating a 'personnel merry-go-round', replacing some leaders before they could become established in a position.[154] In February 1982 Kiselev criticised showiness and a superficial approach to questions, and observed that 'not all leaders who engage in falsification and fraud have been replaced'.[155]

The course of discussion of party affairs in Belorussia was broadly similar to that in the other republics during the second half of the 1960s. During the 1970s and early 1980s, while the criticism of standard bureaucratic party failings remained prominent, this was supplemented by a harsher tone suggesting abuses rather than mistakes and raising broader questions about central policy under Brezhnev. This seems to have been fuelled by Masherov, appearing to be somewhat moderated in the short period after his death. But while Masherov's vigorous criticism of personnel problems in the second half of the 1970s stands out as remarkable for the time, even this tone of harsher criticism did not amount to the sort of campaign evident in the early 1960s and later in the 1980s in Central Asia and Kazakhstan.

THE BREZHNEV PATTERN

Throughout the Brezhnev period there was a big increase in the autonomy of republican leaders from central control. While qualifications were made by the centre to the basic policy of administrative stability, in no case studied here was there any central intervention similar to Khrushchev's policy of pressuring leading personnel on the ground. Visits by the central leadership increasingly became ceremonial not substantive, reflecting the actual growth in the authority of republican leaderships. Significant policy differences in the Brezhnev period concerning the key problem of personnel mistakes existed between republican leaderships in various regions of the USSR. In Central Asia criticism of personnel mistakes and poor party supervision was largely ritualistic. Harsh criticism of irregular methods of party supervision and abuses of authority by officials was relatively rare in Uzbekistan and Tajikistan under Brezhnev, coinciding mainly with the period in the late 1960s and early 1970s when there was relatively strong central criticism of such abuses. In Kazakhstan there was a similar pattern during this period, though the general tone of criticism in the late 1960s was more radical than in Central Asia. During the mid-1970s there continued to be more qualifications of the 'trust in cadres' principle in Kazakhstan than in Central Asia, but there was no sustained campaign against abuses. By the early 1980s corruption was acknowledged in Kazakhstan, but, as in Central Asia, it was described officially as only an isolated problem. In Ukraine and Belorussia there was initial resistance from republican leaders to the 'trust in cadres' policy, which did not occur in Central Asia or Kazakhstan. After Shelest's replacement by Shcherbitsky in 1972, the nature of criticism in Ukraine was relaxed, and by the late 1970s it resembled Kazakhstan, though with greater attention to problems of economic fraud. In contrast to previous periods of harsh criticism under Khrushchev, the most sustained criticism of personnel abuses throughout the Brezhnev period occurred in Belorussia in the second half of the 1970s. Indeed this was the only republic where the criticism of personnel problems during the Brezhnev period bore some similarity in tone to the criticism under Khrushchev and Gorbachev.

4 Radicalism During the 1980s

The 1980s saw a surge of centrally sponsored reform in the Soviet Union. Initiated by Yuri Andropov even before he became General Secretary, this reformist urge could not be halted by his short-term successor Konstantin Chernenko, and took off with a vengeance under Mikhail Gorbachev. The Gorbachev period witnessed a process of radicalisation of reform culminating in the escape of that reform from central control and the resultant collapse of the USSR. Initially the reform publicly sponsored by Gorbachev was strictly limited in scope, encompassing change in the economic sphere with only limited attention being given to political matters. However, under the influence of various pressures, this focus soon widened, until by late in the 1980s many in the leadership acknowledged the need for wholesale change in the Soviet system.

From the outset, the central leadership recognised that change at lower levels was essential. This is reflected in the early prominence given to corruption in various parts of the Soviet Union, including Kazakhstan, Kirgizia, Turkmenistan, Moldavia, Uzbekistan and Azerbaijan.[1] Within six weeks of becoming General Secretary, Gorbachev had called for the elimination of those leaders who conducted personnel policy on the basis of 'personal loyalty, servility and protectionism'.[2] During the summer of 1984, the Rashidov affair in Uzbekistan had burst onto the public scene (see Chapter 6) with reports of widespread personnel abuses, including protectionism, favouring of people from the same region of origin and arrogance, combined with forgery and attempts to defraud the state.[3] These reports became more specific in the lead up to the XXVII CPSU Congress in February–March 1986, with Rashidov's 'depraved style' blamed for the protection of 'major state criminals' and the cruel persecution of 'honest communists who tried to expose the offenders and speak the truth'.[4] From 1986 the extent of corruption in the country began to be revealed publicly.[5] Gorbachev's initial response to this problem was to replace many republican and oblast leaders. By the end of 1986 five of the 14 republican party leaders had been replaced (in Georgia, Kirgizia, Tajikistan, Turkmenistan and Kazakhstan[6]), while between March 1985 and July 1986 50 kraikom and obkom first secretaries (of a total of 157) had been replaced (following the 40 replaced in 1983 and 1984). Yet reports about corruption continued at a high level in 1986,[7] including some which involved relatively recent appointments, like Usmankhodzhaev who had succeeded Rashidov in late 1983.[8] It was partly in response to this persistence of corruption (concerns about economic reform were also important) that Gorbachev first called for democratisation of the party in January 1987, and then allowed a major relaxation of censorship under the renewed meaning of 'glasnost'.[9] This concern with the problems of lower-level personnel policy was maintained into the post-XIX Conference period, when the changes Gorbachev made to party personnel procedures and the growth of other problems pushed this issue from the forefront of his attention.

UZBEKISTAN

In the period between Brezhnev's death and the election of Gorbachev, the emphasis on economic leadership by party organs remained paramount, but this did include vigorous and harsh criticism of the performance of party leaders. In January 1983 the CC CPUz called on party organisations to struggle against uneconomic practice, slackness, squandering and waste of socialist property, eyewash, drunkenness and hooliganism, while the following month the plunder of socialist property, bribery and speculation came under criticism.[10] All of this demanded increased criticism and self-criticism in party life, a theme which remained throughout the year. During 1984 attention was directed to the way in which officials who had been involved in serious failings like deception, eyewash and abuse of official position were often merely transferred to another post.[11] At the XVI plenum of the CC CPUz[12] there was strong criticism of the way in which party organs had not struggled against the squandering of state means, deception and eyewash, abuse of official position, embezzlement, bribery, showiness and self-praise. In some areas there had been familyness, localism and protectionism along with the abuse of official position. In obkom plena following the CC plenum, there was criticism[13] of the lack of collegial leadership, amoralism, appointments on the basis of kinship and common region of origin, subjectivism, arrogance, an insulting attitude to people, forgery, eyewash, deception, false reporting, and 'victorious' reports only on paper. The vigour of these sorts of criticism was maintained intermittently throughout the remainder of the interregnum. Despite the claimed introduction of some measures to deal with these abuses, problems remained; there was still formalism and showiness in work as well as abuse of position, moral degradation and the ignoring of unsatisfactory conduct by individual leaders.[14] In early 1985 party committees were still being called upon[15] to eliminate from cadre work protectionism, selection on the basis of kin, common region of origin and considerations of personal devotion. Such failings continued to be criticised in the following months.[16]

The vigour of the criticism mounted during the interregnum was maintained following Gorbachev's succession to the party leadership. In late March 1985 at the CC CPUz plenum there was criticism of protectionism and the placement of leading workers on the basis of personal devotion, friendship, kinship or common region of origin, the promotion of people who have compromised themselves and the weakness of the struggle against money-grubbing, accumulation, abuse of official position, embezzlement, bribery, deception and eyewash, official misdemeanours, and a private property psychology.[17] At the local party conferences in late 1985 and early 1986 continuing cases of fraud were reported in Tashkent gorkom and many obkoms, such as Kashkadar (where the oblast leadership had been completely changed), Fergana, Surkhandar'ia, Navoi, Khorezm and Bukhara, as well as Tashkent, where the obkom had positively evaluated corrupt raikom secretaries.[18] A liberal attitude towards those who had compromised themselves, deception, the squandering of socialist property, embezzlement, mutual guarantees, familyness and clannish behaviour, localism, reliance upon those from the same region, abuse of office, money-grubbing, moral decay, false reporting and bribery were all reported to be deficiencies that needed to be combated.

At the XXI CPUz Congress in January 1986 Usmankhodzhaev claimed[19] that most abuses did not occur on the initiative of party organisations, instead attributing blame to his predecessor, Sharaf Rashidov. He argued that in the last years there had been crude infringements of party norms and morals and of Soviet laws, and serious deficiencies in the leadership of the economy. There was widespread false reporting, bribery and plunder, promotion on the basis of personal devotion, servility and protectionism, and weak criticism and self-criticism (quoting Gorbachev from April 1985). Successes were attributed to the leader, with the cult of the leader hiding the real state of affairs in the republic. A depraved style prevailed in the party, with showiness and self-glorification, ignorance of criticism and self-criticism, and the loss of modesty and of party and human decency led to intrigue, dodging of responsibility, formalism, indifference, abuse of official position and embezzlement. Promotion occurred on the basis of kinship, common region of origin, personal devotion and mercenary considerations. Under such conditions all types of self-seekers and rascals, bribe-takers, embezzlers and traitors to the party's cause prospered. In an attempt to exculpate himself, Usmankhodzhaev declared that those in leading posts at the time found themselves under the hypnotism of Rashidov's personality and were unable to oppose his will.

At the XXVII CPSU Congress[20] Usmankhodzhaev agreed with the criticisms of Uzbekistan made by Gorbachev in his speech, and again attacked the nature of Rashidov's leadership in similar, if less detailed, terms to those above. He also declared that a healthy atmosphere now prevailed in the republic, but in May a CC CPUz decision charged that Rashidov was in significant measure personally responsible for the 'atmosphere of showiness, complacency and anything goes ... deception of the government and localism, the promotion of cadres ... in many cases ... on the basis of kinship, common region of origin, personal devotion and servility and were often prompted by considerations of profit'.[21] By July[22] Usmankhodzhaev was complaining about how in some party committees, the issuing of numerous documents and giving of speeches supplanted real leadership over lower-level bodies. There were decisions made by single people, a dictatorial style, showiness and a sense of indisputability. Complacency and cover-ups and abuse of official position were also noted in the press, as was the creation of an illusion of well-being due to the functioning of nepotism in the appointment of ideological officials.[23]

While 90 local leaders were removed in Bukhara obkom during 1985 and 1986, deception, a rejection of change and a lack of collegiality remained prevalent.[24] It was claimed that party officials often were not characterised by collegiality and frankness, by demandingness and consistency in the adoption of decisions and supervision over their implementation. There was a lack of personal responsibility and of democracy in the functioning of many party organs. A few weeks later, a strengthening of socialist legality and of criticism and self-criticism was called for in the face of many cases of false reporting, deception, embezzlement, bribery and other cases of abuse of position.[25]

These sorts of charges continued to be made in February and March 1987. The need for a stronger struggle against protectionism, national conceit, bribery, familyness and favouritism towards those sharing region of origin, despite the replacement of 750 leaders during 1986 including eight obkom secretaries and 100 gorkom and raikom secretaries, was noted at the IV CC CPUz plenum in February 1987.[26] This message was reiterated in March, but reports followed of more fraud, abuse of position, familyness, promotion on the basis of region of origin and personal devotion, servility, suppression of criticism, deception, false reporting, nepotism, formalism, mutual guarantees, a liberal attitude to those who infringe, reliance upon a 'nomenklatura circle' who move from post to post, and a restriction of political reform in obkoms previously criticised.[27] The level of fraud was said to have increased in the last half of 1986 and the first quarter of 1987.[28]

In the middle of the year there was another flurry of discussion of abuses in party life, particularly following the publication of the CC CPSU decision on the situation in the Tashkent oblast party organisation.[29] The discussion noted that the obkom was not operating satisfactorily. The rate of party entry had been artificially forced with the result that many people who were unsuitable were able to enter the party. Some collectives had developed an atmosphere that everything was permitted and mutual guarantees existed that led to abuse of power and moral decline; many people who had entered the party were subsequently expelled for criminal activities. Protectionism and acceptance of timeservers into the party remained widespread according to the second secretary Anishchev in August 1987. He declared that the problems that had been identified in Tashkent were present throughout the republic, mentioning specifically formalism, protectionism, kin and common region of origin favouritism. Too many party committees were too tolerant of abuses and deficiencies.[30] Yet despite these well-publicised problems, in local party conferences during the last part of the year, only eight raikom and two gorkom secretaries were sacked, even though 184 report and election meetings were so disorganised that they had to be repeated.[31] One reason for this may have been the high turnover of officials which had already occurred. Half the workers in the CC CPUz apparat, 40 per cent of obkom, gorkom and raikom secretaries and 45 per cent of ispolkom chairmen were sacked during 1986 and 1987, according to Anishchev, who thought the nomenklatura system of appointments from above needed to be kept in order to ensure that suitable people remained in top jobs.[32]

In his first major speech as first secretary in early 1988, Usmankhodzhaev's successor Nishanov criticised the former leadership in Uzbekistan for failing to struggle with corruption in the cotton industry, and singled out the leaders of Bukhara, Kashkadar, Khorezm, Surkhandar'ia and Tashkent obkoms and Karakalpak kraikom for defrauding the state. He called for a struggle against embezzlement, false reporting, deception, eyewash and bribery, and said that the cadre corps had to be cleansed from the rust of corruption, from the idea that everything is permitted, from mutual guarantees. He criticised the attempts to promote 'comfortable' people based on kinship and common region of origin, and called for the elimination of 'vozhdism' and areas free from criticism. He said the bureaucratic style of the organisational-party work department, which used telephone leadership now more than in the past, was unsatisfactory.[33] The resolutions from this CC CPUz plenum said the Bureau and Secretariat must support the democratisation of party life, with more attention to glasnost' and increased participation of members of elected organs in decision-making.[34]

During 1988 there was increasing criticism of Rashidov's

legacy in Uzbekistan. The press published criticism of self-serving nomenklatura officials from an ordinary worker, who said the continued circulation of failed officials between armchairs in Tashkent had caused stagnation, abuses and crimes. He said that the 'high bureaucratic elite' was characterised by localism, bribery, corruption, the growth of family dynasties and kinship clans, and the party had become littered with careerists, eyewashers, toadies and those engaged in pokazuka.[35] Oblast officials in Andizhan, Samarkand and Nukus were still able to control completely the process of selecting delegates to the XIX CPSU Conference,[36] while in August an article in the press called for a decisive struggle against pokazuka, mutual guarantees, protectionism and organised crime in cadre policy.[37] In response to the increasingly critical coverage of Uzbekistan in the central press, Nishanov in an interview in September 1988 tried to present a positive picture of the party as overcoming the problems that flowed from the Rashidov cadre policy based on common region of origin and kin relations, and democratising itself with many new leaders elected,[38] but in October the first secretaries of Samarkand and Bukhara obkoms were sacked for abusing their positions, and criticism was renewed of the practice of selecting personnel based on kinship, clan, common region of origin and on the principle 'I am for you, you are for me'.[39] This was followed by the reprinting from *Izvestiia* of a major expose of corruption under Rashidov.[40]

In contrast to Nishanov's claims, the actual democratisation of party life in Uzbekistan was limited. Only 12 gorkom and raikom secretaries (including five first secretaries) were elected on a competitive basis in 1988, and only two-thirds of PPO secretaries and members of gorkom and raikom bureaux in Tashkent city were elected from two or more candidates.[41] Only two months before the March 1989 elections, the chairman of the Uzbek Supreme Soviet Khabibullaev was exposed as corrupt and allowed to shift to academic work after repenting.[42] A month later the second secretary of Tashkent obkom reasserted the need for vetting by 'the most authoritative communists' of candidates for election to the Congress of People's Deputies, and decried the growth of 'meeting democracy'.[43] After the elections Nishanov, in his last report before moving to Moscow as chairman of the Soviet of Nationalities, acknowledged that the party apparatus in parts of Uzbekistan continued to operate in the old way, through paper creation and telephone orders.[44] He viewed the disturbances in Fergana in early June 1989 as evidence of the isolation of the party from society and its inability to both eliminate corruption and stop the rise of new opponents like the Birlik movement. He also criticised those who sought to cover up their false reporting, embezzlement, bribery, and abuse of position.[45] In the first half of 1989, the level and vigour of criticism seems to have declined compared with what it had been in 1987–88. Following Karimov's replacement of Nishanov in June 1989, there seems to have been a further significant downgrading of discussion of intra-party affairs.

The discussion of the unrest in Fergana in the CC CPUz Bureau blamed the oblast organs, especially the obkom bureau, for allowing nationalist and corrupt elements to use ethnic differences and religious sentiment to destabilise the socio-political situation in Uzbekistan. Protectionism had produced an atmosphere of mutual backscratching amongst local officials who permitted all sorts of abuses and did not act against discredited leaders.[46] In August Karimov said criticism of the party was linked to social and economic problems which the restructuring of the party apparatus had not resolved.[47] Personnel work was still limited by an unhealthy moral-psychological climate, with party members divided into superiors and inferiors.[48] Whilst Karimov supported the elimination of Article 6 in early January 1990, he opposed fractionalism and warned after the republican elections that oppositional activity would not be tolerated.[49] Under Karimov the calls for economic independence and republican sovereignty made by Nishanov and other Uzbek speakers at the Congress of People's Deputies in June 1989 were repeated and extended.[50] But the Uzbek party continued to experience problems of poor quality supervision with oblast officials demanding reports from gorkom and raikom workers rather than helping them solve vital social and economic problems.[51] Protectionism was still tolerated, so that while more local officials were being elected on a competitive basis, tendencies of localism and the emergence of cliques were often apparent in the election of leading organs.[52] The use of multi-candidate elections within the party developed only to a low level in Uzbekistan before the top leaders became most concerned about emerging opponents who sought to challenge the established hierarchy of power in the republic. The reorganisations of the party apparatus in 1989 neither resolved the old problem of inadequate party supervision, nor enabled party officials to acquire new forms of political influence necessary for open political competition. By 1991 Karimov was reinstating many corrupt officials sacked in the mid-1980s, as well as repressing the Birlik movement more severely than informal groups were being repressed elsewhere in the USSR.[53] This showed that despite a sustained campaign of severe criticism which developed in Uzbekistan during the 1980s and reached exceptional intensity during early 1988, the tradition of protecting failed officials remained strongly entrenched.

TAJIKISTAN

Throughout most of 1983 little attention was devoted to problems in the personnel area, although there was some criticism of unsatisfactory leadership by higher-standing party organs and insufficient activity in the struggle against such blights as misappropriation of socialist property, bribery, speculation, parasitism and other infringements of Soviet law.[54] Party organs had to be demanding rather than adopt a liberal attitude to such deficiencies. Throughout 1984 party work was generally portrayed as being in a healthy state, although in August there was criticism of the way in which a liberal attitude to cadres had allowed infringements and abuses, the reporting of officials who had compromised themselves, and attempts to suppress criticism and self-criticism.[55] But such criticism was not the main tenor of party discussion during this period.

At the end of March 1985 the CC CPT discussed the cadre question. First secretary Nabiev noted shortcomings in cadre policy whereby some who held leading posts had sought to deceive party and state, to use official position for personal ends, were not self-critical, were immodest and infringed discipline. There was complacency over shortcomings, a lack of criticism, and cadre questions were resolved by a narrow circle of people, behind closed doors.[56] For most of the rest of the year, discussion of the party was restricted to its role in economic leadership, although in December there was criticism of formalism and paper-creation, haste in cadre promotions, and immodesty and personal enrichment among leading cadres.[57] At the beginning of 1986, new first secretary Makhkamov criticised the way in which many leading party organs were not aware of the real state of affairs at lower levels, how some people had sought to use their official positions for profitable ends, the toleration of abuses and slackness, localism, the promotion of workers on the basis of personal devotion, kinship and common region of origin, and the tendency in some party organs to paper-creation and speech-making.[58] In April, Gorno-Badakhshan oblast party leaders were called upon to do away with conducting their work behind closed doors and exercising telephone leadership.[59]

In early 1987 there was criticism of the way in which party organs were complacent about false reporting and eyewash, the lack of criticism and abuses.[60] Makhkamov claimed the CC CPT was struggling with abuses of privilege, false reporting, abuse of office and protectionism. He said that there were still cases of protectionism, favouring those from the same region, localism and the formation on these bases of kinship-family groupings, of mutual guarantees; local leaders still took care of 'necessary' or 'comfortable' people.[61] This picture was confirmed by reports of local party plena,[62] although these were less negative than in Uzbekistan and there seems to have been an effort to emphasise positive aspects of party performance. There was little stringent criticism of the party during the rest of the year, although in December there was criticism of tolerance towards abuses, personal immodesty, criminal acts and the enjoyment of special privileges, and of infringements of collectivism in leadership and the lack of practical leadership given by higher-standing bodies; localism, protectionism and favouritism toward those from the same region were also present.[63]

There was resistance to democratisation of the party in Tajikistan, where protectionism, appointment on the basis of kinship and common region of origin, petty tutelage and podmena continued due to the persistence of old methods of appointment. Paper-creation, excessive speech-making, and the conduct of business behind closed doors still occurred, while a liberal attitude to criminal acts and abuses such as false reporting, embezzlement and economic mismanagement was still present. While 130 out of 427 nomenklatura workers in Ordzhonikidzeabad gorkom had been replaced in two years, only eight new officials had faced competitive election.[64] The absence of a demanding approach towards those who had discredited themselves and the failure to respond to cases of false reporting, distortion, embezzlement and other infringements were criticised in June.[65] In November a gorkom secretary was removed for groupism, a development that was linked with the improved working of the party committee.[66] However, elsewhere there was still said to be a commandist approach with work conducted behind closed doors.[67] For the remainder of the period there was little discussion of party life despite the measures introduced in January 1989 to restructure the party apparatus.[68] The head of the CPT organisational-party work department claimed in September 1988 that between a third and a half of PPO secretaries had just faced competitive election, a fact which was still stressed after the March 1989 elections to the Congress of People's Deputies.[69] Yet only a handful of gorkom and raikom secretaries had faced competitive election in 1988 (seven including two first secretaries compared to three including one first secretary in 1987).[70] The reduction during 1989 in the republican and obkom apparatus failed to eliminate corruption and could not prevent the manifestation of nepotism, protectionism, localism and nationalism during public elections, nor avert the anti-party protests which erupted in February 1990.[71] The level and vigour of criticism generally in Tajikistan was lower than in Uzbekistan over the same period, particularly during 1984–85 before the replacement of Nabiev as first secretary, but it matches the Uzbekistan pattern in tailing off significantly in 1989.

KAZAKHSTAN

Little attention was devoted to party life in the Kazakh press during the interregnum. There were reports of bribery of law and order officials, the sacking of nomenklatura officials for incompetence and corruption, and falsification and abuse of position,[72] as well as some complaints about weak leadership from above, but there was no continuing discussion of serious deficiencies in the party's internal operating regime.

In March 1985 Kunaev claimed that the existence 'of abuse of official positions, of protectionism, careerism and other unfavourable conduct' was limited to only 'isolated leading communists'. In May he said this was being dealt with through the intervention of the republican CC.[73] This message that corruption was under control was also espoused by the obkom leaders of Dzhambul and Chimkent, two of the most notoriously corrupt oblasts. In the latter the former obkom boss was accused of allowing 'the moving around of failed officials from one leading chair to another', abuse of official positions, personal immodesty, infringement of party ethics, and allowing pilfering, falsification and speculation.[74] But by late 1985 the need for 'more objective and reliable information from the localities' was noted, and Kunaev even referred to 'a noticeable desire to hush up faults and smooth over sharp issues' at some party conferences.[75] Pressure for reform intensified in December 1985, when the continuation of 'croneyism and nepotistic ties' and abuse of position in Alma Ata, Pavlodar, Chimkent and Ural obkoms were reported despite the large numbers of nomenklatura officials sacked during 1984 and 1985; in Alma Ata 28 out of 107 officials replaced had faced criminal charges, while in Chimkent abuses continued even after 480 officials on the obkom nomenklatura had been sacked.[76] In February 1986, at the last plenum before the KCP Congress, Kunaev said the sacking in the past five years of more than 500 officials on the CC nomenklatura had been necessary to overcome 'a degeneration and constipation of personnel'.[77] While acknowledging the existence of serious personnel mistakes in the recent past, he implied that they no longer constituted a major concern in Kazakhstan.

At the XVI KCP Congress in February 1986, Nazarbaev described the party's situation in much more serious terms. He said that 'there are still negative consequences from the established style in the oblasts, which has not been overcome, of thrusting forth isolated successes and eulogising raion and oblast officialdom for inessential services. All of this has become possible because the leadership of the republic has not stamped out such useless methods of work promptly and in a fundamentally party-interested way.' After attacking corrupt party leaders and law and order officials for 'entering into conspiracies with plunderers of national wealth', Nazarbaev said serious personnel mistakes were a result of the lack of collegiality in the republican CC apparatus.[78] There was criticism by long-standing Kustanai obkom boss Demidenko of republican officials for ordering just as many unnecessary reports from obkoms as before, even using special couriers to avoid registration.[79] Nazarbaev continued his attack on Kunaev at the XXVII CPSU Congress, saying that 'under the pretext of stability, there was created a stagnation of officials in high posts. This gave rise to conditions of eulogising and anything goes, which put such leaders beyond criticism, so that in places the requirement of a careful attitude toward personnel was distorted by the forgiving and permitting of everything, which led to infringements of party and state discipline.'[80] This message was reinforced during a May visit to Kazakhstan by CC secretary Dobrynin, who called for 'the decisive elimination of protectionism and of the atmosphere of permissiveness and "infallibility" created sometimes around certain leading persons'.[81] Kunaev reiterated his view on the need to trust personnel at the IV CC KCP plenum in late August, but fraud, abuse of position by leading personnel, the armchair style of leadership, deception and a lack of practical leadership continued to be reported as widespread around the time of his removal in December 1986.[82]

Following criticism of the 'prolonged' lack of openness and democratic norms in the KCP, the new leader Kolbin began 1987 with a strong attack on protectionism, saying: 'We must decisively root out the principle "I am for you, you are for me".' He rebuked old leaders who had 'turned into the kind of homegrown prince whose habit is not to work but to "be royal"', so much so that they had forgotten how to prepare their own speeches.[83] He called for the regularisation of party meetings, insisting that specific party meetings be held only on Tuesdays and Thursdays, with party plena held only on Saturdays, to make sure party officials increased their organisational work in order to improve the parlous economic state of Kazakhstan.[84] Two sessions of the CC KCP Bureau were held within a week, at which the sacking of two raikom first secretaries for podmena and one for nepotism was discussed.[85] Kolbin told the next plenum, held on the Saturday after his attacks on protectionism and nepotism, that immodest leaders would be sacked, and it was decided that all senior party officials must undergo a process of certification to determine their suitability for leading work; replacing officials only by someone from the same nationality was to be eliminated.[86] Despite the fact that the official charged with ensuring this was only a deputy head of the CC propaganda department,[87] this was a much more intensive procedure than the exchange of party documents in the early 1970s had been. In February 1987 reports continued about protectionism, 'local vozhdism', fraud, embezzlement, nepotism and corruption.[88] Kolbin told obkom first secretaries at the end of that month that ordinary people wanted an end to 'the manifestation of family "dynasties" of leading officials', and he warned them against manipulating competitive elections through personal contacts.[89] Whatever the extent of popular support for his new Russian broom, Kolbin clearly made a major effort to overcome the poor supervision and corruption characteristic of the KCP under Kunaev. His criticism of personnel affairs was much more thorough and systematic than the practice of Russian leaders in Kazakhstan in the second half of the 1950s, and was a clear contrast with the Brezhnev-era exchange of party documents in the early 1970s. It is comparable only with Yusupov's brief attack in 1963 and 1964 on the narrowness and closed nature even then of the nomenklatura in Kazakhstan.

Discussion of Gorbachev's first proposals for political reform coincided in Kazakhstan with these attacks on Kunaev. There was, according to a letter cited by Kolbin at the VIII CC KCP plenum in March, 'a whole layer who were willy nilly interested in retaining their caste privileges and who did not flinch from using the poisonous weapon of nationalism for this purpose'. He blamed the riots in Alma Ata at the time of his appointment on those involved in protectionism, which had become a pervasive breeding ground for bribery, cliquishness and toadyism.[90] Nazarbaev accused Kunaev of having sanctioned 'a multitude of abuses', explaining that 'it became a habit to resolve the most important questions secretly, amongst a narrow circle, behind closed doors and without collegiality', so that even obkom leaders were chosen without considering the views of all CC Bureau members.[91] Unsurprisingly, there was little support for Kolbin from obkom leaders, many of whom were waiting to see what would happen and continuing to use old methods, including protectionism and paper-chasing, but the discussion of Kolbin's charges did include criticism of the prevalence of protectionism, nepotism, 'one man rule', bribery, liberalism and a lack of criticism.[92] The lack of support for radical reform amongst officials in Kazakhstan was reflected in the attempt in May to distinguish between 'the resistance of those who in their egoistic interests try to retain an outdated order and privileges' and those who just 'commit disinterested mistakes and need to be given a chance to correct themselves'.[93] Kolbin acknowledged in mid-1987 that there had been only a few isolated cases of gorkom and raikom secretaries being chosen from more than one candidate. While continuing to attack nepotism and a 'clan approach', he also criticised 'isolated people' in the party who wanted 'to deny the past and lump all leading personnel and the whole party apparat together, attempting to counterpose them to the party masses'.[94] Yet for the remainder of 1987 there were still references to abuse of position, the pilfering of party resources, those who had 'adapted their whole life in order to defend their unlimited power', and to cover-ups and showiness.[95] The introduction of glasnost' into Kazakhstan was clearly complicated by the protests against Kolbin's appointment. Whilst he was able to make the work of the party apparatus much more public, this alone did not satisfy unidentified critics who complained:

> What sort of objectivity can you speak of if, in regard to the events of 17–18 December, the local and central press have spoken only about insignificant clashes. Yet more than a few lives were sacrificed there. There is not a word about this, because all the newspapers are under party control. Therefore public opinion will not be objective.[96]

Within six months of his appointment Kolbin was expressing dissatisfaction with the new definition of criticism 'as the freedom to say anything you want anywhere you want'.[97] He was attempting to achieve the impossible, by using public discontent with economic and social problems to attack corrupt networks of power, while lacking personal authority or public support in Kazakhstan.

The last two years of Kolbin's leadership coincided with the radicalisation of Gorbachev's policies after the successful introduction of glasnost' in the central press, but in Kazakhstan there was little sign of political change. The lack of support for reform from party officials afraid of election campaigns was noted in late 1987, when they were told to recognise that 'a return to the old, secret method of selecting leaders is already out of the question'.[98] By January 1988 Kolbin's new rules for party meetings had not reduced the old practice of obkoms requesting far too many reports from raikom officials.[99] The sacking of an obkom boss for protectionism was still reported as due to his ill health, not problems with restructuring, while officials responsible for the December 1986 disturbances were said to have 'merged with the criminal world'.[100] Kolbin continued to criticise Kunaev's legacy even a year after launching his reform drive, but he also engaged in self-criticism: he admitted having displayed elements of 'diktat' toward republican officials, and having given 'such a quantity of instructions that subordinates are not always able to fulfil them', and he also acknowledged that there was some formalism, passivity and protectionism in many party bodies.[101] In the notoriously corrupt Chimkent oblast, 97.9 per cent of people surveyed thought that negative phenomena persisted, with secrecy and 'the law of changing armchairs' still protecting disgraced officials.[102] Criticism of Kunaev for having chosen personnel 'according to clan membership, according to whose representatives were in key positions at the top of the "pyramids"' continued in May and June 1988 from ideology secretary Dzhaninbekov and Kolbin, who also attributed Kunaev's survival to 'protectionism at the highest level' from Brezhnev.[103] Such comments reflected the bribery, protectionism, pilfering and deception of the state that continued at obkom level, especially in the law and order organs. This was not restricted merely to southern parts of Kazakhstan; croneyism was reported as widespread in the largely Russian oblast of North Kazakhstan.[104]

After the XIX Conference Kolbin called rather tamely for more personal responsibility from officials, lamenting the great passivity in lower-level party ranks.[105] There was now 'playing with democracy' in oblasts like Chimkent, but these were 'farcical elections for the people' which did not stop corrupt officials retaining office; this may have been linked to the sort of personnel policy evident in some areas where appointments were made by a narrow circle of people and failed people were transferred from one post to another.[106] Kolbin said in November 1988 that the new democracy was not genuine:

> we have had some bad experiences when two or three candidates have been put forward for alternative elections. Under pressure from apolitical forces reliable people have refused to participate in the electoral contest. This has left just one candidate, the one who the shadowy forces struggled for, and as a result the electors have had no real choice.[107]

The continuation of inadequate party supervision with few effective links with lower levels and the resulting commandism was a major theme in oblast party conferences in late 1988.[108]

A feature article in February 1989 by G. Kozlov, deputy director of the Party History Institute in Alma Ata, analysed problems of podmena, which he said resulted from confusion between the authority of party bodies at different levels, and was made worse by a strong tendency toward centralism, which had weakened political leadership while protecting 'a closed caste of professional bureaucrats who practically could not be sacked'.[109] Whilst this analysis called for more radical change than had occurred in Kazakhstan, the criticism of centralism may have been an oblique reference to Kolbin's failure to achieve significant political reform. In Kolbin's last speech as KCP leader in May 1989 he claimed that the cleansing of corrupt elements had been completed, and said that the second stage of increasing the role of the CC was still occurring. Yet in the discussion of his report there was mention of continued serious personnel mistakes, with some formerly disgraced officials still being promoted to leading posts, liberal and unprincipled personnel decisions, and bossing and reliance on a narrow circle of people.[110]

Nazarbaev replaced Kolbin on 22 June 1989.[111] In July the difficulty of introducing political methods of work in the party was attributed by a consultant to the CC KCP organisational party work department to 'the technocratic approach in personnel policy', which Nazarbaev subsequently criticised at the XVII CC KCP plenum in November.[112] After the outbreaks of popular unrest in the town of Novyi Uzen' and the miners' strike in Karaganda in July, gorkom leaders called for a further reduction in the lists of nomenklatura posts they had to supervise, and better practical examples from their superiors about working in the new conditions.[113] Kozlov now warned against 'identifying decentralisation with democracy' and called for more collective responsibility on the part of local officials and an end to the 'paternalistic practice of leadership' from their superiors. He said that the whole Novyi Uzen' gorkom and apparat should have been sacked, not just the first secretary.[114] At the November plenum the ideology secretary Dzhaninbekov noted the 'lack of trust toward party organs' but disputed the widespread idea of 'a mass exodus from the party'. Responding to 'calls for renouncing the party nomenklatura in general', he said it should remain but be 'reduced to a minimum, determining only the main, key decisions'. He also said 'the pernicious practice' of podmena was continuing, and announced that the 'unjustified standardisation' of Kazakh cultural life would now end.[115] Nazarbaev rebuked party members 'inclined to separatism' from the Union in early 1990, while revealing that the Politburo would soon reconsider its resolution on the protests of December 1986 in which 'the whole Kazakh people were indiscriminately accused of nationalism'.[116]

The lack of reform in the party apparatus in Kazakhstan was openly discussed in the first half of 1990. One raikom boss said the party apparatus was stagnant, complaining that 'still nothing worthwhile has been formulated about methods of party work in the new conditions'.[117] In Aktiubinsk the obkom viewed the democratisation of party life as just 'an ordinary propaganda campaign'.[118] Nazarbaev criticised this and other obkoms at the XIX CC KCP plenum in February 1990 for allowing local party leaders to 'still continue to act as the directors of cities and districts'. He acknowledged that the existing hierarchical system of selecting leaders was 'especially unpopular amongst ordinary communists', noting their calls for fewer layers in the party apparatus.[119] The passivity of lower party organs was mentioned again at a conference of PPOs in March, where Nazarbaev called for 'an end to the practice of forming party committees according to official positions'. He said 'the current crisis in the party' was caused mainly by 'the contradiction between the initiatives coming from "above" and the passivity "below"'. He criticised raikoms for the old fault of continuing to override PPOs, and suggested that the rise of 'destabilising forces' confronting the party could only be opposed by local officials 'through parliamentary means'. While the new first secretary of Abai gorkom in Karaganda oblast was praised by Nazarbaev for finding 'a common language' between party officials and striking miners, he complained that many PPO secretaries continued to 'wait for instructions from above', having lost political influence in their collectives.[120]

Despite recently creating a republican presidency to overcome 'the shortage of executive power' and weakness of authority, Nazarbaev stressed that party committees 'must not drop responsibility for the placement of leading personnel', saying that while the control function of the nomenklatura list would cease, party officials would still be obliged to struggle for their candidates through election campaigns.[121] Yet reorganisation of the party apparatus had not improved party work, while competitive elections were still few and far between.[122] In late May second secretary Anufriev said many party officials now refused to fill leadership positions, party committees avoided discussing urgent problems, and at some local party conferences slogans of openness, democracy and pluralism had masked 'attempts to decide things according to parochial interests and kin relations'.[123] The failure of party reform in Kazakhstan was very evident at the XVII and last KCP Congress in early June 1990, when local party officials accused the CC departments of ignoring the situation on the ground and continuing to operate secretly.[124] Nazarbaev now presented a very critical evaluation of previous reforms, saying Kolbin's leadership was marked by 'a reactivated form of the command-adminstrative system, which sharply blocked any views or opinions other than those of the chief leader'.[125]

Thus there were three quite different republican leaderships in Kazakhstan during Gorbachev's leadership. Initially, the old cliques coordinated by Kunaev continued their rule, despite increased central pressure for personnel renewal from the summer of 1985. This central pressure for reform was endorsed by Council of Ministers chairman Nazarbaev, who attacked privileges for corrupt leaders at both the XVI KCP Congress and the XXVII CPSU Congress in early 1986.[126] Kunaev responded with traditional criticism of the central ministries, and reiterated Brezhnev's slogan of trusting personnel.[127] The replacement in December 1986 of Kunaev by Kolbin, a Russian with experience as second secretary to Shevardnadze in Georgia but no links to Kazakhstan, provoked substantial anti-Russian unrest in Alma Ata and oblast capitals, in which several people were killed.[128] The manner of Kolbin's appointment, at a plenum that lasted 18 minutes and was described by Nazarbaev in January 1990 as typifying 'the worst traditions of stagnation', severely undermined his authority from the beginning.[129] When Kolbin returned to Moscow in June 1989 he acknowledged that disagreements within the republican leadership were partly attributable to his own character, yet still claimed some short-term goals had been achieved.[130] However, despite the vigour of the criticism he encouraged in 1987-88, it is difficult to avoid the conclusion that the same problems remained unresolved. Nazarbaev, who became the new Kazakh leader, was described by the outsider Kolbin as someone with a lot of administrative experience 'here, in the republic, who knows exactly what has been done and what must be done now in order to purposively and consistently deepen and develop restructuring in the republic'.[131] This statement reflected the strength of informal power networks in Kazakhstan, which Kolbin was unable to operate. Whilst he made the local party apparatus work more regularly and efficiently than it had under Kunaev, this by itself did not enable the substantial change required to resolve social and economic problems.

UKRAINE

Ukraine was not marked by extensive criticism of the state of affairs in the party during the interregnum. Most criticism was of the way some party organs spent more time on paperwork than exercising real leadership and of making decisions in ignorance of the real situation on the ground.[132] There were also references to a narrow departmental approach, parochialism and protectionism,[133] bossing, fraud, abuse of official position, and people using official positions for selfish purposes.[134] But these were not major themes in discussions of the party at this time. The tone of criticism was quite moderate during the first half of the 1980s.

In March 1985 Shcherbitsky recognised that there were deficiencies in performance, but his view of these seems to have been very mild: there was a tendency in the agricultural sphere to take decisions behind closed doors, the problem of protectionism was often only addressed following higher-level intervention, and party organs needed to be more aware of the real situation on the ground.[135] Four months later, he criticised a liberal attitude in personnel work.[136] At the end of the year he called for 'the most decisive, unceasing struggle with showiness, window-dressing and any kind of beautification of reality and eyewash'.[137] This was linked with the weakness of practical leadership by higher-standing bodies. The treatment accorded party deficiencies in 1986 was similarly restricted. It was acknowledged that poor personnel work was common in the party. In some raikoms collegiality had been infringed.[138] In mid-year there was criticism of obkoms tolerating officials who had 'been fooling around with their work, breaking party ethics and CPSU rules', of failure to dismiss officials who had defrauded the state, and of methods of leadership involving the conduct of business behind closed doors.[139] Apart from these occasional references to serious deficiencies, discussion of the party concentrated on economic leadership and some administrative matters.

In February 1987 the first secretary of Voroshilovgrad obkom was sacked as a result of a scandal about the persecution of a journalist from *Soviet Miner*.[140] The old bosses of Dnepropetrovsk and L'vov obkoms were sacked in March, because of mistakes 'in selecting personnel for the law and order organs' and for protecting corrupt officials. They were replaced by Ivashko and Pogrebniak, reformers who had been CC CPU secretaries, the latter for over a decade.[141] While Shcherbitsky affirmed the importance of 'continuity' of officials soon after these changes, saying 60 per cent of obkom secretaries and 88 per cent of gorkom and raikom secretaries had been replaced during 1981–85, he acknowledged some 'personnel stagnation' in 'particular places'.[142] At this time there was some criticism of a leading party official who had had a liberal attitude to those who abused their positions and for having 'exaggerated his worth', and obkom leaders who had not responded to and even hid major abuses.[143] There was also criticism of the behind-closed-doors-directive style of work in Kiev gorkom and the fact that in Volynsk people who had infringed party and state discipline remained on the obkom nomenklatura despite earlier criticism of this from above.[144] The first public criticism of Shcherbitsky and second secretary Titarenko was made at the CC CPU plenum in late March 1987 by Zhitomir obkom first secretary V.M. Kavun, who said they were partly to blame for abuses in Voroshilovgrad, Dnepropetrovsk and Lv'ov.[145] At the July plenum Kiev obkom first secretary Revenko signalled new pressure on personnel: 'It is no secret that so far we have sacked only those who we can no longer put up with. But there are many others who have been given a chance and are not using it.'[146]

Shcherbitsky acknowledged in July 1987 the new need to 'renounce outright' podmena and 'to establish in practice genuinely political methods of leadership, based on primary party organisations and labour collectives'.[147] Subsequent reports confirmed that podmena remained a big problem in Donetsk, Nikolaev, Kharkov as well as other oblasts.[148] Differences over glasnost' and the need for more reform emerged during November between Shcherbitsky and CC CPSU ideology secretary Medvedev, who saw 'no cause for panic' or any reason 'to limit or smother democratic processes' after Gorbachev's speech re-evaluating Soviet history, saying the centre would intervene 'where necessary'.[149] Shcherbitsky spoke in late 1987 of giving existing officials 'a second wind', claiming that 'the tasks of restructuring must be resolved largely with the personnel we have now. We must value them, respect them and help them reach the level of contemporary requirements.'[150] At the January 1988 plenum he said only 10 per cent of gorkom and raikom leaders selected in the past year were chosen from more than one candidate, while criticising 'the dilution of ideological criteria' in the media and admitting he was overburdened with work.[151] Calls from several obkom leaders for a devolution of power over personnel were made at this plenum, but not followed up.[152] Six months later CC CPU secretary Kachura stated at the XIX Conference that podmena was difficult to overcome on the ground due to 'the very structure of party committees', adding that it characterised the CC CPSU.[153] From mid-1988 the 'need to oppose more actively manifestations of national nihilism' increasingly worried the republican leadership.[154] In October Pogrebniak said the only way to respond to the growing threat to party control in western Ukraine was to 'speak about the blank spots of our history'.

Ivashko said 'some officials of the CC CPU apparat and republican bodies' should be sacked, and Revenko said more regular information must be supplied to lower party organs.[155] Shcherbitsky said in November that the CC CPU apparat was ineffective because of 'a superficial approach to things and still insufficient links to gorkoms, raikoms and PPOs', but he claimed that party committees could not be occupied now with 'some kind of "pure" organisational, political and ideological work', ignoring responsibility for solving economic problems.[156] This instruction reinforced Kachura's criticism that the cause of inadequate party supervision was the structure of the party, not just the abuses of particular leaders.

Ivashko became second secretary in December 1988, after four obkom first secretaries were replaced in the autumn.[157] He chaired the commission on party work established with the reorganisation of the CC apparat, with a brief to strengthen organisational work.[158] This was not a radical move to stop podmena, since it was reasserted in January that 'no one can remain outside the control of a party organisation'.[159] The strength of party resistance to change in Ukraine before the March 1989 elections was symbolised by the choice of the recently retired Prime Minister Liashko, one of the last of the Brezhnev generation, to head a special Supreme Soviet commission investigating repression under Stalin.[160] When Gorbachev visited the Donbass in late February, he stressed that personnel work, while now 'more complicated', remained 'decisive', urging the promotion of 'energetic and talented people'.[161] Shcherbitsky responded by noting that 148 gorkom and raikom secretaries and 10 obkom secretaries had just been replaced at recent party conferences, while Ivashko claimed podmena was being overcome because 'the processes of democratisation have enveloped all rungs of the party'.[162] This claim, which contradicted the view expressed nine months earlier by Kachura (see above), was contradicted by a CC CPU Politburo discussion in mid-April, which admitted that 'many party committees have put off restructuring their work and the demarcation of functions with soviet and economic organs, have not focused on key directions of the economic reforms and are slowly moving over to political methods of leadership'.[163] The lack of preparedness of officials for the elections is evident from figures in Shcherbitsky's last major speech, to a CC

CPU plenum in May 1989. He said 'only 15 per cent' of gorkom and raikom secretaries had been selected from more than one candidate, with only 11 per cent of first secretaries and only one obkom secretary chosen in this way. Shcherbitsky's response was to urge discipline, saying it was 'especially important to raise the responsibility of the leaders of editorial collectives'.[164] Most local party officials at this plenum attacked the lack of direction from Moscow, not Shcherbitsky, and endorsed his call for discipline in strong terms.[165] Ivashko affirmed this view at a session of the CC CPU state and law commission in late May, but in July another view was expressed by the ideology department head Kravchuk, who said bluntly: 'party committees must not separate themselves from autonomous associations with a Chinese wall, but rather extend their work with them, appreciate their goals and be able to persuade and direct the initiative of the people to the benefit of restructuring'.[166] This difference assumed practical importance in July with the miners' strikes that Shcherbitsky described as much better organised than party committees, blaming obkom bosses for allowing such a 'real threat of a weakening of the leading role of the CPSU in restructuring' to emerge.[167] Kavun, the first to criticise Shcherbitsky in 1987, now thought demoralisation amongst party officials could be remedied only by clear central directives and decisive use of the mass media as 'an effective instrument of the party and the state'.[168] After the strikes, the growth of Ukrainian nationalism led by Rukh continued despite warnings from new KGB boss Golushko and the head of the Kiev military district Gromov, who called for 'more decisive and energetic action' against 'attempts to split society'.[169] When Shcherbitsky was replaced, obkom leaders in Ukraine were divided on whether his replacement should be confirmed unanimously or chosen by a vote. While a vote was won easily by Ivashko against an economic secretary Gurenko, such elections were still reported as a novelty at gorkom level.[170] Ivashko soon appointed Kravchuk to take over as ideology secretary, but this did not stop divisions between reformists and conservatives at the following plena in October and November.[171] Gurenko, now second secretary and head of the commission into repressions under Stalin, reported in December on a dispute in a raikom in Kherson oblast between the first secretary and the ideology chief, as a result of which the whole raikom resigned.[172] At the end of 1989 the new head of the CC CPU ideology department, Popovich, said, discussing personnel turnover since 1985: 'far from all of us have come to realise the difficulty and I would even say the precariousness of the current political situation'.[173] Whilst some leaders like Kravchuk were able to manage discontent for a while, the purpose of the party apparatus as a structure of supervision was not only failing to be realised, but increasingly impossible even to imagine.

It is clear that the style of criticism in Ukraine during the 1980s was very mild. Even when the language used was at its most extreme, in 1987, this did not signify recognition of major problems with the way the party was operating. After that date, there was virtually no harsh criticism of the state of the party's domestic life and procedures from the republican party leadership, although isolated expressions of stronger criticism focusing on the rise of political opposition to the party became more evident after Shcherbitsky's replacement in late 1989.

BELORUSSIA

In Belorussia during the interregnum, most comment on the party related to seemingly routine administrative problems rather than abuses. Leadership by resolution and by generating paper was noted, with the accompanying consequence of failing to give concrete leadership to lower-level party organs.[174] There were also isolated references to falsification, abuse of official position and the pilfering of socialist property, to deception and covering up the real situation, and to personnel who had got beyond criticism, or had degenerated and abused their posts.[175] These references were similar to those in Ukraine, Kazakhstan and Tajikistan, but fell far short of the major campaign which was beginning in Uzbekistan.

There was little discussion of party questions in 1985. In April first secretary Sliun'kov reported that while some officials had been sacked for abusing their positions, others had been reappointed to leading posts;[176] there were also reports from other areas of abuses, the reappointment of failed officials and leadership by directive,[177] but these were not very numerous. At the XXX Congress in January 1986 Sliun'kov said that podmena was widespread, and added that 'there are more than a few cases of leading officials conducting themselves improperly and abusing official positions'; some officials had been dismissed for defrauding the state.[178] The congress resolution[179] called on party committees to 'conduct an unceasing struggle with showiness and clamouring. Fraud, abuse of official positions, careerism, an aspiration toward personal enrichment, croneyism and protectionism must be decisively stamped out. Figures who take the path of deceiving the state, pilfering and trampling on the norms of socialist morals must be sacked.' Such abuses were discussed by the Bureau throughout 1986, although the main emphasis of discussion of party matters concerned economic work.[180] At a plenum of the Minsk obkom in November it was observed that 'in many districts the pernicious practice of reassigning officials from one leading chair to another has not been stopped'.[181] The resolution of the last plenum that Sliun'kov reported to noted that there was no improvement in leadership of PPOs by higher party organs (a reliance on paper leadership continued, with the introduction of generalised decisions which bear little relationship to the actual situation), or a principled evaluation of falsification and fraud.[182]

This did not stop Sliun'kov's return to Moscow at the January 1987 CC CPSU plenum. His replacement Sokolov reported in March 1987 that in the past five years 75 officials in the republican CC nomenklatura had been sacked, 41 of these for abuses. Subjectivism and cliques were being overcome, but there were still many mistakes; promotion still chiefly came from within the narrow circle of the nomenklatura. There was very little democratisation of the party and replacements were chosen by a narrow circle of officials.[183] The resolution from the plenum addressed by Sokolov[184] noted that subjectivism and croneyism in promoting leaders had not been eliminated and that there had been abuse of position by members of the CC nomenklatura. Obkom plena revealed fraud and scepticism about political reform, and also passivity and a lack of practical leadership from above.[185] A second secretary of Grodno obkom was sacked for improper conduct in July, and a raikom boss was sacked in September for choosing personnel on the basis of friendship and falsifying economic results, as well as sexual immoralities which he tried to hide behind the appearance of a model leader.[186] In late December 1987 an editoral complained that some party committees 'now try to reduce everything to decorative changes, not affecting the habitual style and rhythm of life'.[187] Old problems of poor party supervision such as weak links between higher and lower party organs and telephone leadership remained, while competitive elections for party officials were not being used widely.[188]

Sokolov responded at the January 1988 plenum by calling on CC officials to give better leadership and exercise more control, while local party leaders criticised the CC for seeking too many reports and called for greater freedom for obkoms, gorkoms and raikoms to determine the structure and staff of their apparatus independent of the CC. One speaker declared: 'many officials are turning their official positions and the goods they have been trusted with into a source of personal enrichment'.[189] A discussion in mid-1988 found that party committees proceeded according to old stereotypes, with reports saturated with figures instead of analysis and officials having little knowledge of changes on the ground.[190] In July it was revealed that many leaders tried to persist with old methods because they could not cope with glasnost'.[191] The Minsk obkom had not changed its bureaucratic style of administration, nor controlled abuses by officials.[192] In August 1988 there were reports about a leader ignoring collegiality in personnel work and the existence of subjectivity in the promotion of people to leading posts.[193] Restructuring of party committees following the XIX CPSU Conference decision began in Belorussia, but this failed to prevent continued cases of lower party organs 'willingly or unwillingly copying the command line of obkom apparat officials'.[194] Only 12 per cent of PPO secretaries had been elected by secret ballot, and because of confusion about elections there had been an unjustified growth in positions to satisfy all candidates.[195]

Several months after the March 1989 all-union elections, a conference in the CC BCP noted that secret ballots were rarely used within the party, and that 'the weakest point in the activity of lower party branches is their inability to do specific things'.[196] There was increasing criticism from these branches in late 1989 of the failure of higher party organs to consult them about the new Programme to be used in the elections to a new Supreme Soviet.[197] This was followed by further criticism from the ideology secretary of Minsk obkom of the secrecy of party decisions, including the role of the nomenklatura approach to personnel, which created the impression of shady deals agreed behind people's backs.[198] The resolution of personnel matters by a narrow circle, liberalism and the relocation of discredited officials from one post to another was still occurring in early 1990.[199] The first use of competitive elections at obkom level in Belorussia did not occur until 1990, when it was already clear that 'they are not a panacea for many failings in personnel work'. It was observed that: 'The practice of electing leaders in conditions ensuring the opportunity of not formally but really choosing the most authoritative and suitable people professionally and morally has still not become a habitual, obligatory rule for all intra-party, state and social life.'[200] The need for changes to the party's Rules was raised, not only to make election on an alternative basis mandatory, 'but also to remove the step by step process of forming leading party organs, since the current hierarchical procedure gives the apparat unlimited opportunities to influence the process of elections'.[201] Whilst competitive elections for top party positions were used in March, this was already several months after similar elections in Ukraine, and by then the divisions within the BCP had grown between the bulk of party officials resisting political change and those in the Democratic Platform who wanted to take over from the old incumbents.[202] Increasing anger came from local party officials toward the initiators of political reform in Moscow, but this did not help the conservative republican leadership faced with new competitors for power.

THE POST-BREZHNEV PATTERN

This review of the situation throughout most of the 1980s shows a resurgence of higher-level criticism in the early part of the decade, reaching new heights after 1985. As in the Khrushchev period, the pattern is not standard across all republics. In Uzbekistan high levels of vigorous criticism of personnel abuses emerged as early as 1983 and continued at such a level into 1989, with leading party figures being openly accused of corruption and criminal activity. Levels of criticism were lower in

Tajikistan, but between 1986 and 1988 they did reach levels higher than had been customary with charges of personal abuse and criminal activity recurring. Higher levels of criticism occurred in Kazakhstan in 1985, escalated in 1987 and then tailed off in 1989. In Ukraine and Belorussia, levels of criticism did not increase substantially. Much of the reporting in these two republics emphasised old themes and eschewed the sorts of accusatory and threatening language evident in the other three republics. While some of the comment in these two republics did take on a greater urgency than normal, it did not constitute the sort of campaign that occurred in Central Asia and Kazakhstan.

This survey of the pattern of reporting during the Khrushchev and post-Brezhnev periods shows some consistency in the geographical patterns during the two campaign periods, at the end of the 1950s to the early 1960s and in the 1980s. In both periods, Uzbekistan experienced the highest levels of vigorous criticism while Ukraine and Belorussia were least affected in this way. Tajikistan also experienced high levels of criticism during both periods, while in Kazakhstan criticism was stronger in the mid-1980s than the 1960s, although even in the 1960s it was still stronger than in the two Slavic republics. Furthermore, similar patterns of language were used. In the two Central Asian republics during both periods, the language was threatening and accusatory, emphasising fraud, criminality and deception. The main focus was not on bureaucratic incompetence or official mismanagement, but on conscious criminal design. This tenor was also evident in Kazakhstan during the mid-1980s, but was less in evidence during the earlier period. In contrast, in Ukraine and Belorussia in the 1980s the tone of the criticism was much more one of inadvertant failure, bureaucratic mismanagement, and mainly of honest people doing their best in a difficult situation. In fact, it was little more than a continuation of the principal themes evident throughout the Brezhnev period. How are these patterns to be explained?

5 Why this Pattern?

The pattern of discussion of problems in intra-party functioning in the republican press is clear. Throughout the whole period there was a continuing current of criticism of the performance of lower-level leaders, but during most of this time that criticism was standardised and did not portend a threat to lower-level incumbents generally. However, there were two periods when the level and vigour of criticism were sharply raised and the sense of threat became more tangible. In the initial years of the Khrushchev period up until 1959, the discussion was couched in more moderate language, suggesting administrative sloppiness and mistakes rather than crimes. From 1959 into 1962, the language was more vigorous and the symbolism reflected a more serious malaise within the party; problems were due less to mistakes than to the conscious decisions of personnel, with crime rather than error being at the heart. Following Khrushchev's ouster, the language and symbolism were once again moderated, with less emphasis upon abuse of position and power and more on personnel oversight and administrative mistakes. The harsh critical tone returned with Andropov, and was escalated under Gorbachev.[1]

This pattern was not standard across all republics surveyed.[2] While generally the tone and language of those more moderate phases (1953–58 and 1963–82) were common to all republics analysed, the more vigorous criticism was much more prominent in some republics than others. In general terms, criticism tended to be more vigorous in republics in the following rank order: Uzbekistan, Tajikistan, Kazakhstan, Ukraine and Belorussia. Although such a rank ordering cannot reflect fine grades of distinction, the greater vigour of the criticism in Uzbekistan and Tajikistan compared with the other three republics, and in particular Ukraine and Belorussia, is clearly established. The question is why these temporal and geographical patterns occurred.

THE ROLE OF ALL-UNION POLITICS

One of the enduring characteristics of the study of Soviet politics has been the relative neglect of politics below the all-union level. While this was for a long time largely a result of paucity of information and relative inaccessibility of sites,[3] it also reflects the dominance held by the totalitarian paradigm over Western approaches to Soviet affairs. Totalitarianism allowed for no autonomy on the part of lower-level political figures, and relegated local political life to the realm of the unimportant. Even when alternative approaches shook the dominance of the totalitarian paradigm, like the emergence of a school of social history[4] and theories which recognised the existence of elements of plurality within the Soviet system,[5] politics below the all-union level remained relatively low on the research agenda. Both the course of politics below the all-union level and the nature of the relationship between politics at these different levels of the Soviet system thus remained largely unexplored. But there clearly was a relationship between the course of political life at each of these levels, and this was reflected in the timing of the more vigorous criticism of party leaders: those phases when criticism at the republican level was at its most severe and vigorous coincided roughly with periods when similar language was being used at the centre, chiefly by the party leader. When the language at the centre was more moderate, so too was it less extreme in the republics.

Khrushchev's Campaign Pressure

Khrushchev was always an interventionist First Secretary. His abrupt, often biting interruptions of speakers were a constant feature of party plena and like gatherings following the consolidation of his position with the defeat of the anti-party group in 1957. But even before this, the highly interventionist profile he adopted in policy issues was evident. His career before Stalin's death was characterised by continuing personal involvement not just in the broad sweep of policy-making, but often in the minutiae of policy implementation. This sort of level of involvement was maintained after he became First Secretary. Moreover, he was a person of infectious enthusiasms and strong views, a combination which, when combined with the powers his office entailed, could lead to policy havoc. The course of policy under Khrushchev was idiosyncratic, with national policy frequently being moulded by the First Secretary's latest fads and enthusiasms, often associated with ideas whose relevance to the Soviet situation was questionable at best. The cultivation of the Virgin Lands, the campaign for corn, and the fostering of chemicals were three instances from different times in Khrushchev's career which reflect his personal effect upon the policy agenda. Once he had become convinced that a particular course of policy should be followed, he often then mounted a personal campaign to oversee its implementation. Involving both speeches and visits to particular areas of relevance to the policy, Khrushchev vigorously and without concern for the sensitivities and sensibilities of those around him pursued the course he favoured.

This sort of style was highly interventionist. Khrushchev was not reluctant to tell farmers how they should farm, including giving lectures on the virtues of particular methods of planting, growing or harvesting the crop. He was particularly severe on what he perceived to be deficiencies in performance, often using colourful language to convey the blunt message that people were not performing up to expectations. Khrushchev's hectoring, interventionist style created an environment in which the threat of criticism from above was always present. For many this threat would not have been imminent; the physical size of the country and the demands of office made a visit by Khrushchev unlikely. However, the style he set could encourage other, lower-level leaders to adopt similar approaches, thereby injecting an element of uncertainty into many people's professional lives. While this level may have been significantly lower than that which existed under Stalin, it was nevertheless a feature of the lives of many officials at all levels.

This interventionist style occurred against a general background portending change to some of the established patterns of party life. Most important here was the emphasis upon the principle of collectivism in leadership following Stalin's death, a principle which implied a move away from an individual leadership style towards a more truly committee style of decision-making. This was reinforced by the de-Stalinisation campaign explicitly launched at the XX Congress with its open attribution of blame for the problems experienced during Stalin's rule to his personalised leadership style. This was a clear signal about the dangers of individual leadership unchecked by the collective wisdom both of one's peers and the party in general. This had direct relevance to contemporary party officials and the way they performed in office. Furthermore, the campaign encouraged by Khrushchev from 1958 to increase levels of popular participation in political life, especially through the recruitment of unpaid volunteers and activists into decision-making, supervisory and implementation roles,[6] was a clear attempt to bring pressure to bear on non-performing officials. This became more marked in 1961.[7] In this context, then, levels of uncertainty for party leaders were increased not only by the propensity for interventionism on the part of the First Secretary, but by the changing party norms which seemed to suggest closer monitoring of individual leadership performance.

Until the end of 1960, the leadership's comments on the performance of party officials remained relatively restrained. There was criticism of the way in which party organs exercised leadership over agriculture, how they had a superficial, bureaucratic approach which prevented them from gaining an intimate knowledge of events on the ground.[8] Party organs were accused of spending more time on the composition of resolutions and the holding of meetings than of giving real assistance to production.[9] At the XX Congress in 1956, Khrushchev[10] noted that some party officials 'who did not justify the high confidence placed in them by the party were removed from the CC', a reference to tensions within the elite rather than the performance of party officials generally. He then went on to call upon party organisations to develop criticism and self-criticism, to review the results of work with a critical eye, and resolutely to combat self-delusion, boasting and conceit. He said many of the shortcomings that should be eliminated were the result of complacency and a tendency to give a doctored picture of the real state of affairs. He criticised the way in which in the past cadres had given 'armchair leadership' to the economy. Party personnel were often 'engaged not so much in the work of organisation, as in the collection of all manner of data, statistical returns and information', while some party workers 'instead of being daily amidst the masses, confine themselves to their offices, produce reams of resolutions, while life passes them by'. As well as stating that the performance of party officials should be judged by the success of the economic unit for which the person was responsible, Khrushchev criticised shortcomings in cadre selection and training. There was unnecessary shifting of officials from one job to another, with party bodies confining themselves to a formal study of cadres and sometimes promoting and shifting people without taking into account their political and other qualifications.

There were instances when a more critical tone was evident, as in comments on cadre work within the Kirgiz party in October 1958.[11] Party organs were accused of serious errors in the selection and promotion of cadres. They were said to have conducted inadequate study of their cadres, of being unacquainted with rising young workers who deserved promotion, instead tolerating the continued holding of responsible positions by incapable people who were poor organisers and showed no promise as leaders. Some party organisations artificially shifted people around, thereby creating a narrow clique of so-called irreplaceable workers. Furthermore 'Party organs insufficiently educate cadres in the spirit of high ideinost', adopt a liberal attitude to party workers who do not meet their obligations, infringe the interests of the state, allow immodesty in personal behaviour, and misuse their official position.' Many of the points made in this decision are unremarkable, reflecting continuing deficiencies in the functioning of the cadre selection process. However, the charges that there were party workers who infringed the interests of the state, allowed personal immodesty and misused their positions could be hints of something more serious. Alternatively they could be read in a more benign fashion; instead of reflecting unacceptable, even criminal, behaviour by party workers, they may simply represent a reassertion of the familiar charge that party organs and their workers were not exercising sufficiently vigilant 'kontrol'' over their counterparts in the economy.

This latter interpretation is supported by the absence of vigorous charges in the addresses Khrushchev gave to the CC plena of June and December 1958.[12] Similarly some of the published reports from the report and election campaign conducted in the party at this time complain about the performance of party officials in less threatening terms: one party bureau was accused of lacking self-criticism and being cut off from the masses and, while higher-standing bodies knew about this state of affairs, they did nothing to remedy it; in another case party officials were accused of shutting themselves up in their offices, losing contact with the masses, cutting themselves off from life behind mountains of paper, and being more interested in holding sessions and passing resolutions.[13] But it was also noted that the report and election campaign showed that party organs were intolerant towards manifestations of negligence, conceit and violations of democratic principles in party life.[14]

A growing concern among at least a part of the all-union leadership at this time was the danger of localism. The immediate stimulus for this concern was the establishment of the sovnarkhozy in 1957.[15] Khrushchev had noted the danger that these could stimulate localism at the time he championed their establishment;[16] the concentration of economic authority at the regional level in theory seemed to greatly increase the propensity for regional autarchy and the breakdown of central control. The answer to this for Khrushchev was to be increased supervision and monitoring. In this context, local party organisations, supplemented after 1958 by an expanded role for volunteers and activists, were meant to exercise increased control over state and economic organs in order to combat such tendencies.[17] The problem was that many suspected local party leaders were more likely to support their regional colleagues against the centre than vice versa. It was this concern which strengthened the centre's worries about localism. According to a report from September 1958,[18] there had been instances of localism by state officials, in the form of such things as padding plan fulfilment reports, concealing and squandering raw materials and attempting to adopt reduced plans by underreporting actual performance. Such action placed local needs above national needs. The report continued that party organs must combat localism and all manifestations of anti-state practices. Yet there were party workers who not only failed to defend the general interests of the state, but often promoted anti-state practices; they supported the incorrect proposals of managerial officials and sometimes even forced such officials to carry out work not included in the plan in order to suit local interests.

Localism was not a major concern in Khrushchev's address to the XXI Congress in January 1959.[19] He called for the promotion of both experienced workers and talented youth, for avoidance of the situation where there was the incorrect evaluation of officials and where those who could not manage their assigned tasks and were isolated from the life of the people held responsible posts for a long period of time; some party organs were accused of moving such people from place to place. He said that the CC trained cadres in, *inter alia*, demandingness, refusal to tolerate shortcomings, and criticism and self-criticism. At the CC plenum in June 1959[20] he called for increased supervision, including public supervision, over production and output,[21] and discussed instances of localism on the part of managers, principally through manipulation of the production process. At the end of year plenum[22] Khrushchev criticised failures on the part of producers to meet their obligations and called on party organisations to exercise effective supervision in order to overcome this. He also criticised the performance of Kazakhstan and its first secretary Beliaev, who was soon to be removed. This fed into the campaign against local nationalism which emerged in 1959 and which laid the groundwork for a broad recentralisation of powers between 1960 and 1963.[23] The plenum also saw laudation of the performance of Riazan oblast (see below).

The public stance taken by Khrushchev hardened considerably in 1960. There were a number of reasons for this. Of particular importance here was the apparent deterioration in Khrushchev's position within the leadership. The changes to the leadership between May and July 1960 appear to have weakened Khrushchev, or at least strengthened the position of those (Kozlov and Suslov) whose views on various policy issues differed from those of Khrushchev.[24] At the same time a series of setbacks occurred in policy spheres either directly associated with Khrushchev personally or for which he had to take responsibility. Among these were the U2 incident in May, the collapse of the summit with the US two weeks later, and the sharp deterioration in relations with the Chinese reflected most clearly in the withdrawal of Soviet technicians from China in July. But perhaps most important was the situation in agriculture, that sphere of the economy in which Khrushchev had taken the most abiding personal interest. The results of agricultural policy in 1959 and 1960 had been very disappointing; the harvest had been mediocre and stockbreeding was in decline. What made this even worse were the revelations that came to light in autumn 1960 about the situation in Riazan oblast.

In 1958 the leadership of Riazan oblast had promised to triple in one year the amount of meat the oblast delivered to the state.[25] In February 1959 Khrushchev visited Riazan and gave his personal blessing to this endeavour.[26] Just prior to the December 1959 CC plenum, it was announced that this target had been achieved. At the plenum Khrushchev lauded the achievement of the oblast, disclosed that the initial publication of the oblast's pledge had been made on his instruction, and announced that Riazan first secretary Larionov would be made a Hero of Socialist Labour.[27] Khrushchev thus personally associated himself directly and unambiguously with the performance of Riazan. Unfortunately for Khrushchev, in September 1960 Larionov died (reputedly by suicide), after which it became clear that the Riazan achievement was a result of a combination of organisational malpractice (much of the Riazan breeding stock was slaughtered to reach the meat target, while many beasts were imported from surrounding oblasts in an attempt to maintain production) and false reporting. The much heralded triumph of Riazan turned out to be a case of gigantic fraud, deception and false reporting.

Although the full details did not become publicly available for some time, the Riazan case was a major embarrassment for Khrushchev within leadership circles. However, it also provided him with the means of counter-attacking: the problem with agriculture was not that the policy was faulty, but that it was being sabotaged by many of those on the ground. Riazan was only one case among many of officials using falsification and swindling to undermine production targets.[28] Furthermore, as Riazan showed, party officials were prominent in this. Khrushchev now launched a drive against falsifiers, with party leaders directly in his sights.

At the January 1961 plenum Khrushchev hectored the speakers and in particular castigated oblast leaders. The theses he presented called for the purging of deficient officials, of those who refused 'to break out of the vicious circle of their own ideas'. His speech[29] discussed the failure of various regions to fulfil their obligations. He claimed that careerists had entered the party and sought to establish their authority through dishonest machinations. He called on the party to struggle with such people 'who had a party card in their pocket' because they brought shame to the party. Those who failed to fulfil their plans and obligations were labelled enemies of the socialist state. They were accused of not being concerned for the situation in the region, kolkhoz or oblast, but of being on the look out only for their own best interests. Those who infringed the decisions of party and state must be excluded from the party and brought before the court. Khrushchev's words, including his emphasis upon the importance of unpaid functionaries and mass monitoring of administrative performance, constituted a significantly sharper attack on party officials than had been made before.

Following the plenum Khrushchev embarked on a series of trips to different parts of the country where he criticised those who embellished matters and concealed their mistakes; for example, the Kirov obkom first secretary had known about cases of report-padding but had refused to take any action.[30] According to a report in the party's organisational journal,[31] there were some officials who engaged in machinations, falsified accounts and deceived the state. They were careerists who engaged in hoodwinking and falsification of reports, distortion, report-padding and bribery. The report warned against appeasement of such deceivers of the state and against any conspiracy of silence. It said that some officials had failed to draw the lessons from the January plenum and continued to show a lack of principle in cases of hoodwinking. This theme was also prominent in the report about the removal of Tajik leader Ul'dzhabaev in April 1961 discussed below.[32] It was also reflected in the Supreme Soviet decree in May making report-padding subject to three years imprisonment.[33] The accompanying commentary referred to the recently uncovered cases of report-padding and hoodwinking, and said that these flourished where inner-party democracy was being violated, criticism and self-criticism were not developed, and personnel were chosen on the basis of neighbourhood ties, kinship and personal loyalty.[34]

This theme was not maintained consistently in central discussions of party affairs during succeeding months. Nevertheless, in the period leading up to the XXII Congress in October 1961, major leadership changes were made: in the 12 months from October 1960, 55 of the 114 oblast and krai first secretaries were purged;[35] so too was Tajik first secretary Ul'dzhabaev, who was explicitly charged with the sort of abuses against which

Khrushchev had railed in January. Furthermore, in the precongress discussions, one participant argued that there was a need for an independent supervisory machine below the oblast level so that 'control' was not dependent upon the local party apparatus and independent supervision could thus be exercised over local party officials.[36] Khrushchev returned to this theme at the XXII Congress in October. In his speech to the congress[37] Khrushchev declared that in the period of the cult of the individual there had been harmful methods used in the party – high-handed administrative methods, the hushing up of shortcomings, indecision in work and fear of anything new. There had been many toadies, hosanna-singers (yes men) and falsifiers. He then said the party combats (in present tense) violators of party and state discipline, people who deceive the party and state. He went on to argue that the work of party officials should be judged on the basis of the concrete results of the production units for which they were responsible, and where those units did not fulfil their plans, the party leaders should be removed. Reflecting his loss of faith in the capacity of the party apparatus effectively to exercise supervisory functions, he called for a reduction in the apparatus of party bodies and an expansion in the use of volunteers, including a heightened role for the public in supervision of the apparatus.[38] He attacked local party officials who 'awaited directions and instructions from above on each and every occasion' and thereby failed to exercise their own initiative. Noting that the falsification of reports and other acts of deception will always be condemned, he declared that 'It is quite impermissible for a leading party post to be held by one who falsifies reports or is a hide-bound bureaucrat.' He noted the need for greater system in the way local party bodies rendered account to higher bodies. The resolution on Khrushchev's report[39] declared that there was no place in party leadership positions for those 'out-of-date and conceited persons who have lost their feel for life, who are devoid of ideas and principles'. Moreover the party wages an 'implacable fight against those who violate party and state discipline, against people who set out to deceive the party and state, against toadies, hosanna-singers, eyewashers and bureaucrats'.[40] This was a clear attack on the performance of many in the party apparat.

The attack explicitly launched by Khrushchev at the January

1961 plenum and reaffirmed at the congress, and the distrust of the independence and performance of local officials that this signified, was codified in the new version of the party's Rules adopted at the XXII Congress. Many of the additions made to the Rules at this time, when taken together, reflect both Khrushchev's unease and his methods of dealing with the problem. The campaign which had begun in the late 1950s to stimulate popular activism and involve the masses in supervision of officials had its echoes in the Rules in the demand that party members become more involved in all aspects of public life, including the need to 'boldly expose shortcomings and strive to eliminate them, struggle against ostentation, conceit, complacency and localism, give a decisive rebuff to all attempts at the suppression of criticism, resist all actions causing damage to the party and state, and report them to party organs up to the CC CPSU' (#2). In accord with this, the responsibilities of PPOs were enumerated and expanded, with the addition of the injunction that 'on the basis of the wide development of criticism and self-criticism [the PPO] leads the struggle against manifestations of bureaucratism, localism and violations of state discipline, suppresses attempts to deceive the state, and takes measures against slackness, extravagance and wastefulness in enterprises, kolkhozes and institutions' (#58). The Rules also strengthened the role of the aktiv in supervising local life (#30). The higher levels of activism thereby demanded were underpinned by a newly expounded conception of the qualities demanded of party members, the so-called 'moral code of the builder of communism'. As well as possessing such qualities as devotion to communism and the motherland, collectivism, humaneness, honesty and fraternal solidarity, the communist must be intolerant of violations of public interests and irreconcilable to injustice, parasitism, dishonesty, careerism and money-grubbing (#58).

While relying on the involvement of committed communists, the Rules also reflected an attempt to introduce formal means of dealing with the problem. The Rules now declared that those 'guilty of suppressing criticism and persecuting critics must be called to strict account by the party, right up to expulsion from the CPSU' (#3), while party members who had committed a criminal misdemeanour were now subject not only to expulsion from the party, but also to prosecution in accordance with the law (#12). The higher level of demandingness toward individual party officials was associated with renewed emphasis upon collectivity in leadership, a principle explicitly counterposed to individualist leadership (signified by reference to the cult of personality) and violations of intraparty democracy (#28), and with the 'systematic renewal' of party organs and limits on tenure, including specific turnover targets for party organs (#25). This emphasis upon individual office-holders was reinforced by strengthened reporting procedures: the outline of the principle of democratic centralism was changed to provide for party organs to make periodic reports not only to their party organisations but also to higher-standing party organs (#19), while party organs were enjoined systematically to inform party organisations about their work in the period between congresses and conferences (#29). All of these changes to the Rules suggest an increased commitment to combating the sort of abuses Khrushchev had criticised at the January plenum.

In a discussion of agriculture at the March 1962 plenum[41] Khrushchev barely mentioned this theme, although he did note that carrying a party card was not real evidence that a person was acting the way a party member should. At the November plenum at which the bifurcation of the party apparatus was adopted, Khrushchev argued[42] that the bifurcation would enable the party to concentrate more satisfactorily on both the industrial and agricultural sectors of the economy. He also noted the need to verify the actual state of affairs at lower levels and said that supervision within the party was unsatisfactory. Hence the creation of a new control organ, the Committee for Party-State Control,[43] and the continuing emphasis on mass surveillance of local officials. An important task of the newly established organs of supervision was said to be suppression of eyewash, report-padding, localism,[44] bribery,[45] waste and embezzlement of state materials. He said that such activity had been common in the economy, and he noted that embezzlement had been widespread in Uzbekistan. In places bribery had been conducted by leading workers with a party card in their pocket. Party committees were called upon not to accept such abuses by party members.

These themes were not raised in Khrushchev's speeches to CC plena in 1963 and 1964.[46] Nor were party decisions

Why this Pattern? 113

generally characterised by such sentiments, although there were references to some of these matters from time to time. When *Pravda* published the regulations establishing the new Committee for Party-State Control in January 1963,[47] they included the need to put 'a decisive end to violations of party and state discipline, to manifestations of localism, narrow departmentalism, and hoodwinking; report-padding, mismanagement and extravagance ... wage a ruthless fight against bureaucratism and red tape, bribe-taking, speculation and abuse of office'. There is no evidence that in practice party officials were much affected by the CPSC.[48] In March 1963 there was a report that there had been cases of report-padding, hoodwinking and deception in Azerbaijan, and the party head had not always called officials to account.[49] In April 1963 Khrushchev criticised the localism of the territorial party structure.[50] Kazakh authorities led by Yusupov criticised the way in which party organs often limited themselves in personnel matters to a narrow circle. Some Bureau members, including former first secretary Kunaev, were accused of considering kinship, regional preference and personal loyalty more important than political and business qualities in promotion questions.[51] A decision from May 1963 on cadre work in Donetsk oblast[52] criticised violations of the principle of the selection of cadres on the basis of political and professional qualifications, reliance on a narrow circle for promotions, and the shifting from one position to another of people who have failed and compromised themselves. A CC resolution on ideological work in Tashkent[53] noted that some officials embarked on the path of deception and violation of discipline. Some officials ruled by administrative fiat, were contemptuous of popular complaints, criticisms, comments and proposals, avoided personal meetings with subordinates and the public, and were haughty, callous and rude towards people. There were also reports of people who had abused their positions being protected by party committees.[54] But these reports were isolated instances of serious charges; there was not in 1963 or 1964 the sort of campaign that had been evident in 1961.

Khrushchev's most threatening language toward party officials was thus limited mainly to 1961, with the vigour tailing off in 1962. This was clearly part of a broader campaign directed against localism, fraud, dissimulation, falsification and deception on the part of regional officials. This had always been a problem from the beginning of the Soviet state (see Chapter 6), but it became a pressing issue at this time because of the effect of the sovnarkhoz reform, the poor performance in agriculture, and the political implications of both of these for Khrushchev personally. It is probable that the pressure imposed by Khrushchev for better performance itself stimulated such activity; the greater the pressure lower-level leaders came under, the more likely they were to seek to protect themselves through both false reporting and the direction of effort into satisfying superiors by generating reports than by taking direct action to improve production. Khrushchev became convinced that he could not entirely trust the party apparatus to exercise its supervisory functions, hence his encouragement of 'popular control' and warning about the way the masses would not put up with poor performance by officials. He also strengthened the legal apparatus; during 1961 the large-scale pilfering of state or public property was made a capital offence, as was so-called 'indirect theft' (report-padding and abuse of authority).[55] Khrushchev levelled charges of anti-state behaviour against officials, including for the first time party officials.[56] Khrushchev was thereby targeting party officials and increasing the level of threat to them by openly identifying them as a category who were not performing. The period of his most vigorous attacks appears to have been shorter than the similar period in Uzbekistan but to more closely match those of the other republics.

The sort of campaign which Khrushchev waged in the early 1960s was not sustained until his removal in October 1964. It clearly flagged in 1962–63 and disappeared in the following year. Nor was this sort of campaign targeting party officials revived under Brezhnev. This does not mean that the Brezhnev regime was not officially concerned about some of the problems that Khrushchev had identified, but its concern was not directly translated into threats against party officials.

Brezhnev's Trust in Cadres

Throughout the Brezhnev period the Soviet press continued to be characterised by reports of and complaints about the way in which economic performance was adversely affected by unacceptable activity by individuals and groups. The sort of actions identified in press reports were not new; they were the same complaints that had been heard in the press since the 1930s. They included podmena (substitutionism), poor guidance of the economy, lack of attention to the verification of implementation of decisions, lack of criticism and self-criticism, weak intra-party democracy and poor leadership by higher-standing bodies over lower. Sometimes there were also more serious charges, including the padding and over-reporting of production, eyewash, bribery, turning a blind eye to abuses, theft, embezzlement, use of state resources for private means, speculation and nepotism/croneyism. Such charges, often discussed in the West in terms of corruption,[57] were not new to Soviet discourse. The focus on the economy as the location of such deficiencies and upon economic figures as the main culprits was also not new. Nor was the general treatment of party figures. But what made the approach to the role of party figures in such activity difficult to avoid was the role the party was meant to play in the economy during this period.

While it is impossible to quantify the extent of party involvement in economic affairs during different periods of Soviet rule, it is clear that under Brezhnev its involvement was meant to be extensive. Certainly it was not meant to ignore its educational/mobilisational role, but it is difficult to disagree with the conclusion of one student of this when he declares 'that economic affairs were central to the routine functioning of the CPSU during the Brezhnev years'.[58] What is important is the nature of that involvement.

One of the primary themes of the Brezhnev regime was the need to escape the arbitrary and idiosyncratic approach characteristic of the Khrushchev period. He was critical of the 'hasty reorganisations', 'subjectivism', 'voluntarism' and 'harebrained schemes' of Khrushchev, and promised cadres that they would no longer have to suffer arbitrary, personalistic rule.[59] In accord with his attempt to bring a greater degree of regularity to the functioning of the Soviet politico-administrative system, and thereby to insert the party more fully into the production process,[60] a development fuelled by the failure of the Kosygin reforms in the mid-1960s, he also sought to bring regularity and stability to the Soviet (including the party's) personnel system. The result was a policy of 'stability of cadres'.

The essence of this policy was captured in the phrase that came generally to be used when discussing personnel questions, 'trust in cadres', and will be discussed below. The emphasis on regularity implicit in this notion also applied to the processes of decision-making and administration. The imposition of regular routine upon such processes, added to the continuing emphasis that the party had an important role to play in the economy, projected the party into the economic sphere as an institutional entity with broadly defined functions to perform. Instead of checking up on subordinates through aggressive interventions into problem areas as in the Khrushchev period, party organs were expected to achieve results through the regular coordination of the work of economic agencies. Furthermore, given the emphasis upon the continuing need to promote party officials with high levels of technical qualifications and the specific emphasis upon the need for the party continually to verify that decisions, including those relating to economic matters, have been carried out, it became increasingly difficult to separate economic performance from party performance. In this context, it is significant that throughout the Brezhnev period an attempt was made to distinguish the party and its officials from the worst abuses occurring in the economic sphere.

Clear evidence of this aim is to be found in the press and in Brezhnev's speeches, particularly his keynote addresses to successive party congresses and the resolutions adopted at those congresses. The initial emphasis in the press was on reassuring cadres by rejecting the threatening language of the Khrushchev era and by emphasising that the centre trusted officials at lower levels competently and honestly to carry out their tasks.[61] Despite a call by Kosygin in December 1964 for the replacement of officials who did not respond to criticism,[62] the overwhelming thrust of central comment was much more benign towards officials.

At the XXIII Congress in March–April 1966, Brezhnev discussed various aspects of party life.[63] Among other points, he noted the importance of higher party organs keeping in close contact with those below them and of struggling against the narrow departmental approach that was common under the old-style government ministries (i.e. those prior to the abolition of the sovnarkhozy). In a formal statement of what was to be the regime's policy on officials, he also referred to 'complete trust in cadres' as part of the principle of democratic centralism. He emphasised the importance of collective leadership and noted the role of criticism and self-criticism in the correction of communists who had deviated from the party Rules and in the prevention of faults in work from becoming aggravated. He said those who suppress criticism should be subject to the severest penalties. He argued that the development of intra-party democracy presupposed the simultaneous improvement of intra-party discipline. There was also a need to enhance communists' sense of responsibility for the situation in their party organisations and to be exacting toward all members so as not to allow a liberal attitude to those who contravene party and state discipline, forget their duty to the party, and think party membership should bring them certain privileges. Brezhnev also discussed changes in the party Rules which he believed would increase the responsibility of communists for the activity of their party organisation, the addition to the Rules of the sentence 'The party rids itself of all persons who infringe the Programme and Rules of the CPSU and who, by their conduct, compromise the lofty title of communist', and the removal of mandatory turnover levels (thereby giving greater security of tenure). Many of the main points of his address were repeated in the congress resolution,[64] which also declared 'Party and soviet organisations and economic organs must conduct a decisive struggle for strengthening state discipline, for eradicating bureaucratic methods of leadership, a narrow departmental approach to affairs, and localism.'

Brezhnev's address to the congress was important for the official articulation of the principle of 'trust in cadres', and, despite the rhetoric about discipline and the party ridding itself of those who acted in an unacceptable fashion, the general tone was not one that portended a threat to lower-level leaders. The message that this sort of presentation of cadre policy conveyed was that lower-level cadres were not self-seekers out to abuse their positions for personal gain. Rather they were honourable people who were trying, often under difficult conditions, to achieve the best results for the Soviet system and party.[65] They may make mistakes, but rarely did they commit crimes. Furthermore, it was assumed that the administrative hierarchy would produce better results if officials were trusted and respected rather than pressured as under Khrushchev. Consequently the centre had faith in its lower-level functionaries and understood the difficulties they faced. Under these conditions, although the centre would be demanding in its expectations of performance, as long as officials acted to the best of their ablities, did not make major mistakes, and served the central leadership loyally, they would not be demoted or removed. In practice, while officials were responsible for the economic performance of their regions, they tended not to be removed for poor economic performance unless it was accompanied by political scandal occasioned by corruption or favouritism. Thus officials at all levels gained a guarantee of security of tenure, in principle linked to performance, but in practice often regardless of the quality of service. Even when Brezhnev used more vigorous language in his June 1966 election speech, in which he referred to the need to combat bureaucratism and formalism, strengthen socialist legality and combat hooligans, criminals, bureaucrats, idlers, parasites, and plunderers of public wealth,[66] he was not referring to party officials and thereby casting a shadow over 'trust in cadres'. While the central approach to lower-level party cadres was to avoid administrative pressure upon them, this did not mean that the centre did not have high expectations of them. In May 1966 Brezhnev referred to the need for 'high responsibility and demandingness toward cadres',[67] while in March 1968 he explicitly revised the notion of 'trust in cadres'.[68] He declared that 'trust in and respect for cadres must invariably be combined with high demandingness towards them. The party, while trusting its cadres... will stringently penalise any violation of party or state discipline, regardless of positions held or past services.' This was associated with the need for iron party discipline.

Towards the end of the 1960s there was some vigorous criticism of problems in the Soviet administrative structure, but these related principally to the state ministries. At the December 1969 plenum Brezhnev criticised the inertia in the ministries, the waste of resources and the ministerial lack of responsibility.[69] He appealed for frankness in the public revelation of shortcomings[70] and believed that better party oversight was a potent weapon against such problems. But it was acknowledged at this time that there were also some problems within the party itself. In a discussion of the work of the CC of the Tajik Communist Party in December 1968,[71] it was claimed that supervision over the work of cadres was poorly conducted, leading in some cases to those in charge of economic bodies (including enterprises) losing the feeling of responsibility for the work entrusted to them, violating party and state discipline and failing to combat the squandering and embezzlement of socialist property. They often engaged in fraud themselves, distorting data in reports in order to cover up shortcomings and create an outward show of a satisfactory state of affairs. Party committees often failed to give a principled evaluation of such phenomena and failed to speak openly with responsible personnel about their shortcomings and errors in a party-like manner. Some 12 months later in a discussion of the conduct of party meetings in Yaroslavl,[72] meetings were accused of failing to mobilise communists for the struggle against violations of state and labour discipline and public order, and against drunkenness, embezzlement of socialist property,[73] squandering and other anti-social phenomena.

At the XXIV Congress in March–April 1971 Brezhnev's comments were a bit more pointed.[74] In discussing law and order and respect for legality, Brezhnev specifically referred to the importance of this for officials. While discussing 'Moulding the New Man', prior to the section of the speech devoted specifically to the party, Brezhnev called for an uncompromising struggle with survivals of the past 'such as money-grubbing, bribery, parasitism, slander, anonymous letters, drunkenness and the like'.[75] Turning to the party, he declared that the party rids itself of those who violate its Programme and Rules. Party organisations have drawn the correct conclusions from the XXIII Congress instructions and have begun more resolutely to get rid of those who violate party or state discipline, or abuse their office, or whose behaviour casts a slur on the title 'communist'. There must be no conciliatory attitude toward those who behave incorrectly. He noted that criticism and self-criticism had been further developed, but there were some party leaders who lacked restraint and tact and the ability to accept criticism and react accordingly. Those who underestimate or ignore criticism are doomed to failure. He repeated the view that the development of intra-party democracy is inseparable from the strengthening of party discipline, and then went on to argue that it was time for an exchange of party cards, the last having occurred 17 years earlier. In support of this view he said that there are some party members who are not real political fighters. When they come across shortcomings and other negative phenomena, they pretend to notice nothing and ignore it. There are some whose activity is solely for show, for creating an outward impression. They exhort and talk a lot, but remain on the sidelines. The party cannot accept passivity and indifference. Turning to cadre work, he said that the promotion of young promising people was combined with regard for veteran cadres, and that the practice had been 'to combine trust and respect for people with principled demandingness'. He criticised those who believed that they knew everything, issued instructions on all questions and ordered people about instead of using the experience and knowledge of others. He also noted that the party had long had skilled cadres who were able to resolve problems within their competence, and said that more trust must be placed in them with correspondingly more asked of them. Collective leadership and personal responsibility were essential, as was effective control. Cadres who violated discipline, failed to draw conclusions from criticism and behaved incorrectly must suffer the necessary consequences. Furthermore he said that leading posts are not reserved for anybody forever.

The tougher stance toward cadres evident at this congress led into the exchange of party documents and the anti-corruption campaign in the Caucasus at this time.[76] It also saw significant criticisms of some party organisations, the two best examples being of the party in Tbilisi in February 1972 and in Tambov in February 1975. The review of the work of the Tbilisi gorkom[77] was significant because it preceded the replacement of the Georgian leader Mzhavanadze by Shevardnadze in September of that year and the subsequent drive against corruption launched by the new first secretary.[78] After criticising the gorkom's poor leadership in the economic sphere, the decision went on to declare that in the resolution of cadre questions there was sometimes a lack of principle, liberalism and a failure to take into account the opinion of the collective and the party organisation. Weak workers who are unable to organise things are sometimes put into responsible posts. The gorkom has been unable successfully to combine confidence in cadres with demandingness of them, but has a tolerant attitude to those who badly carry out their responsibilities, allow bureaucratism and a scornful attitude to the enquiries and needs of workers. The gorkom, and raikoms, gave insufficient leadership to and showed insufficient interest in the PPOs. The city party organisation has only weakly led the struggle against such phenomena as embezzlement of state property, speculation, bribery and parasitism. A decisive struggle must be waged against departmental narrow-mindedness and manifestations of localism. Leninist principles must be implemented in the selection, placement and training of cadres to ensure that all sectors of life are headed by politically trained, competent and capable organisers. Personnel must have a feeling for the new and be able critically to evaluate what has been achieved. Demandingness and the personal responsibility of leading cadres for the work entrusted to them are to be enhanced, and personnel are to be made strictly responsible for violating party and state discipline and abusing their official positions. There must be undeviating observation of the Leninist norms of party life, steady development of intra-party democracy and the principles of criticism and self-criticism.

In June 1976 the results of the implementation of the earlier decision on Tbilisi gorkom were evaluated.[79] It was declared that significant progress had been made in overcoming the problems identified in 1972. The Georgian CC was said to have waged a decisive struggle for the strict observance of Leninist principles in the selection, placement and training of cadres. In solving cadre questions, the principle of collegiality was being confirmed, as was the taking into account of the opinion of party members and working collectives. This was making it possible to avoid errors that had existed until recently in evaluating personnel, promoting them on the basis of personal loyalty, family or friendship ties. While criticism and self-criticism and verification of implementation had improved, there was still a need to go further. Leading cadres must be taught to solve all questions from the perspective of party positions and general state interests. Criticism and self-criticism must be developed, and must ensure self-critical analysis of achievements and shortcomings. There has been an uncompromising struggle waged against relapses into philistine, petit-bourgeois psychology, nationalist manifestations, money-grubbing, outdated and harmful customs, manners and religious prejudices. Active struggle must continue against infiltration of bourgeois ideology, private property tendencies and other remnants of the past. While the new Georgian leadership was praised for successfully controlling corruption in the republic, the general warning to other party organisations was limited by the fact that Mzhavanadze had been allowed to retire from office without punishment.[80]

The discussion of the state of criticism and self-criticism in the Tambov oblast party organisation[81] noted that more would have been achieved in the economic, cultural and educational spheres had the party made better use of criticism and self-criticism. The party organisation had failed to analyse its own work in this way. Proper demandingness was not required of cadres who failed to ensure fulfilment of economic plans and assignments. There was a liberal attitude toward people who violated party and state discipline and misused their offices. There was little criticism of shortcomings and failings, and a lack of a sufficient response to cases of an incorrect attitude to criticism, to suppression of criticism and the persecution of those making such criticism. There must be decisive opposition to those who, by citing 'objective' reasons, cover up their failure to meet plan targets and mistakes in organisational and educational work. Suppression of criticism must be ended and those punished who fail to respond properly to criticism, interpret just rebukes as undermining their authority, place personal self-esteem above public interests, and take vengeance on those who criticise them. Three years later[82] Tambov obkom was declared not to have drawn the necessary conclusions from the earlier decision. Deficiencies in organisational and political work remained and there was little effective criticism and self-criticism.

At the XXV Congress in 1976, Brezhnev[83] declared that the aims of the exchange of party cards had been achieved. One result was that communists had become more exacting toward each other and an atmosphere of intolerance to breaches of the Rules had developed. Care had been taken to ensure that no one unworthy of the lofty title 'communist' remained in the party. Those 347 000 who did not receive new party cards were people who had departed from the rules of party life, breached discipline, and lost touch with their party organisation. He said that a Leninist style of work eschewed subjectivism, implied a high degree of demandingness with respect to oneself and others, ruled out self-complacency, and was opposed to manifestations of red tape and formalism. He noted the importance of criticism and self-criticism (referring to the decision on Tambov in this regard) and said that this meant that every aspect of the activity of an organisation should be given an objective evaluation, that existing shortcomings should be subjected to all-round analysis in order to eliminate them, and that there should be no liberal attitude toward shortcomings or those who allow them. 'Trust and respect for people should go hand in hand with a high demandingness towards those responsible for assignments.' Any incorrect response to criticism should evoke a sharp and swift response from party organs. He then emphasised the importance of supervision and verification of adopted decisions, saying that sometimes successive decisions were adopted on the same question. Is this not, he asked rhetorically, a case of a liberal attitude toward non-fulfilment? Defensively he noted that he had raised this question not because there was some sort of crisis in the party regarding fulfilment and criticism and self-criticism, but because these were essential for success. Turning to cadre policy, he said that many young promising cadres had been promoted, but there had been no frequent replacement of cadres. Cadres had been moved when necessary. However, cadre stability did not mean leaving in leading posts those who failed to pull their weight or cope with their duties, those who displayed irresponsibility and lived on their old merits, believing that their post would of itself ensure them of prestige and respect. Those who had lost the capacity critically to assess their ability, had lost touch with the masses, bred toadies and bootlickers, and had lost the trust of communists could not be party members. Brezhnev also declared that law in the economic sphere must be better at countering cases of defrauding the state, doctoring the accounts, theft of socialist property, undue zeal in giving priority to local interests and such problems. Furthermore, there were still departures from the socialist rules of morality – acquisitiveness, proprietary tendencies, hooliganism, red tape and indifference to one's fellow humans.

Brezhnev's comments on the deficiencies of officials show how the earlier claims for the success of the 1972–75 exchange of party documents were exaggerated. Following this congress, there was increased public pressure placed upon state ministries and ministers in various sectors of the economy,[84] but this applied overwhelmingly to those in the state rather than the party. There was some recognition of problems in the party: abuse of official position,[85] suppression of criticism[86] and nepotism[87] were noted, but these were minor themes in press discussion in the late 1970s.

At the XXVI Congress in 1981, Brezhnev[88] reported that the CC had had to criticise the work of some party committees and their leaders, and where this did not help, had come to organisational conclusions. He reported that almost 300 000 people had been excluded from the party since the XXV Congress for actions inconsistent with being a communist, and declared that the attitude towards those who acted in an unworthy fashion or infringed party Rules or morals was 'implacable'. He criticised the way in which some specialists who entered the party apparatus from production lacked sufficient political experience and carried administrative-economic methods into party work. He also emphasised the importance of the verification of implementation and the struggle against infringements of party and state discipline, but noted that for a significant number of party organisations verification retained only a narrow place in their work. Supervision had to be systematic and simultaneously from above and below. Party meetings must be the scene of deep and serious discussion of contemporary questions, not people sitting for hours listening to pre-arranged speakers. While noting that there was no place for anonymous letters, he called for a deepening of criticism and self-criticism and the confirmation in all party organisations of the spirit of self-criticism and intolerance towards shortcomings. Any attempt at the persecution of those who made criticisms must be decisively rebuffed. While discussing the economy, he said that not one case of abuse, waste or lack of discipline should escape popular control. Generally the speech devoted little attention to deficiencies in the work of the party or its cadres.

Brezhnev's comments at successive congresses concerning party cadres reflect a tougher stance at the XXIV and XXV Congresses in 1971 and 1976 than at either of the other two. This may reflect the exchange of party cards which was conducted between these two meetings. However, it does not represent a major centrally sponsored campaign of criticism of lower-level party officials; there appears to be no clear and sustained pattern in the more general comments to be found in central party decisions about the situation in and performance of lower-level party organs at this time, nor was the essential guarantee of security of tenure which underpinned the whole period shaken. Throughout the Brezhnev period the main thrust of commentary on the party was addressed to its role in the economy and the need for it to give effective leadership over economic cadres.[89] There were also complaints about deficiencies in admission procedures to the party,[90] the need for a strengthening of criticism and self-criticism,[91] poor cadre selection,[92] and the need for more improved verification of implementation.[93] Sometimes party organs were also accused of having little knowledge or concern about the situation at lower levels of the party; they were accused of being isolated from the real conditions of life.[94] There were also complaints about the way in which party meetings were organised and run, and in particular how the agenda and conduct of the meetings was dominated by the leadership while the rank-and-file were for the most part passive.[95] There were some charges that party organisations and members had adopted a liberal attitude to violations of party and state discipline or the party's Programme and Rules.[96] This usually involved a failure to punish such violations. Some party organisations were accused of tolerating shortcomings in work,[97] often but not always in the economic sphere, and of failing correctly to evaluate and act against 'negative phenomena',[98] once again often in the economic sphere. These sorts of complaints concerned deficiencies in the normal, day-to-day functioning of the party and occurred throughout the party's post-war history. In themselves, they did not constitute charges of illegal, criminal or malfeasant acts by party members.

Generally the Brezhnev period did not see much criticism of the activity of party organs or their cadres. Even when there were discussions of deficiencies in party operations, including references to problems like abuse of position, suppression of criticism and violation of established norms, the language did not approach the vigour of that used by Khrushchev in 1961. It did not represent a major assault on local officials; indeed the impression is less that party officials were committing crimes than that their major failing was not reacting sufficiently strongly to the failings of others. Throughout this period the discussion of malfeasant behaviour is almost wholly confined to the economic/state sphere, not the party. This is further reflected in the rationale for the exchange of party documents begun in 1972.[99] This was not justified in terms of coming to grips with criminal activity by party members, but of getting rid of those who were instrumental in the shortcomings in the party's functioning and who did not satisfy the high standards of being a party member. There was clearly no attempt made to emphasise criminal or malfeasant behaviour on the part of party officials, regardless of the performance of their economic and state counterparts. This was consistent with the cadre policy championed by Brezhnev.

The effect of this policy was evident in the turnover rates for party leaders. Over the period of Brezhnev's rule the occupants of leading party offices changed almost completely (by 1971 nearly 75 per cent of oblast first secretaries had been replaced since Brezhnev came to power[100]) but the rate of turnover was significantly reduced compared with that under Khrushchev; according to one student, the turnover rate of obkom first secretaries for 1955–64 was 20 per cent per annum, and for 1964–78 10 per cent per annum.[101] Within the Russian Republic, of 72 obkom first secretaries 43 were replaced between October 1965 and February 1971, 19 between February 1971 and September 1976, and nine between September 1977 and February 1982.[102] The turnover in republican politburos and secretariats was generally lower under Brezhnev than under Khrushchev.[103] In the 14 posts of republican party first secretary there were 25 changes in the 12 years of Khrushchev and 14 in the 18 years of Brezhnev; the turnover of first secretaries under Khrushchev was three times the rate of the turnover under Brezhnev (see below). Stability of cadres was firmly entrenched as practice as well as policy.

Another aspect of the Brezhnev personnel policy partly reinforced this. Under Khrushchev the pattern of appointment to regional posts had generally involved the appointment into the region of someone from outside. This reflected in part a central desire to reduce the possibility of the growth of regional loyalty and to increase the propensity to give central or

Table 5.1. *Percentage of obkom first secretaries appointed from within the oblast*[104]

	1953–64	1964–78
RSFSR	41.0	72.2
Ukraine	60.9	44.2
Kazakhstan	19.5	22.2
Uzbekistan	27.3	28.6
Belorussia	50.0	33.3
Total	40.5	49.2

national interests priority over those of the region. Generally under Brezhnev, the pattern of appointment was different, particularly in the Russian Republic. When posts became vacant, and of course this occurred much less frequently because of the stability of cadres policy, the general pattern was to appoint from within the existing region, usually the deputy of the recent incumbent. This pattern and its republican variations is shown in Table 5.1.

The impact of this regional variation, with internal promotion less in evidence outside the Russian Soviet Federated Socialist Republic (RSFSR), is moderated by the fact that in those republics with more important oblasts (i.e. those whose first secretary was normally a member of the CC CPSU), internal promotion was more likely than in the oblasts of lesser significance.[105] In any event this policy preference for internal promotion, explicitly supported by Brezhnev at the XXIV Congress in 1971,[106] reinforced the impression embedded in the stability of cadres notion: local officials could be trusted and were not under attack from the centre. This was the major continuing theme throughout the Brezhnev period, notwithstanding some isolated instances of more vigorous criticism.

The End of Trust in Cadres

This message began to change towards the end of the 1970s when KGB chief Yuri Andropov began an anti-corruption campaign which, in retrospect, seems to have been aimed at weakening the position of Brezhnev. The first official sign of this campaign was a CC resolution published in August 1979.[107]

Among the major concerns of the new law and order campaign were to be mismanagement, wastefulness, report-padding, eyewash (hoodwinking), parasitism and speculation. These sorts of concerns clearly showed that the campaign was to be directed against, *inter alia*, officials who were taking advantage of their positions to act in an unacceptable fashion. This was confirmed in a secret CC letter sent to republican and local party committees in November 1981[108] and the report of a meeting of the Politburo in December 1982.[109] It was reflected too in some of Andropov's speeches. At the CC plenum following Brezhnev's death, Andropov criticised the poor leadership of the economy and called for the elimination of departmentalism and localism; he also called for cadres who were politically healthy.[110] In the June 1983 plenum he directly criticised instances of the use of state and public property and official position for personal enrichment.[111] Furthermore, throughout this period he vigorously espoused a discipline campaign designed to strengthen discipline in both production and in society at large. The regular publication of reports of Politburo meetings which began in 1982[112] reinforced this message by projecting an image of a vigorous central leadership actively giving guidance to society as a whole.

The discipline and anti-corruption campaigns clearly had officials as their major targets. While there was no explicit identification of party officials as being any more guilty than their counterparts in the state or other official structures, the course of the campaign showed that prominent party personages were not immune. After considerable skirmishing, Krasnodar kraikom first secretary and long-time Brezhnev associate Medunov was dismissed from his position in July 1982, and 11 months later he was removed from the CC. At the same time Minister of Internal Affairs and Brezhnev confidante Shchelokov was also removed from the CC. Throughout 1981 and 1982 increasingly investigations began to draw close to members of Brezhnev's own family, his daughter Galina and her husband Yuri Churbanov.[113] Finally there was the Uzbek cotton scandal which first blew up in mid-1984 but did not reach its denouement until some four to five years later (see Chapter 6). This involved cases of massive over-reporting of the cotton harvest, added to widescale nepotism, privilege and corruption in Uzbekistan. Some prominence was also given to anti-corruption campaigns in Georgia and Kazakhstan at this time.[114] The important thing about all of these campaigns is that they clearly included party officials. This group was not considered immune, but as investigation showed, was often as enveloped in corruption as its state counterparts.

This campaign was continued after Andropov died. In March 1984 Chernenko spoke out against the squandering of state funds, eyewash, abuse of office, bribery and embezzlement,[115] and it was under Chernenko that the Uzbek affair became public. The effect of this campaign was clear in personnel changes. According to one study,[116] during Andropov's brief time in office (12 November 1982–9 February 1984) there were 30 changes of obkom first secretary in the USSR (22 per cent) and under Chernenko (13 February 1984–10 March 1985) there were 13 (9 per cent); under Andropov there were three new republican first secretaries (in Azerbaijan, Uzbekistan and Belorussia, although none were removed for disciplinary reasons: Azeri leader Aliev was promoted, the other two died) and none under Chernenko. The level of changes as a result of the scandal in Uzbekistan was even greater.[117] By publicly bringing down a significant number of the party's leading officials and by bringing the scandal close to Brezhnev's family, thereby showing that even the party General Secretary could not defend his closest associates, this campaign was a clear central warning to party leaders at all levels and marked a new high in attacks upon their positions. This was to be extended under Gorbachev.

From the outset Gorbachev hinted that the campaign begun under Andropov would continue, but this time there was greater concentration upon party officials than there had been earlier. In his first speech following Chernenko's death Gorbachev reaffirmed the need for order, the cleansing from life of alien phenomena and the strengthening of socialist legality.[118] Two days later he said that the 'strict observance of order and legality, and a strengthening of labour, state and party discipline' would be at the centre of attention, and there would be a struggle against showiness, empty words, boastfulness and a lack of responsibility.[119] At the April 1985 CC plenum he criticised the way in which many local leaderships were working, 'false idealisation', and the conduct of personnel policy on the basis of 'personal loyalty, servility and protectionism'.[120] In

November 1985 he strongly criticised the way in which local and regional party leaders hid things from the CC by showiness, embellishing reality and providing false and distorted information.[121] In the lead up to the XXVII Congress in February 1986, the republican party congresses generally were characterised by criticism of former and even some current republican leaders. In his address to the congress,[122] Gorbachev criticised window-dressing, showiness and harassment of critics. He also criticised the state of affairs in Uzbekistan, where he said they spoke only of successes, papered over shortcomings, responded irritably to criticism, people were concerned only for their own well-being and careerism, there was toadyism and 'unbridled laudation' of those senior in rank, embezzlement, bribery and gross transgressions of socialist legality. A number of republican leaders also raised corruption as an important issue in their addresses to the congress. The congress resolution[123] called for the elimination of flattery, servility and toadyism from the party and for the struggle against irresponsibility, permissiveness and breaches of party and administrative discipline, ethics and morality. It also declared that the party would not accept the practice of protectionism, or promoting cadres because of personal devotion or because they came from the same town or locality.

The level of threat implicit in this sort of language seems to have escalated towards the end of 1986 and early 1987 with increasing press coverage at this time of corruption in various republics: Kazakhstan, Kirgizia, Turkmenistan, Moldavia, Uzbekistan and Azerbaijan all featured prominently in such exposés.[124] In January 1987 at the CC plenum Gorbachev was scathing about the problems at the lower levels of the party.[125] He criticised the party's conservatism and inertia, its lenience and lack of demandingness, toadyism and personal adulation, red tape, formalism, intolerance and suppression of criticism, careerism, administration by decree, permissiveness, mutual cover-ups, departmentalism, parochialism, nationalism, substitutionism, a weakening of the role of party meetings and elected bodies, embezzlement, bribery, report-padding, violations of discipline, and the filling of positions with those unfit to hold office. He pointed in particular to the degeneration of personnel and breaches of law in Uzbekistan, Moldavia, Turkmenistan, Kazakhstan, Krasnodar krai, Rostov oblast and

Moscow. Gorbachev's speech was an indictment of lower-level party officialdom and laid the basis for his espousing of policies of 'democratisation' as a means of dealing with these problems. The following months saw press reports repeating many of the charges made by Gorbachev at the plenum.[126] The existence of a 'closed ruling elite' in which leaders, often linked by personal loyalty or common regional origins, 'take turns holding a range of nomenklatura posts' was decried at a CC plenum in Azerbaijan in April 1987.[127] In July it was declared in Kazakhstan that the appointment of 'careerists, sycophants and toadies' to 'a considerable number of key posts' had led to 'a moral degeneration of a proportion of personnel'.[128] This theme was reiterated in February 1988, when a report of a CC plenum in Kazakhstan said the obstruction of personnel change by protectionism, nepotism and the omnipotence of old bonds was continuing.[129] It is clear that at this time there was a major centrally inspired campaign against deficient performance at lower levels of the party.

Gorbachev's answer to the malaise that he identified at lower party levels was 'democratisation', but this policy was not given any real teeth until the XIX Conference of the party in mid-1988.[130] In his speech Gorbachev was less severe on lower-level party leaders than he had been, although he did refer to a command style of leadership, the development of a sense of infallibility among some leaders, and the abuse of power and moral degeneration. The conference made a number of decisions of far-reaching consequence for the future of the Soviet system, including the introduction of secret ballot multi-candidate elections in the party and a restriction of two five-year terms in elected party office, except in certain exceptional cases. The importance of these decisions has been overshadowed by that establishing a new state structure, but within the context of Gorbachev's continuing attack on lower-level party leaders, these decisions were highly significant. The introduction of multi-candidate secret ballot elections (even if permissible rather than mandatory) threatened to deny local party leaders the power they had traditionally been able to exercise through their manipulation of the nomenklatura system. Rank-and-file communists might now have control over their leaders instead of those leaders being effectively out of the control of their nominal constituents. Furthermore, the limit placed on

Table 5.2. Turnover rates of obkom first secretaries

	No.	%
3–12/85	27	20
1986	19	14
1987	24	17
1–8/88	12	9

tenure threatened to rob them of one of the major perks of office. Within the context of the criticism of privileges[131] that was to be heard at this time, the decisions of the conference were potentially a severe blow against local power holders.

In the period following the conference, the decisions taken by that body were enacted. In practice, a small minority of party officials actually had to face competition in election for party office, and there is no evidence that many party leaders lost office as a result of this decision. However, the reduction in the party's capacity to conduct a centralised personnel policy resulting from the conference-induced organisational changes to the secretarial apparatus at central and lower levels[132] was a real blow at the power base upon which most leaders rested. Their positions were further called into question by the erosion of the party's position in Soviet society from early 1989, resulting from the expansion of the political arena and the entry of new forces, and the gradual disintegration and loss of confidence of the party as a whole. In the minds of many of these lower leaders, such developments were a direct result of Gorbachev's policies.[133] This was so even though after the middle of 1988 Gorbachev's rhetoric lacked the same sort of direct threats common prior to the conference.

Thus in the first three years of his rule Gorbachev explicitly attacked lower-level party leaders. His language was even more threatening than that of Khrushchev had been, and his complaints about abuses and shortcomings more vigorous. His vigour is also reflected in the turnover rates of republican and obkom first secretaries.[134] By the time of the XIX Conference, 11 of the 14 republican first secretaries had been replaced since Gorbachev had come to power,[135] while the turnover of obkom first secretaries had also been extensive.[136]

At all levels of the system in the first three years in office in particular, Gorbachev wielded the cadres weapon to bring about mass changes. Furthermore, until 1988 this usually involved the movement into regions of people from the outside, often with recent experience working in Moscow.[137] Clearly Gorbachev was dissatisfied with the performance of many party leaders throughout the country and he sought to remedy this through a combination of exhortation, increased discipline, threats and personnel replacement. There is no evidence that, in terms of individual leaders' performance, this had much effect on the way they carried out their functions. But it did significantly increase the pressure upon them and create an environment in which they were much more vulnerable to public attack.

Central and Republican Patterns

This survey of successive central leaderships' attitudes toward lower-level party leaders shows that there is a rough correspondence between the more vigorous criticism of party leaders in the republican press and similar criticism emanating from the centre. This is shown in Table 5.3. However, the fit is by no means exact nor is the pattern standard across all republics. Republican-level criticism overlapped with that of the centre, but it did not coincide in all cases; the main exception is Uzbekistan, where vigorous criticism started earlier (as suggested in the table), while in the other republics the fit with the central pattern is much more consistent. Furthermore, the sort of language used at the centre was not evident in all republics. In an attempt to explain this, attention must be turned to the republican level.

Table 5.3. *Periodisation of central and republican level criticism*

	Republican	Central
Moderate	1953–58	1953–60
Vigorous	1959–62	1961–62
Moderate	1963–82	1963–82
Vigorous	1983–88	1983–88

REPUBLICAN POLITICS

A common feature of communist politics as it manifested itself across the globe was the use of leadership succession as an excuse for criticism of poor performance by the system as a whole. When a leader had gone, the problems currently being faced could be attributed to his influence, thereby absolving the new leadership and the system more generally from blame for current difficulties. This was evident at the all-union level in the Soviet Union, where Stalin, Khrushchev and Brezhnev were all explicitly blamed by their successors for difficulties being experienced in Soviet society. This tendency was also common at lower levels of the party structure, although it was not an inevitable consequence of leadership succession; at times, sometimes for peculiarly local reasons, leadership changeover was not accompanied by high-level criticism. The issue is whether the general pattern of criticism described above was shaped by local leadership changes.

The link between various periods of criticism and leadership change is suggested by comparing the rate of turnover of all republican party first secretaries with the approximate periodisation of the course of criticism. Table 5.4 gives the total number of first secretaries replaced during each period from 1953 to the end of 1988, the average annual percentage of turnovers in each period, and the average annual number of turnovers in each period.

The two periods of most vigorous criticism were also the periods in which the highest levels of turnover occurred. The clarity of this picture is obscured somewhat by the figures for the initial 1953–58 period. However, the comparatively high figures for this period are explained by three factors peculiar to it:

Table 5.4. Turnover of first secretaries

Period	Number	Average annual %	Average annual no.
1953–58	14	4.2	2.3
1959–62	10	4.5	2.5
1963–82	16	1.4	0.8
1983–88	16	4.8	2.6

1. The initial attempt to break with the Stalinist period, manifested in the replacement of Stalinist republican leaders. In 1953 alone there were four cases of replacement (Armenia, Azerbaijan, Georgia and Ukraine), while the replacement of first secretaries in Uzbekistan in December 1955 and Tajikistan in May 1956 can also be seen as removing holdovers from the Stalinist past.[138]
2. The shakeout associated with the defeat of the anti-party group in 1957. In December 1957 three new first secretaries were appointed in Kazakhstan, Ukraine and Uzbekistan, with Kirichenko and Mukhitdinov from the latter two republics both being promoted to Moscow to strengthen Khrushchev. The 1955 removal of Ponomarenko in Kazakhstan was also related to the demotion of his patron and Khrushchev challenger Malenkov in February 1955.
3. During this period there were four changes of leadership in Kazakhstan, a level of turnover unparalleled in post-Stalin times. These are discussed below.

This means that there were special circumstances responsible for the high level of turnover during this initial period, and if the effect of these is discounted, the approximate coincidence between high turnover and vigorous criticism is evident.[139]

All of the leadership changes in the five republics studied are outlined in Table 5.5. If republican leadership changes were instrumental in shaping the outbreaks of more vigorous criticism, those changes would have to have taken place either shortly before the criticism began or during its course. The potentially relevant leadership changes were:

Uzbekistan: Kamalov/Rashidov, Rashidov/Usmankhodzhaev, Usmankhodzhaev/Nishanov
Tajikistan: Ul'dzhabaev/Rasulov, Rasulov/Nabiev, Nabiev/Makhkamov
Kazakhstan: Beliaev/Kunaev, Kunaev/Yusupov, Kunaev/Kolbin
Ukraine: –
Belorussia: Masherov/Kiselev, Kiselev/Sliun'kov, Sliun'kov/Sokolov

Comparison of this pattern of leadership changes with the 1959–62 period of vigorous criticism of local leaderships helps to explain one of the features of the pattern of criticism. The

Table 5.5. *Republican leadership successions*

Uzbekistan	Tajikistan	Kazakhstan	Ukraine	Belorussia
Niiazov	Gafurov	Shaiakhmetov	Melnikov	Patolichev
		2/54	4/53	
		Ponomarenko	Kirichenko	
12/55		5/55		
Mukhitdinov		Brezhnev		
	5/56	3/56		7/56
	Ul'dzhabaev	Yakovlev		Mazurov
12/57		12/57	12/57	
Kamalov		Beliaev	Podgornyi	
3/59				
Rashidov				
		1/60		
		Kunaev		
	4/61			
	Rasulov			
		12/62		
		Yusupov		
			6/63	
			Shelest	
		12/64		
		Kunaev		
				3/65
				Masherov
			5/72	
			Shcherbitsky	
				10/80
				Kiselev
	4/82			
	Nabiev			
10/83				1/83
Usmankhod-				Sliun'kov
zhaev				
	12/85			
	Makhkamov			
		12/86		
		Kolbin		
				2/87
				Sokolov
1/88				
Nishanov				
6/89		6/89	9/89	
Karimov		Nazarbaev	Ivashko	
			7/90	
			Gurenko	

relative weakness of the criticism in Ukraine and Belorussia during 1959–62 may partly be due to the absence of relevant leadership changes near this period. In Belorussia, although the replacement of Patolichev by Mazurov in July 1956 had been preceded by public criticism of the leadership under Patolichev,[140] by 1959–60 more than three years had elapsed. Such a period would have made attempts to link current problems with the former leader difficult to sustain. Furthermore Patolichev was Minister for Foreign Trade from 1958 to 1985, a position which probably discouraged criticism from within his former bailiwick. In Ukraine, when Kirichenko was replaced by Podgornyi in December 1957, the former was taken to Moscow to become a CC secretary, and although he lost this post in May 1960 (apparently as a scapegoat for the agricultural failure of 1959[141]), his position at the centre and support from Khrushchev were probably sufficient to dissuade his Ukrainian successor from engaging in full-scale criticism of his period in Kiev at the outset of his tenure. Although such criticism could conceivably have been mounted following Kirichenko's fall from grace, it would have appeared odd given the quiescence immediately following his departure from Kiev. Thus in both Belorussia and Ukraine there was not a suitable leadership succession upon which significant criticism could hang.

The situation in Kazakhstan was a little more complex, with two leadership changes occurring in 1960 and 1962. The former change, which saw Kunaev replace Beliaev, was clearly linked to Khrushchev. There had been criticism of the state of affairs in Kazakhstan in both the central and republican press for some time, and Khrushchev had personally been openly critical of the state of agriculture in the republic. The Virgin Lands scheme had been his initiative and, despite the opening of new land, the size of the harvest in Kazakhstan had declined. Khrushchev held first secretary Beliaev directly responsible.[142] The Kazakh CC removed Beliaev at its January plenum, with Brezhnev in attendance. He was replaced by Kunaev, who only held this post for two years before being shifted to chairmanship of the Council of Ministers (whence he had come) to make way for Yusupov. The means of removal of Beliaev clearly opened him up to criticism sanctioned from above. Similarly the shifting of Kunaev seemed to set Kunaev up as a likely target for vigorous local criticism; it followed Khrushchev's criticism of Kazakhstan at the November 1962 CC CPSU plenum[143] and criticism of Kunaev for personnel mistakes and for allowing abuses to occur.[144] But Kunaev was less vulnerable than Khrushchev's criticism may suggest because he was still in a position to exercise significant power at the republican level; Brezhnev's continuing support was probably also significant here. Nevertheless, even the effect of his position and high-level support was not sufficient to prevent all such criticism from occurring; his long-standing rivalry with Yusupov, reflected in the latter's criticisms during 1961, fuelled similar criticisms in the year following Kunaev's displacement.

There was only one succession in Tajikistan, from Ul'dzhabaev to Rasulov in April 1961. The plenum at which this occurred was witness to scathing attacks on Ul'dzhabaev.[145] Along with the chairman of the Council of Ministers (Dodkhudoev) he was openly accused of hiding his failings through eyewash, deception and report-padding. Cadres had been selected on the basis of locality, friendship and personal devotion, which gave rise to familyness, mutual guarantees and suppression of criticism. Ul'dzhabaev was accused of using this network of personal protection to profit from criminal activity, and was not only removed as republican first secretary, but expelled from the party. The image presented of Ul'dzhabaev, in particular using deception to hide his failings, accorded perfectly with the model Khrushchev had been attacking since the Riazan affair came to light. This may in part explain the vigour of the criticism. But probably also important was the apparent rivalry between Ul'dzhabaev and his successor Rasulov. In August 1960 Rasulov had been dropped from his positions as member of the CC Bureau (a post he had held since 1954) and CC secretary. This may have meant that he was content to see criticism of his predecessor, to whom he may have felt he owed little. Rasulov used the criticism campaign to promote supporters in place of those allied to his former rival Ul'dzhabaev and to demonstrate his reliability to Moscow by reinforcing the central campaign of criticism of Ul'dzhabaev.

In Uzbekistan, where the criticism was most vigorous, there was one instance of leadership succession, from Kamalov to Rashidov, which occurred in 1959 before the development of the major central campaign against local officials in 1961. In domestic Uzbek affairs, Kamalov had been a principal rival of his predecessor Mukhitdinov.[146] When the latter was moved to Moscow in 1957, he continued to meddle in Uzbek affairs in an attempt to unsettle his former opponent. In attempting to do this, one of Mukhitdinov's main supporters was Rashidov. In this way, Rashidov and Kamalov were established rivals, with the result that Rashidov had little incentive to try to curb criticism of his predecessor once he became first secretary.[147] Indeed, he pursued this vigorously, using the criticism campaign and accompanying personnel changes to place his own supporters in positions of responsibility in the republic. Thus in the Uzbek case there was clearly a coincidence of interests between the centre, whose views would have been shaped by its Uzbek 'expert' Mukhitdinov prior to his fall at the end of 1959, and the new republican leader in attacking Kamalov.[148]

The removal of republican first secretaries in this period was not confined to those discussed above. In addition, during this time there were leadership changes in Turkmenistan (Babaev/Karaev 12/58 and Karaev/Ovezov 5/60 – Babaev died), Azerbaijan (Mustafeev/Akhundov 7/59), Latvia (Kalnberzin/Pel'she 11/59), Armenia (Tovmasian/Zarobian 12/60), Kirgizia (Razzakov/Usubaliev 5/61), and Moldavia (Serdiuk/Bodiul 5/61). In the period between March 1959 and May 1961, changes of first secretary occurred in nine of the 14 union republics that had republican parties; the exceptions were Belorussia, Estonia, Georgia, Lithuania and Ukraine. This is a significant level of turnover and reflects a major centrally inspired reshuffling of personnel in the lead-up to the XXII Congress. This is what Michel Tatu refers to as the 'Pre-Congress Purge'[149] and reflects attempts by central politicians to consolidate themselves prior to the congress.

The second period of more vigorous criticism (1983–88) also witnessed significant levels of turnover among republican party first secretaries. In the republics in which we are interested, the following leadership successions occurred:

Uzbekistan: Rashidov/Usmankhodzhaev, Usmankhodzhaev/Nishanov
Tajikistan: Nabiev/Makhkamov
Kazakhstan: Kunaev/Kolbin
Ukraine: –
Belorussia: Kiselev/Sliun'kov, Sliun'kov/Sokolov

The replacement of Rashidov by Usmankhodzhaev was occasioned by the former's death in November 1983. However, it also occurred in the early stages of the public airing of the Uzbek affair, and Rashidov's death provided the opportunity for Andropov to shift in someone in an attempt to combat the abuses of which this affair consisted. Usmankhodzhaev had served in the Bureau under Rashidov for some years, but did not come from the same locality as Rashidov and most of those who formed the ruling clique around the first secretary. Furthermore he had served the 1969–72 period in Moscow, presumably where he had come under the notice of those around Andropov in 1983.[150] With the expectation from the centre that Usmankhodzhaev should prosecute the anti-corruption campaign in Uzbekistan, the fact that he was not an established close member of Rashidov's clique may have made satisfying this expectation somewhat easier than it might otherwise have been. However, as a prominent politician throughout much of the Rashidov period, Usmankhodzhaev also had an interest in seeking to ensure that the campaign did not escape control. He sought to limit the unrolling of the anti-corruption campaign, in particular by making Rashidov its main focus. Within the context of the removal of virtually all of the leading Uzbek politicians who survived from the Rashidov era, this was becoming increasingly difficult the further the campaign went. This was especially the case given the attitude of chairman of the Supreme Soviet Rafik Nishanov, who had been removed from high office and sent into disgrace under Rashidov but had come back at the time of his death. In the words of one scholar, he 'seemed to relish the opportunity to demolish the "Rashidov myth"'.[151] When the seemingly inexorable logic of the removal of Rashidov-era leaders reached its conclusion with the replacement of Usmankhodzhaev by Nishanov, the latter could allow full vent to be given to the criticism of the former leader. With the subsequent arrest, charge with corruption and sentence to 12 years imprisonment of Usmankhodzhaev, fuel was given to the anti-corruption campaign in Uzbekistan.

In Tajikistan, Nabiev had come to power as a result of the death of his predecessor in April 1982. More vigorous criticism in the republic does not appear to have begun until 1984–85, clearly under impetus from the centre. It was in December 1985 that Makhkamov replaced Nabiev, who officially retired on pension despite being only 55 years of age. The conduct of the Tajik economy had been under criticism for some time, but as Makhkamov had been chairman of the Council of Ministers since 1982, any criticism directed at Nabiev on this basis would have been a double-edged sword. But because Makhkamov had not earlier held a full-time party post, criticism of leadership in that realm was less likely to involve the new first secretary. At the XXVII CPSU Congress Makhkamov gave a speech in which he was very critical of corruption and saw it as a major issue, and his continued tenure of the Tajik first secretaryship until the twilight of Soviet power, gaining membership of the central Politburo at the XXVIII Congress in July 1990 in his capacity as Tajik leader, suggests that he continued to play a role deemed satisfactory by the centre. Once again local ambition plus central stimulus was instrumental in structuring criticism.

In Kazakhstan, the long-time Brezhnev associate Dinmukhamed Kunaev was replaced by Gennadi Kolbin in December 1986. Kolbin's appointment was a conscious move by the Gorbachev leadership to promote into the leading position in Kazakhstan an outsider who could be relied upon to follow the centre's wishes and clean up the mess that was perceived to exist there. Kolbin was a Russian with no links to the republic. He was clearly sent to break up the personal machine of Kunaev which had controlled the republic since the mid-1960s, and despite the public disturbances on his appointment, he proceeded to attack that machine with vigour. Thus he was willing to pursue an anti-corruption course not only because of the bidding of his central supporters, but also because destroying the power and reputation of his predecessor was the best way of establishing his own authority. This was, therefore, a case of a new leader vigorously sponsoring a campaign of criticism both in support of a central policy change and in order to strengthen his own position in the republic. But Kolbin's position was not as clear-cut as this may suggest. It was complicated by the growing prominence of Council of Ministers chairman Nazarbaev, who had been appointed in 1984 after having, in the words of one obkom boss, risen 'as quickly as yeast' in the early 1980s.[152] As Nazarbaev and Kolbin manoeuvred for advantage, they both had interests in developing strong criticisms of Kunaev's legacy.

But the situation was even more complicated than this

suggests. High levels of criticism occurred in Kazakhstan well before Kunaev's removal and while Kolbin was still located outside the republic, in Ul'ianovsk. Central criticism of corruption in Kazakhstan had occurred since 1984, and with the critical comments made by Gorbachev about the state of low-level personnel affairs in 1985 and 1986, it is clear that pressure was mounting in the republic. It seems that Kunaev's response was to seek to deflect blame by joining in that criticism and using it as a cover to suggest that he was acting vigorously to eliminate the negative aspects of life in the republic. The personal role he played in giving voice to that criticism suggests that this was a conscious tactic. Although in political terms the success of this tactic was undercut in part by Nazarbaev's increasingly critical attitude to Kunaev,[153] it did serve to swell the wave of criticism that was growing around the republic. So here was a case of a republican leader falling in behind a centrally inspired campaign in an endeavour to protect his position, which must have seemed increasingly shaky in the light of the death of Brezhnev, the subsequent anti-corruption campaign targeting Kazakhstan among other republics, and the stance adopted by Nazarbaev.

In Ukraine, where criticism was muted, there were no changes of first secretary until September 1989, reflecting the strength of the hold Shcherbitsky had in the republic and his prominence in Moscow. Furthermore, the absence of the sort of threatening language evident in both the central press and the republican press in those republics where a campaign occurred shows the ability of the Ukrainian leader to control the tenor of reporting in the republic when his position was not under threat. The contrast between the strong campaign against Kunaev and the lack of such criticism of Shcherbitsky, also a long-standing member of the Brezhnev Politburo, is clear.

In Belorussia too the criticism was much less vigorous than it was in either of the Central Asian republics or Kazakhstan. There were two leadership changes, Kiselev to Sliun'kov and Sliun'kov to Sokolov. The former succession was brought on by Kiselev's death. Sliun'kov had spent the previous eight years working in Moscow, but in domestic Belorussian politics he had been part of a different faction to his predecessor. Upon coming to power, he proceeded to foster the rise of members of his faction at the expense of others,[154] but despite the obvious circumstances that seemed to favour such a development, this was not accompanied by a vigorous campaign to impugn the name of his predecessor. When Sliun'kov was promoted to Moscow as CC secretary in February 1987, he was replaced by Sokolov. Despite the fact that the latter was not a member of the same faction as Sliun'kov, again there was no public retribution. Gorbachev's former association with and public support for Sliun'kov, added to possible domestic Belorussian factors in the form of implicit agreements associated with cross-factional coalition building,[155] explains the absence of vigorous criticism under Sokolov. It also shows the ability of these first secretaries to control the content of the republican press.

What sort of pattern does this suggest? Criticism of a predecessor seems to be most vigorous when three things are combined: a central campaign emphasising criticism, a change of leader at the republican level which brings to power someone who was not an intimate of his predecessor, with the former leader not promoted and thereby made relatively invulnerable. This was clearly reflected in those instances where criticism was most severe (Uzbekistan in March 1959 and October 1983, Tajikistan in April 1961 and December 1985, and Kazakhstan in January 1960 and December 1986) and was not in those instances where criticism was more muted (Ukraine and Belorussia throughout the period; Kazakhstan in December 1962 is a special case). Without a leadership change, there is no scapegoat for local-level criticism. However, without the green-light from the centre, there seems to have been a marked reluctance to engage in open and forthright criticism, even if the new incumbent was politically opposed to his predecessor. This is shown by a glance at the leadership successions prior to 1982 and not yet discussed (there is no consideration of those occurring after 1988 because by then the rules of intra-party politics had changed fundamentally). The relevant successions were as follows:

Uzbekistan: Niiazov/Mukhitdinov, Mukhitdinov/Kamalov
Tajikistan: Gafurov/Ul'dzhabaev
Kazakhstan: Shaiakhmetov/Ponomarenko, Ponomarenko/ Brezhnev, Brezhnev/Yakovlev, Yakovlev/Beliaev, Yusupov/ Kunaev

Ukraine: Melnikov/Kirichenko, Kirichenko/Podgornyi, Podgornyi/Shelest, Shelest/Shcherbitsky
Belorussia: Patolichev/Mazurov, Mazurov/Masherov, Masherov/Kiselev

In Uzbekistan, the replacement of Niiazov by Mukhitdinov was engineered by Khrushchev personally, while the emergence of Kamalov as first secretary was a result of the promotion of Mukhitdinov to Moscow. In both cases the position of first secretary was filled by a rival of the immediate past incumbent.[156] Immediately following Niiazov's ouster, there was some criticism of, among other things, cadre policy in some regions being conducted on the basis of friendship, nepotism and region,[157] and this was associated directly with the central Uzbek leadership. At the XIII Congress of the CPUz, Mukhitdinov openly attacked Niiazov,[158] but no sustained campaign emerged. In the case of the Kamalov succession, while there was some criticism of economic leadership,[159] any propensity to criticise would probably have been blunted by recognition of the powerful position Mukhitdinov seemed to have in Moscow.

In Tajikistan there was only one succession, when the long-time first secretary Bobodzhan Gafurov (he had become first secretary in 1946 and was the longest serving in the region) was replaced by Tursumbai Ul'dzhabaev. Gafurov may have been removed as part of the general de-Stalinisation following the XX Congress, but there appears to have been no personal animus on the part of Khrushchev towards him.[160] Gafurov was appointed Director of the Institute of Oriental Studies in Moscow at a time when its political importance increased substantially.[161] Ul'dzhabaev came from the same district as Gafurov and appears to have been assisted in his career by the person he replaced,[162] and so had little reason to foster criticism of his predecessor.

In Kazakhstan there were four changes of first secretary in four years beginning with the shift of Ponomarenko into the republic in 1954. The original replacement of Shaiakhmetov by Ponomarenko was part of Khrushchev's drive to launch the Virgin Lands scheme; Shaiakhmetov and his deputy had been resistant to this, so Khrushchev moved Ponomarenko and Brezhnev into the republic to replace them at the head of the party.[163] There was some criticism of leadership at this time, with Shaiakhmetov being accused of nationalism, lack of attention to the real situation on the ground, nepotism and localism in personnel matters, and bureaucratic methods of leadership,[164] but it was not very vigorous.[165] Within a short period Ponomarenko was replaced by his deputy and Khrushchev client Brezhnev. As a client of Malenkov, Ponomarenko's fall was due to the demotion of his patron; he became ambassador to Warsaw. While again there was some criticism of the leadership at different levels of the republic following his fall, there was no concerted or vigorous campaign. In February 1956 Brezhnev returned to Moscow as a CC secretary, being replaced by his deputy Yakovlev. With Brezhnev's star on the ascendant, he was not vulnerable to a major criticism campaign. However, the continuing crop failure in the Virgin Lands did make Yakovlev vulnerable, but there was barely a ripple of criticism in the Kazakh press when he was replaced by Beliaev in December 1957. In December 1964, following continuing agricultural disappointment but more importantly the replacement of Khrushchev by Brezhnev, Yusupov was replaced by Brezhnev ally Kunaev. No vigorous criticism ensued, despite the seemingly favourable conditions of a failed first secretary plus support for the new incumbent from Moscow.

In Ukraine Melnikov was replaced three months after Stalin's death. He was charged with poor leadership, errors in cadre selection and incorrect implementation of the party's nationality policy, charges which amounted to a criticism of his pursuit of the Stalinist policies in nationality affairs.[166] The replacement of Kirichenko by Podgornyi in December 1957 was occasioned by the former's promotion to the post of secretary of the CC CPSU, and therefore to a position which would have dissuaded Podgornyi from criticising his predecessor had he wished to do so. Similarly Podgornyi's replacement by Shelest in June 1963 saw the former move to Moscow to become a CC secretary, and thereby gain relative immunity to criticism in Ukraine. By contrast, the replacement of Shelest by Shcherbitsky in May 1972 was clearly a demotion for Shelest as a result of his opposition to a series of policies pursued by the Brezhnev leadership over the preceding years;[167] the criticism of personnel sponsored by Shelest in the period before his removal and noted in Chapter 3 was more vigorous than that voiced by the centre, and may have been one factor here. There was some criticism of Shelest following his removal,[168] but this focused on nationality policy and did not approach the levels of a significant campaign.

In Belorussia the replacement of Patolichev by Mazurov in July 1956 had been preceded by criticism of the republican leadership at the BCP Congress in January 1956, so the way seemed clear for further criticism once Patolichev had gone. Furthermore, although Patolichev became Minister for Foreign Trade, he was not one of Khrushchev's close colleagues[169] and would therefore not have enjoyed his personal protection. But there was no vigorous criticism campaign, despite the seeming opportunity for one to develop. The Mazurov/Masherov succession came about as a result of the former's promotion to Moscow for his support for the move against Khrushchev,[170] and therefore into a position from which criticism could be discouraged. In any case, he was replaced by his deputy, who was also a member of the same 'Partisan' faction in Belorussia,[171] and who therefore probably had little reason to pursue a campaign of criticism. Nevertheless, comment on personnel matters in Belorussia during the 1970s was sharper than we might have expected, even though it was not sufficient to label it a full-blown campaign. The harshness of the tone, reflecting doubts about the thrust of the 'trust in cadres' policy, is related to the tension that developed between Brezhnev and Mazurov in Moscow (leading to the latter's dismissal in November 1978), a tension translated into Belorussia by the attempt of a pro-Brezhnev group to undermine Masherov's leadership.[172] The harshness of tone was related to this struggle. The Masherov/Kiselev succession followed the death of Masherov in an automobile accident. The circumstances surrounding this were mysterious, and it is possible that he was killed for political reasons.[173] He was replaced by Kiselev, who was a client of Brezhnev and therefore not a member of the 'Partisan' faction. Thus, favourable grounds seemed to exist for the unrolling of a criticism campaign, but no full-blown campaign developed.

This brief survey of leadership changes outside the periods of most vigorous criticism suggests the importance of a centrally sanctioned campaign for the mounting of such criticism at the republican level. Even when there may have been personal, domestic republican or centrally based antagonisms between successor and former incumbent, as in the cases of the

Niiazov/Mukhitdinov, Mukhitdinov/Kamalov, Shaiakhmetov/ Ponomarenko, Ponomarenko/Brezhnev, Yakovlev/Beliaev, Yusupov/Kunaev, Shelest/Shcherbitsky and Masherov/Kiselev successions, criticism was at best muted and there was no widespread criticism campaign in the republic. Only when such a campaign was centrally sanctioned, for central political reasons, was a republican campaign forthcoming.

But it is important to recognise too that, even during the periods of heightened criticism, this did not take a consistent pattern across all republics. The criticism was much less potent and vigorous in Ukraine and Belorussia than it was in the other three republics. The absence of a leadership change in the early 1960s in both republics and in Ukraine in the early 1980s is one factor here, although this should not have prevented all criticism from occurring. In Belorussia there was a leadership succession (Kiselev/Sliun'kov) which seemed to have the ingredients to trigger a widespread criticism campaign; not only did it coincide with the Brezhnev/Andropov succession in Moscow, but in Belorussia it involved the wholesale replacement of the pro-Brezhnev faction led by Kiselev by the faction headed by Sliun'kov and focused on Minsk.[174] But it did not produce a vigorous criticism campaign. This suggests that, even when there was a centrally inspired criticism campaign, republican leaders had some room for manoeuvre in how they responded to that campaign, particularly if they were not vulnerable themselves; the Kunaev–Shcherbitsky comparison makes this clear. They did not slavishly have to follow the lead from Moscow, although there was clearly some need to trim their sails to keep the centre happy. Crucial here was the political structure which existed in the republic, and this is discussed in the following chapter.

Thus the pattern that emerges here seems clear, if somewhat messy. High levels of vigorous criticism are most likely in a republic where:

* a vigorous central campaign of criticism is underway;
* a change of republican first secretary occurs which:
    - brings to power someone not closely associated with the former incumbent;
    - the former incumbent does not enjoy the support of a high-level patron in Moscow;

– the former incumbent does not occupy a position which makes him relatively invulnerable to criticism.

If either of these main conditions is absent, criticism is likely to remain closer to the routine level and to lack the vigour of the more exceptional periods. But comparison of the major periods of vigorous criticism at the republican and central levels (see Table 5.3) shows that these periods did not exactly coincide. With the exception of the initial period of vigorous criticism at the republican level (1959–62), this pattern is consistent with the lower levels taking their lead from the centre. Standardised patterns of criticism are pursued except when the centre seeks independently to stimulate criticism at a higher level, as it did in 1983.[175] Once the centre decided to raise the tempo of criticism, republics fell into line, with those experiencing recent appropriate leadership changes most active in doing so. This timetable is consistent with republican leaders seeking to avoid bringing undue central attention to themselves as well as with the sort of local power structure discussed in the following chapter. However, the earlier period of vigorous criticism does not appear to be consistent with this pattern because the outbreak of vigorous criticism at the republican level seems to predate that of the centre. This suggests a relative primacy for republican-level events, and if we look at the three republics where criticism was most robust, it is clear that there were republican level factors at work: in Uzbekistan the Kamalov/Rashidov succession (March 1959) was preceded by a prolonged struggle fuelled in part by Mukhitdinov in Moscow, in Tajikistan tensions had been present within the leadership prior to the Ul'dzhabaev/Rasulov succession (witness Rasulov's demotion in August 1960), and in Kazakhstan the Beliaev/Kunaev succession (January 1960) was preceded by central concern at the course of economic development in the republic, a point local opponents were pleased to take up. Clearly republican-level developments were important in the generation of vigorous criticism, although central agreement was necessary for it to achieve a full flowering. Important in understanding the role of republican-level developments is analysis of the power structure at this level, and it is to this which we must now turn.

6 The Pattern of Power

The discussion of the more vigorous periods of criticism in Chapters 2 and 4 shows that there were certain sorts of formulations which kept recurring in party discussions of leadership failings. While the similar nature of such formulations may reflect editorial policy, and in particular a desire to be guided by the sort of language used by political leaders, it also reflects a certain commonality of problems across both different parts of the country and different time periods. The issue here is the extent to which the criticism accurately reflects the situation at which it is directed, and therefore the degree to which it is indicative of the real nature of problems within the party structure.

CRITICISM AND CORRUPTION

The most extensive and vigorous bout of criticism was directed at the state of affairs in the Uzbek republic in the early 1980s. An early warning of this affair was the despatch of an official of the Procurator's Office in 1980 to investigate corruption in the republic,[1] an activity which was blocked by Uzbek first secretary Sharaf Rashidov. However, in Rashidov's final months and with Andropov's national anti-corruption campaign unrolling, the pressure began to build; further central investigators were sent in 1983, and between July 1983 and May 1984 five officials were expelled from the Uzbek CC. The affair really burst onto the scene at the June 1984 plenum of the Uzbek CC,[2] and it attracted open criticism at the XXVII Congress of the CPSU in February 1986.[3] Echoes of this continued into 1991 with the controversy over the actions of the two chief investigators sent to Uzbekistan, Telman Gdlian and Nikolai Ivanov,[4] but the main thrust of criticism of Uzbekistan subsided following the replacement of Uzbek first secretary Usmankhodzhaev by Nishanov in January 1988 and the more general discussion of corruption at the XIX Conference in June–July of that year.

The origins of the Uzbek affair lay in the cotton harvest.

Investigations showed that since 1978, Uzbek officials had been engaged in a major exercise of report-padding. Between 1978 and 1983, officials had reported each year that the crop was between 500 000 and 900 000 tonnes greater than it was, with the result that over this period Moscow paid Uzbekistan more than one billion roubles for some 4.5 million tonnes of raw cotton that existed only on paper.[5] This fabrication of production was unusual not just because of the scale of the over-reporting, but because of the extent of those involved. The network of those implicated spread far beyond those types of officials usually involved in such activities, heads of production units, district and perhaps oblast leaders. In Uzbekistan the network of involvement spread all the way up the Uzbek political structure, including the party first secretary and the chairman of the Council of Ministers, and even included leading officials in Moscow. This was clearly far more wide-ranging than the normal cases of report-padding criticised in the press.

While the extent of falsification and fraud alone would have made the Uzbek affair something of a *cause célèbre*, what gave it its real impact was the extent of the network of informal power relations it revealed. At the heart of this was party first secretary Sharaf Rashidov and the politico-administrative structure he headed. Following his consolidation of power in the 1960s,[6] Rashidov was able to build a political machine resting principally upon personal associations mediated through nepotism, friendship and shared region of origin. This political machine permeated and effectively displaced the formal political structure as the principal mechanism for running affairs in Uzbekistan. While its original currency was personal relationships, what oiled the wheels of its functioning was the proceeds of what was vigorously lambasted in the Soviet press as corruption. The 'cotton scandal' was one aspect of this. The economy of the republic was largely taken over by Rashidov's informal machine, and while some of the proceeds of the economy continued to be directed into public purposes like housing and education, a significant part was siphoned off into the pockets of officials. Much of this was spent on further development of illegal economic activity, but a considerable portion also went into sustaining a luxurious lifestyle. Rashidov and those in key positions below him led a style of life which the ordinary member of the nomenklatura with their own privileged lifestyle, let alone the Soviet citizen, could barely imagine.[7] Mutual protection and cover-up, allied to the inclusion in this network of responsible people in all walks of life in the republic including the law enforcement organs, were the main defences of this informal structure.[8] The whole economy and public life of the republic was subverted by Rashidov and his supporters whose connections and alliances spanned the various official institutions and, in practice, effectively displaced them. In turn Rashidov was firmly supported by a patron in Moscow, party General Secretary Brezhnev.

The extent of the republican-level involvement in the Rashidov machine is reflected in the casualties of the purge mounted by Moscow from 1984. Rashidov himself was discredited posthumously and his body removed from its place of honour in the mausoleum in Tashkent. Among those indicted were the chairs of the Council of Ministers and Supreme Soviet, the Minister and Deputies of Internal Affairs, Ministry of Internal Affairs officials in many regions of Uzbekistan, and many managers of production enterprises in the republic. Between 1981 and 1986 some three-quarters of the CC were removed. In 1986 alone, some 750 people in leadership positions were replaced, including eight obkom secretaries, 100 gorkom and raikom secretaries, 40 gorispolkom and raiispolkom chairmen, and 18 ministers and other agency heads. Some 90 per cent of directors of state and collective farms were replaced, while during the period of the purge the net depletion of party ranks (expulsions and terminations less admissions – it is unclear whether the figure includes deaths) was in the tens of thousands.[9] More than half of the CC CPSU and CPUz nomenklatura in Uzbekistan was replaced.[10] Also arrested and ultimately imprisoned was USSR First Deputy Minister of Internal Affairs and Brezhnev's son-in-law Yuri Churbanov and, paradoxically, the person who had carried much of the purge in Uzbekistan, Rashidov's replacement as first secretary Usmankhodzhaev.

The Uzbek affair was clearly an important instance of the prosecution of corruption in the USSR. It also raised the question of why this sort of activity had taken on such a scale in Uzbekistan. The answer offered by many has been couched in cultural terms. The crux of this sort of explanation has been to argue that the cultural norms of Central Asian society have facilitated the development and strengthening of such patterns of behaviour. The continuing strength of kin and clan associations in combination with a highly developed sense of personal and familial obligations is said to have encouraged the formation of strong informal networks which subverted the official structure. Cultural norms emphasising familial and tribal obligations underlay the widespread filling of positions with family members, clansmen and fellow tribesmen, and strengthened the tendency for mutual assistance and protection. Such norms were said also to be instrumental in encouraging people to look 'instinctively for leadership to a chieftain and his council of elders'.[11] In the view of one observer,[12] the effect of these traditional social bonds was strengthened by the way in which Central Asians used them as a means of rebuffing the assimilationist policies fostered by the centre.

It is not clear how important such cultural factors were. Strong extended family, kinship, tribal and regional bonds, allied to the preservation of cultural norms through the continuing strength of pre-Soviet traditions (of which Islam is probably the most important), would have affected the behaviour patterns of many Uzbeks at all levels of society; certainly Soviet explanations of corruption in Central Asia emphasised the importance of culture.[13] Such traditions would have sustained the types of informal networks which emerged in Uzbekistan. But how important were traditionally based cultural values in structuring the course of Uzbek public life?[14] Although there are significant problems in attempting to use political culture as an explanation for political structures or events,[15] both in terms of establishing the precise content of cultural values and handling the question of causality, it would be naive to assume that cultural values play no part in defining political life. While not having deterministic power, culture does play a part in moulding the contours of politics; although culture cannot determine particular outcomes or patterns of action, it can make particular sorts of results more likely by providing historico-cultural validation for certain sorts of potential patterns and denying it to others. This means that a culture with strong elements of obligation like those sketched above would have both facilitated and sustained the sort of political machine which developed in Uzbekistan. But because culture alone cannot determine an outcome, the development of such informal structures and practices as those brought to light in the Uzbek affair should not be attributed to cultural factors specific to Central Asia alone.

A glance at other major targets of anti-corruption campaigns shows similarities with the Central Asian experience. The public campaign against corruption in Georgia which unrolled in 1972 and involved the replacement of first secretary Vasilii Mzhavanadze by Eduard Shevardnadze, brought to light many of the same abuses evident in Uzbekistan, including the effective division of the republic into spheres of influence run by individuals under the overall patronage of the first secretary.[16] The crackdown on corruption in Azerbaijan following Gaidar Aliev's accession to the first secretaryship in 1969 also brought to light the existence of informal networks of influence and power which were used by incumbents to line their own pockets.[17] While both of these major campaigns threw up the same sort of informal personal structures as had existed in Uzbekistan, the Transcaucasia region is also one where scholars have seen cultural influences not unlike those of Central Asia.[18] However, such cultural claims have not been made of the regions experiencing some other celebrated anti-corruption campaigns in which similar structures and processes have been present. The moves against Brezhnev-client Sergei Medunov in Krasnodar krai culminating in 1983[19] and against N.A. Bondarenko in Rostov in 1984[20] both brought to light networks of corruption resting upon informal personal machines at the service of the local leader and used by that person and his cronies for their own purposes, but without the explanation of tribal culture. Central to all the major corruption campaigns regardless of the area in which they occurred was the informal political machine focused on the party secretary.

A more important factor in showing that the processes and structures in Uzbekistan were not unique is the nature of the charges made against deficient leaderships in all parts of the country during periods when no criticism campaign was being vigorously pursued by Moscow. These criticisms are charted in Chapter 3, but what do they mean? For the purposes of discussion, the two most important areas are leadership and cadre policy, and although during the Brezhnev period the emphasis was on honest cadres doing their best, it was recognised that there were problems.

Leadership

The charges which fit into this category relate to deficiencies in the operation of the formal principles designed to structure leadership roles in the party, and to the abuses that flowed from the subversion of such principles. One set of charges relating to the formal principles complained about the way in which leading party bodies knew very little about the situation prevailing at lower levels, including in party organs at those levels. Complaints about the weakness of links between levels of the party, about rare visits to the localities by party secretaries, telephone and declarative methods of leadership and the weakness of verification of the implementation of party decisions all convey a sense of party organs out of touch with what was happening at lower levels. Associated with this was the charge that party bodies were insufficiently demanding in what they expected of cadres, and often adopted a liberal attitude to infringements of party norms and rules. Sometimes party organs were also accused of taking too much on themselves, either in the form of petty tutelage/podmena (the substitution of party organs for state organs) or of higher organs deciding issues which should be resolved at lower levels. These all involved a failure on the part of higher party organs to exercise satisfactory leadership over those below them.

Another set of charges relating to the formal principles criticised the weakness of collective leadership in party organs. Sometimes this was directly linked with the over-bearing role of a single individual or with the charge that a narrow circle of people decided all issues. This was usually associated with the perceived weakness of criticism and self-criticism, and therefore intra-party democracy, with a bureaucratic style of leadership, and with the weakness of party meetings. Meetings were often said to be held infrequently and, when they were held, to be conducted in a purely formal fashion; this meant that the rank-and-file played little part in the meetings, which were dominated by the leadership with their set speeches and prepared resolutions.

Cadre Policy

Concerns about the conduct of cadre policy fall into three main areas: party entry, party training, and promotion/appointment policy. With regard to party entry, concern was sometimes expressed about the failure of party bodies to ensure the correct class distribution of new members; usually this was a complaint about the weakness of working-class recruitment. But this can be seen as an element in the broader problem, that of failing to take sufficient care about the recruitment process. Complaints about collective rather than individual recruitment, the failure adequately to vet prospective new members, and the general failure to follow specified entry procedures suggested that party entry was not the hurdle it was meant to be.

If quality control was a problem at the point of entry, it was not necessarily overcome once a new member had joined the party. Deficiencies in the conduct of ideological training was a frequent complaint. Another matter for concern was that party bodies did not give sufficient attention to the development of an adequate cadre reserve. This also had implications for promotion/appointment policy.

The failure to develop a cadre reserve meant that the party organ often did not have sufficient capable and trained people available to fill responsible positions when they became vacant. As a result, incompetent or unsuitable people were often appointed to these posts. Alternatively appointments to responsible positions were made from among the same narrow group of leaders each time, thereby creating an illusion of 'irreplaceability' around these people. Another common complaint was that Leninist norms and principles of cadre selection were infringed; people were appointed to responsible positions not on the basis of their professional and political qualifications, but on the basis of their personal or kinship relations with the leader, personal friendship or common place of origin.

These sorts of complaints, which were made across the country and throughout the entire post-Stalin period, regardless of whether major criticism campaigns were being conducted or not, reflect a party structure operating on the basis of practices and principles often quite at variance with those officially prescribed to structure its functioning. They are also quite consistent with the sort of situation which gave birth to the Uzbek and other scandals criticised in the periods of more vigorous criticism under Khrushchev and Gorbachev. The essence of such charges was criminal behaviour. Abuse of office, the use of official position for profit, abuse of power, fraud, embezzlement and bribery were all unacceptable and would have been considered corrupt in most political systems. Careerism and self-seeking were also attributed to party leaders. So too was the tendency to engage in toadyism, bootlicking and favouritism, charges which accused leaders of appointing to responsible positions people who were little more than their creatures. This was usually associated with charges of protectionism, of the way people banded together to support one another and defend themselves against outside attack and criticism, and of familyness, meaning the formation of such protective groups. Localism and parochialism, meaning a tendency to place the interests of one's region before national interests, was often seen as part of this. Another set of criticisms related to the way in which lower-level organs sought to deceive those at higher levels about the true state of affairs in their region. Charges of eyewash, report-padding, falsification, deception, bragging, cover-up, showiness and triumphalism are all typical of this sort of situation and were often linked with the notions of familyness, protectionism and localism already noted.[21]

These two sorts of charges, those relating to mistakes and those relating to abuses, are consistent in the picture they present. The more moderate charges may be seen as less direct and forceful means of describing the same sorts of phenomena openly criticised during the more vigorous bouts of criticism. The absence of severe criticism during the Brezhnev period, particularly concerning Uzbekistan, Tajikistan and Kazakhstan where criticism had been strongest under Khrushchev, reflected a change in the evaluation of local power structures by the centre, not a change in the nature of those structures.

The complaints about the weakness of links between party levels and weak oversight by higher organs over lower reflects the perception by Moscow authorities that party leaders at lower levels were often able to act in whatever way they wished without effective restraint or monitoring from above. The checking and verification mechanisms were not working effectively within the party, leaving the structuring of local political life largely up to the wishes of local elites. As the other complaints related to leadership suggest, such structuring was a long way from the party's official norms.

The complaints about collective leadership reflect a situation in which the local party leadership is not closely accountable to the rank-and-file. Decisions may be dominated by a small clique or even by an individual, party gatherings are infrequent and even when they are held have a purely formal character, the rank-and-file party members exercise no effective control over their leaders, nor do they participate meaningfully in party life. Thus free from such control, local leaders are able to commit abuses, from helping their friends to lining their own pockets, with relative impunity. In order to defend their position and protect themselves and their supporters, they engage in deception of those above them in the party structure.

The criticisms of cadre policy refer to the way in which such local cliques may be built up and developed. The concern about low entry standards was in some cases a euphemism for allowing people into the party regardless of their qualifications but because they support or are in some way associated with the local leadership. The weakness of training courses in the party is understandable in a context where personal loyalty and commitment are considered more important than professional/ideological qualifications. Furthermore, the association of the weakness of the cadre reserve with the claim that instead of new people being promoted into positions of responsibility, local leaderships tended to use the same people, shifting them from post to post, was a pattern consistent with the reliance by local elites upon those loyal to them personally. This was the charge openly made in the complaint about the infringement of Leninist norms in cadre policy.

The sort of construction placed upon these charges here is not, of course, the only meaning that could be attributed to them. In some cases pure incompetence and mismanagement could have been the root of the problem. In others, slackness in adherence to official norms may have been the cause. But it is interesting, and significant, that when these charges, which were made across the country and during all periods, are combined, they are consistent with a picture of local affairs led by family group structures operating through personalised networks of associations rather than the formal hierarchies of party and state bodies, just like those criticised in Uzbekistan: familyness, mutual guarantees, protectionism, nepotism, localism and rule by an unaccountable clique around the first secretary are the common features.

This sort of situation has usually been labelled corruption. Both the Soviet press and Western scholars[22] have tended to discuss this in terms of corruption, and there is an undeniable sense in which this is appropriate. When norms and rules are bent by officials in order to achieve personal gain, it is difficult to conceive of this in any other way than as corruption.[23] However, by defining such activity as corruption, Soviet commentators were able to ignore the systemic aspects of such activity and blame it squarely on the nature of the individuals involved. Many Western commentators recognised the systemic aspects of such behaviour, but while doing this and at the same time labelling it as corruption, they tended to obscure a fundamental reality of the whole situation. If such activity was a result of the logic of the system, as these commentators suggest, it is difficult to argue that it is in some way a corruption of that system. Rather what this means is that such behaviour reflects not the corruption of the system as such, but the lack of synchronisation between the fundamental logic of the system and the formal rules and principles which were ostensibly meant to guide it. In this sense the label corruption imposes a pejorative anti-systemic tag on activity which stems from the nature of the system itself. When this tag is justified is when that activity is directed at personal gain beyond that which is broadly considered acceptable within political circles. When such gain is not excessive (and the definition of this may be difficult to establish clearly and could change over time as well as vary significantly at different layers or in different sectors of the elite) such behaviour was acceptable. In other words what has here been called 'corrupt' was present at all times throughout the system, and was only seen as corrupt by those running the system when in their eyes the private gains became excessive or there was political capital to be gained from exposing and criticising it.

The central point here is that the structuring of local power around clique/family group control was a logical corollary of the way the system developed and functioned and the demands within it. Such a power structure has its roots in the early years of the Soviet regime.

UNCERTAINTY AND DECEPTION

Upon coming to power in the capital, the party sought to extend its influence throughout the country, but in doing so it had to confront a hostile environment. This was not only a result of the way it had come to power and the civil war it had to prosecute until the end of 1920, but also the policies it implemented. Even in solid working-class districts, by 1921 the Bolsheviks had used up much of the political capital they had enjoyed at the time of the October seizure of power. In this sort of threatening environment, where local party leaders had to construct an administrative system while at the same time responding to demands from above, it was a natural response for leaders to place most reliance upon those with whom they were acquainted. Leaders looked to long-time associates, friends and even family in an attempt to construct a system which was reliable. They needed to be able to rely upon and trust those with whom they worked, so personal association seemed a natural basis for cooperation. The importance of this was increased by the underdeveloped nature of the central personnel system in the initial years of Bolshevik rule when the weakness of both the record-keeping system and the institutional machinery to carry out decisions encouraged a reliance upon personal knowledge of and association with potential appointees.[24]

With the consolidation of the system in the 1920s, other pressures emerged contributing to the generation of family group control at lower levels. Significant among these were the sorts of expectations held by the centre about lower-level performance and how it should be evaluated. The leadership in Moscow made heavy demands upon its lower-level officials. During the drive for agricultural collectivisation and forced-pace industrialisation at the beginning of the 1930s in particular, they were expected almost to achieve miracles in terms of levels of collectivisation achieved, crops collected and industrial development fostered. When the tempo and momentum of the 'great transformation' slowed and the system lapsed into a more regularised mode of operation, the demands were none the less emphatic. Now cast in terms of the responsibility of local party leaders for the levels of production achieved in the regions over which they presided, success in party office was judged in terms of satisfying central targets for economic production. Despite the continued injunctions against podmena, success nevertheless depended upon the performance of the local economy, and therefore provided a compelling incentive for party leaders continually to become involved in economic matters. The problem for lower-level leaders was that if they operated according to official rules, they would have to play little more than an ideological, mobilisational role in the regional economy, but if they were to be politically successful, they felt they could not leave economic matters to chance.

The natural response to this situation was twofold. First, party leaders personally became directly involved in managing the economy, often taking decisions of a low-level, even routine nature. Second, they wanted to ensure that they had around them a team of people upon whom they could rely. If their political careers depended upon it, they did not want to have to rely upon those whose loyalty they may have doubted. Nor did they want to rely upon formal procedures, rules and regulations which could get in the way of ensuring that the economy performed successfully. They were reinforced in this by recognition that if there was a choice between obedience to formal rules and instructions on the one hand and achieving plan targets on the other, Moscow preferred the latter. Achievement of the plan target was a defence against charges that rules were broken, but the plea that local figures followed all the rules was no excuse for the failure to meet the specified targets. Thus the development of family group control was an effective method of dealing with a situation of uncertainty: the need to ensure target fulfilment was best met by having an arrangement whereby the local leadership worked coherently and efficiently to foster economic development.

The chances of failure in this were enhanced by another aspect of the Soviet political structure. The orders that came down to lower levels were numerous and not always mutually consistent. In particular, plan details did not always dovetail together in such a way as to provide for local elites a clear blueprint as to what was expected; for example, the plan might not provide for sufficient raw materials to make the quantity of finished goods demanded. Where such instructions were in conflict, local elites may appear to have been given some room for manoeuvre. But the reverse side of this coin is that it also meant that there was an automatic trigger whereby they could be held accountable; if they could not satisfy simultaneous instructions because those instructions were mutually incompatible, they could be charged with infringing orders from above. The prospect of failure was thus always present and always out of the control of local elites. The uncertainty thus created was not ameliorated by the practical fact that the capacity of the centre to exercise effective control was greatly restricted by having to deal with a range of subordinate groups more interested in obstructing than facilitating central control.[25]

The uncertainties for lower-level leaders created by demands from above for successful performance were reinforced by the way in which the Moscow-based leadership periodically sought to extend its control by limiting their autonomy. This was, of course, one aspect of the continuing flow of central instructions, decisions and regulations designed to structure the party's internal operating regime; by increasing the regularity and predictability of the functioning of the party machine, the centre hoped to eliminate the institutional slackness that created room for the exercise of substantial local autonomy. But beside such continuing efforts at institutional tightening were more spectacular direct assaults on the positions of lower-level officials. The bloodless purges of 1929–30 and 1933–34 were explicitly aimed at this. The terror of the second half of the 1930s also had this as one element and clearly increased levels of uncertainty throughout the political structure. Similarly Khrushchev's campaignist approach and emphasis on mass participation in 1959–62, added to the substantial turnover levels of this period, and especially the highly critical tone of 1961, would all have heightened uncertainty among regional elites. The language and actions of the Andropov and Gorbachev leaderships during the 1980s also had this effect. Thus throughout the Soviet period the sense of vulnerability to central pressure and retribution was never far from the political life of local and regional elites.

The perceived need to foster economic development in order to achieve centrally defined plan targets is part of the explanation for why the family groups usually involved the leading figures in all of the major local organisations. Party first secretary, soviet chairman, chairman of the collective or state farm, factory manager, trade union and komsomol leaders usually belonged to the local elite. It could be that such leaders, appointed independently, came together for mutual support and defence. Alternatively they may have been appointed with an eye to ensuring that people of like mind filled the major institutions under the party first secretary's eye. Two and sometimes three other organisations could also be involved in the family groups: the local representative of the security apparatus, the local representative of the party's control organs, and the editor of the local newspaper. Local family groups would endeavour to involve these people in an attempt to control the communications links with Moscow. If the group could monitor all avenues of information leading out of the region, their capacity to deceive the centre in cases of non-fulfilment of targets was increased; it could never be perfect because the centre often sent visiting plenipotentiaries into the regions to provide an independent source of information, and this could never be adequately combated. Thus the family group was an important defence mechanism against failure: not only did it potentially increase the chances of success by ensuring a compatible team ran the region, but it also improved the chances of deceiving the centre should it fail. This is clearly reflected in a comment from Uzbekistan: 'The ability to fulfil the plan at any cost was valued above all else. As a result, such alien and immoral phenomena as report-padding, hoodwinking and bribery have penetrated our lives'.[26]

This question of the deception of Moscow also had a linguistic dimension. Prior to the relaxation of censorship under Gorbachev, the language of public discourse in the Soviet

Union was highly stylised and standardised. Individual words and linguistic formulations had certain overtones independent of their orthological linguistic meanings. The political significance of these formulations was increased by the uncertainties inherent in the system noted above. This manifested itself in practice in the reluctance of political figures at all levels to deviate markedly from the tone of public discourse that prevailed at the time, with the result that the patterns of criticism emanating from Moscow tended to be picked up and replicated at lower levels. Deviations from that discourse were bound to stand out, and potentially to draw attention to the figure responsible. For most people, the notoriety that could ensue was not welcome because it could attract official attention to their performance, thereby potentially triggering central moves against them. Most people therefore abided by the linguistic norms, especially if they were engaged in the sorts of activity that increased their vulnerability to central action. This tendency helps to explain the shadowing of the more vigorous periods of central criticism by those at lower levels of the structure, even when the criticisms were directed at those who were now giving voice to those charges.

Deception of the centre was also aided throughout much of the Soviet period, especially prior to the Second World War, by the poor communications network in the USSR. Many party organisations were regularly connected to their superiors only by means of written communications, often carried by special courier, or by the telephone[27] or telegraph. Access to some party organisations on the part of higher-standing party officers was often difficult, and is reflected in the frequent complaints about the weakness of linkages between different party organs. This sort of situation encouraged the development of family group control. Not only did it make higher-level monitoring of the situation more difficult, but it also forced local elites to rely upon their own resources. If contact with the next higher level in the party structure was difficult, when local problems arose local elites had to find their own solutions. They could not rely on significant assistance from above. The implication was that they should fashion a politico-administrative structure in the region that could handle whatever arose, hence facilitating family group emergence.

The reliance upon the sort of personalised network of which

the family group consisted was also encouraged by the ethos of the party's cadre policy. While it was Stalin who insisted on the principle 'Cadres decide everything', this was the hallmark of personnel policy throughout the life of the Soviet regime. The main message which this principle conveyed was that the personality, qualities, commitment and conviction of individual cadres was more important for the achievement of the regime's goals than the procedures that had been laid down to structure political and administrative life. The identity of individual officials was more important than the regularised procedures which the party was seeking to develop (see below). It follows that personal networks were more highly valued than institutional procedures in the culture of party life.

The institutional structure of the party's cadre policy also facilitated the development of family group control. The nomenklatura system of appointment[28] put significant power of patronage in the hands of party secretaries and officials at all levels of the party. It has long been accepted by observers of the Soviet scene that control over the power to appoint has been a significant weapon in the hands of successive party general/first secretaries at the all-union level. Such power has also existed at lower levels, and although the lower down the hierarchy one went the less extensive the power, even at the city level the gorkom secretary could dispense significant patronage. This sort of power could be used by party secretaries to ensure that offices within their purview were filled by 'appropriate' people.[29] Of course the power of officials at higher levels of the party structure to 'parachute' people into the region was extensive and could be used to upset the plans of local officials and to disrupt the creation of family groups at lower levels, but two facts worked to ameliorate the effect of this:

1. The person parachuted into a region in which he had no contacts could become hostage to the same sorts of considerations discussed above, making for the development of regionally based protective networks; in other words his success too could come to depend upon the success of the region. If this was the case, there would be a strong incentive for the newcomer to become encapsulated into the

existing family group or, if he was vigorously supported from above, to overthrow the existing group and replace it with one of his own. Thus the logic of the local situation could lead to the replacement of one family group by another or to the takeover of an existing family group by a new first secretary.

2. For about half of the post-Stalin period (1964–82) the personnel policy followed by the centre was not intrusive. Brezhnev's 'stability of cadres' policy discussed above, added to the propensity to promote from within regions rather than to cross post from outside, created ideal conditions for the consolidation of family group networks of control. Rather than being used to break up family group control, during this period the personnel mechanism may actually have reinforced it.

Clearly there were strong pressures emanating from within the Soviet party encouraging the structuring of local power around personalised machines in preference to the regularised institutions and norms emanating from the party machinery. But these pressures should have worked throughout all parts of the party and cannot explain why the development of family group control seems to have taken on a more developed form in the Central Asian republics than elsewhere. The cultural norms of the region discussed above are probably important here; they would not only have provided a cultural stimulus by themselves for the development of protective networks of officials, but they would have substantially strengthened the pressures emanating from within the party itself for the growth of such structures. Culture may have been important in another way also. Because of the gulf between the cultural values of this region and those of Russia from where most initial Bolshevik leaders came, it is likely that the sense of isolation the early rulers experienced noted above would have been even stronger in this region. Surrounded by people whose language, culture and civilisation were so different from their own, Russian officials were even more likely to seek support in such protective networks than in the culturally more familiar parts of the Soviet Union. If this was the case, it is likely that the principle of family group control became even more solidly embedded in the party structures of this region at an earlier date than elsewhere. The tradition of family group control may thus have been stronger than in other parts of the country. Furthermore, the effect of the sense of isolation stemming from the cultural strangeness of the region would have been reinforced throughout the entire Soviet period, but especially in its early years, by the difficulties of communication with Moscow. The communications infrastructure of this region was probably more underdeveloped than in any other part of the country with the exception of the far north. Cut off from the centre, local officials had to rely upon their own resources even more than their counterparts in European parts of the country, and therefore had greater incentive to seek the support to be found in family groups. Furthermore, the distance also hindered the centre's attempts at regulation and control, thereby facilitating the development and consolidation of such power structures. And finally, we should not dismiss the importance of personality. While pressures emanating from within the party and from society at large may have promoted this type of power structure, it still needed individuals with the ambition, skill and luck to make the most of the opportunities provided. It may be that in Central Asia, and particularly in Uzbekistan (although Kazakhstan under Kunaev should also be included), there was the coincidence of this type of leader and the pressures noted above. It may be that this combination of factors will go a long way towards explaining the strength of family group control in this area.

THE ORGANISATION OF PRIVILEGE

While the pressures for personalised political machines were powerful in the party, as suggested in Chapter 1, these pressures were not unchallenged. Throughout the Soviet period there were continuing attempts by the centre to bring about a greater degree of regularity in the way in which the machinery of the party functioned.[30] The form they took usually involved a rewriting of the party's Rules and adjustments to the administrative regulations designed to structure its functioning, along with the organisational restructuring of a section of the party's machinery; this often involved the CC Secretariat with corresponding changes being made at lower levels. There was also a continuing stream of communications and injunctions from the centre calling upon lower-level bodies to function in a more regularised fashion and giving them directions about how to achieve this. This sort of activity was accompanied by exhortations about how the monitoring of activity at lower levels had to be improved.

The effect of this sort of activity was to generate pressures from within the party structure for a greater regularisation of its proceedings. As local committees developed their own secretarial apparatus and these began to carry out basic housekeeping functions, they created pressures for bringing a greater degree of regularity into the way the party conducted its business. Pressures for more routinised office procedures, the regularisation of meetings and the keeping of adequate records went with the creation of a machinery of administration in the party. The strength of such pressures should not be exaggerated, but they nevertheless did exist. The result was that throughout the party there was a continuing tension between pressures for the structuring of local relations on the basis of personalised networks and pressures for a higher level of institutionalisation based on organisational norms.[31]

The way this tension was worked out in practice differed from location to location and over time. The principal factors determining the outcome of such tension in particular instances would have included the strength of personality, ambition and disposition of the first secretary, the extent of the support (both local and from higher levels) he possessed, the degree of coherence of the local secretarial apparatus, the sort of pattern that had become entrenched in local lore that shaped the way the local party organisation functioned, and the attitude and degree of interest taken in the particular region by the centre. While the relationship between these factors was highly variable, the pressures making for informal personalised networks seem generally to have been stronger. In some cases, as in the Uzbek scandal noted above, they seem to have completely overwhelmed pressures for organisational institutionalisation. In others, their effect was moderated by these organisational pressures. Cases of the latter were less likely to be subject to the sorts of savage criticism discussed earlier in this work, although leadership changes or changes in other circumstances could lead to the emergence of personalised networks even where organisational institutional patterns had seemed to be established. The pressures for personalised networks were so powerful that they could not be eliminated from the party structure.[32]

This should not be surprising. The personalised model was widely embodied by the patterns of all-union elite politics as well. The models of leadership provided by Stalin, Khrushchev, Andropov and Gorbachev were all of an activist party leader who was not closely constrained by official invocations of the principles of collective leadership. Even Brezhnev, who operated within the broad principles of collectivism, was widely seen as the *primus inter pares* within the Soviet leadership and as the individual who set the tone for the structuring of leadership relations. Furthermore, the history of the consolidation of power by successive party leaders was a history of the development by those leaders of informal networks of supporters and the promotion of such supporters into positions of responsibility. The path to power was widely seen to lie through the generation of the sorts of personal relations which family groups embodied. In this sense the model of leadership provided by the general/first secretary would for the most part have reinforced the propensity of lower-level leaders to play a role largely unencumbered by formal organisational constraints.

The prevalence of family groups throughout the party structure, added to the tradition of similar sorts of phenomena operating at the apex of politics, suggests that the criticism which appeared in the press, despite the specific nature of the charges, was not directed against the family groups as a phenomenon or the structuring of power along these lines. If in practice these were the effective building blocks of the party and their existence was justified by elite example and general party practice, it would be unusual for the centre seriously to criticise them in principle. The championing of criticism of lower-level family groups by those sections of the elite linked with the secretarial apparatus and desirous of building up their institutional power by strengthening principles of organisational institutionalisation was one source of such criticism. Another source lay in the personal political motives of individual elite actors; the campaigns of vigorous criticism fostered by Khrushchev, Andropov and Gorbachev discussed earlier are cases in point. But these are exceptional cases. It is likely that when criticism was directed at lower-level leaders and the way they played out their political role, the critics, at least before Gorbachev, had in mind less the principle of the family group mode of organisation than some of its negative consequences, and in particular the excess which could accompany it.

The main thrust of much of the criticism of lower-level leaders is the abuses that flowed from the way they carried out their responsibilities. Given the centre's preference for the achievement of targets over obedience to rules, the centre seems to have been willing to accept the reality of family groups except where they were associated with activity that was deemed to be unacceptable. The problem is determining exactly where the line lay between what was acceptable and what was unacceptable, particularly given that that line could change unpredictably with changes in central policies and priorities. What seems to have been the principal defining factor determining whether activity was acceptable or not was whether official position was used for personal gain in a way not sanctioned by the party's norms. The association of office-holding with access to privilege was long-established and regularised in the party through the nomenklatura system. This was in part a reaction to the problem of attracting talented people to responsible office in the situation of a deficit economy where access to goods and services was often more valuable than money. Each level of office had attached to it a notional entitlement to certain sorts and amounts of privilege.[33] Where officials used their offices for personal profit outside that which was embedded in the operative norms of the structure of privilege, they were likely to be subject to criticism. Clearly there was some margin here; minor skimming off from the economy was likely to be tolerated in normal circumstances, especially when the region was performing up to central expectations economically. However, if the personal abuse of position became excessive, particularly in a context where economic performance was disappointing, the cry of 'corruption' was more likely to be heard. This was particularly the case if the central leader had invested much political capital in improved economic performance and needed a scapegoat for the failure of his policies.

General norms about what was acceptable and what was not cannot be defined with any certainty, not only because they shifted over time, but because of their nature these are not conducive to precise measurement. What does appear to have been deemed essential throughout most of the Soviet period, at least until the 1970s, was a degree of discretion in the enjoyment of privilege. While access to privileges on the part of elites was widely known among the general populace, it seems to have been accepted that such privilege was not to be flaunted. But under Brezhnev there seems to have been a major shift in regime norms. The less demanding approach to lower-level officials reflected in the 'trust in cadres' policy signified a lowering of pressure on these people which thereby gave them expanded scope to pursue self-enriching activities.[34] Furthermore, such increased opportunity was associated with a more relaxed view about acceptable levels of personally acquisitive and family group behaviour. The result has been the perception of higher levels of corruption under Brezhnev than existed before, and the consequent vigorous reaction of Andropov and Gorbachev. But the essential point about the Brezhnev period is not that corruption suddenly took hold, but that its manifestations became more widespread and publicly visible.

What this means for our understanding of the situation which gave rise to the Uzbek scandal is that while the power structure resting on informal personal networks culminating with Rashidov may have been the most extensive and most characterised by venal pursuit, in essence it was little different from the types of power structures common throughout the rest of the party. It was the scale of the personal enrichment and individual power, the range of people involved, the level of wealth and excess on the part of the principals which distinguished the so-called 'Sharafrashidovshchina' from family group control elsewhere. The essence of family group control of the region was the same.[35]

What were the implications of family group activity for the party? The practical role the party organisation played in each region depended upon the outcome of the tension between the pressures making for family group control and those leading towards organisational institutionalisation. Where the latter were the more powerful, and personal networks were largely restricted to cliques operating within the party's organisational milieu, party institutions could continue to play a major part in structuring the course of local political life. Where family group control was most strongly established, party institutions were less influential in shaping the course of local affairs. When a family group ran a region, party organs might meet regularly, discuss issues and pass resolutions, but such activity was really a formality, a facade behind which the real decision-making took place within the group. The party's public performances simply served to legitimise the outcome of the political dynamics taking place within the family group. Similarly the head of the family group normally was the party first secretary, but although this position gave to the incumbent certain powers, the real basis of his family group power lay elsewhere. It resided in the personal relationships he possessed, in the networks of mutual affiliations and support of which the family group consisted. Official party position may have been significant in the generation of this, but it was not the real source of his power.

This does not mean that the party was unimportant. Legitimation in itself was important for the family group and for maintenance of its power; without the fig-leaf of party legitimation, party group control would have been plainly vulnerable to the charges of abuse of power and corruption. But the party was also important because it was the personnel system within the party which facilitated the appointment of members and potential members of the family group to leading positions within the region. Furthermore, through its control apparatus, the party potentially provided the means for the centre to challenge and even break up family groups. If family groups were to remain secure, therefore, they could not forsake the party. They had to ensure that the party apparatus in their region remained firmly under their control. They also had to ensure that they possesed strong links, usually mediated through the party, to higher-standing officials within the party structure who could act as their patrons and protectors, as Brezhnev had done for Rashidov.[36]

The dominance of family group control thus had important implications for the party as a structure. The latter's formal rules and regulations were always rubbing up against the reality of family group control and because they could not consistently structure internal party behaviour in the face of such a power disposition, the institution as a whole found it difficult to generate organisational principles which possessed normative authority. An instrumental approach to the party's rules, regulations and procedures could not be overcome, with the result that the party found it difficult to develop a sense of its own organisational coherence and integrity. The personal principle which lay at the heart of family group control continued to structure power within the party and to define the main contours of party life. The continuing scope and power of the General Secretary has been the most frequently noted case of this, but the principle applied throughout the party as a whole.

It is the dominance of the personal principle which best marks the party out as an organisation in which power is organised along patrimonial lines.[37] Max Weber discussed patrimonial rule, seeing it as a system in which 'all governmental authority and the corresponding economic rights tend to be treated as privately appropriated economic advantages'.[38] It was a form of society in which, in the words of one commentator on Weber, 'the ruler's retainers held sway over territories allocated to them, in a relationship of mutual dependence with the ruler.... [O]fficeholders are there primarily to perform personal services for the ruler, not as professional specialists.'[39] The position of the patrimonial official derived from personal submission to the ruler, and that official's power rested upon that personal relationship. Or in the words of another writer, 'the power and identity of an institution [is] defined in terms of the leader's political identity and power'.[40] The patrimonial office lacked a separation between private and official spheres, with the result that political power was a form of personal property, although in the Soviet case a peculiar form which could only be appropriated through domination of the party apparatus at particular levels, and which could not be securely exchanged for enduring economic advantage.

The conception of patrimonialism outlined above was thus one in which the leader's power was such that he could appoint people to positions of responsibility within the system, and they would then work in order to sustain and even increase the benefits flowing to the leader while at the same time benefiting themselves from this arrangement.[41] Such a system must almost inevitably have been a segmented one: the supreme leader appointed his subordinates to responsible positions within the structure, and those subordinates appointed yet further layers of their subordinates to lower level positions.

Political machines, resting on networks of mutual support and connected into larger, more over-arching machines also resting on political support, were thus the building blocks of a patrimonial structure. Personal relationships and personal support were the cement of such a structure.

This sort of structure has long been recognised as typical of Stalin's rule: the dictator appointed satraps to the regions who ran those areas for the advantage of themselves, of Stalin and of the system. The leader and supporters came almost to own the structure in the sense not only that they controlled it, but that their own personal interests and those of the structure became effectively fused within the prevailing organisational ethos.[42] This situation continued to exist after Stalin died, carried into the post-Stalin era through the vehicle of the family groups. While these remained the basic building blocks of the Soviet party structure, patrimonialism remained the essence of political power. And while patrimonialism remained the key organising principle of the party, it undercut the attempt to generate genuine infrastructural power; patrimonialism and despotic power went hand in hand.

Conclusion: The Weakness of Infrastructural Power

The preceding analysis has shown that the course and nature of criticism of lower-level party leaderships was moulded by central political priorities and local political realities. When the party First/General Secretary personally mounted a vigorous campaign directly against lower-level leaders, as Khrushchev did at the beginning of the 1960s and Andropov and Gorbachev did in the 1980s, the levels of criticism in the republican press were higher and the charges more severe than at other times. Furthermore, turnover levels tended to increase. But the pattern was not standard across all republics; in those areas where a leadership change had occurred in the recent past or during the campaign, levels of criticism tended to be higher unless there were countervailing, usually centrally related, factors. Where local leaders were not removed, criticism was less harsh. What is particularly interesting about these periods of more intensive criticism is that although the charges tend to be more severe, broadly reflecting misdemeanour rather than mismanagement, the situation they portray at the local level is perfectly consistent with the picture that is presented in the sort of criticisms made in the non-campaign periods. Continuing personalist politics, continuing family group control, low levels of organisational institutionalisation and weak infrastructural power shine through the criticism during all periods. Some explanations for the maintenance of this situation have already been suggested. The tenacity of family group control reflects the fact that this mode of operation served a real need within the party's power structure. Furthermore, while traditional priorities remained paramount, if not unchallenged, there was little incentive for change. A sense of institutional inertia was also evident; the party had always operated this way, and it would need a major effort to change direction. Such an effort was possible following Stalin's death, both as a function of the regularisation of institutional functioning and the change in party leadership.

Conclusion: The Weakness of Infrastructural Power

Pressures for the consolidation of organisational institutionalisation, and thereby usually infrastructural power, are inevitable whenever a political machine survives over an extended period. The basic demand that the machine should function with a modicum of efficiency of itself generates pressures for regularity of procedure, for the consolidation of principles and practices which will provide for those within the structure a high degree of certainty, if not of outcome then of process. This is a process of institution-building, of basing the principles which guide the institution on the needs of the institutional structure itself. By regularising internal procedures, the capacity of the centre to intervene in lower levels of the structure should also be regularised. This does not mean that the centre's power over the lower levels was necessarily increased by being routinised. It may be that such routinisation occurred only in the central organs, or in conjunction with a substantial consolidation of local power; indeed, routinisation may have involved decentralisation of power away from central authorities. Nevertheless, the consolidation of infrastructural power within the political structure is unlikely without institutionalisation.

If the strengthening of infrastructural power involved the routinisation of processes on the basis of institutional or organisational norms, its course would be undercut by the conduct of the organisation's life on the basis of principles other than those institutional or organisational norms. This was the situation in the Communist Party under Stalin. The Stalinist dictatorship continually undercut the pressures for routinisation on the basis of institutional/organisational norms. Despite the emphasis in successive versions of the party Rules, in the party press and in the speeches of party leaders upon principles like collective leadership, the regular meeting of party organs, and democratic centralism, these remained more important at the rhetorical than at the practical level. Stalin's power was highly personalised and the functioning of elite politics was structured around the preferences of the vozhd'. At the post-war height of Stalinist rule, with supreme decision-making taking place in informal groupings of Stalin's cronies and official party organs rarely meeting,[1] and with the institutional integrity of the party undermined by the expansive role still played by the security organs, there was little pressure coming from the centre to strengthen infrastructural power within the party. Throughout the Stalinist period, power remained despotic, with pressures for infrastructural power very weak.

With the death of Stalin, an opportunity arose for a reversal of this situation. The early emphasis upon institutional regularity and upon restoring the party to a position of institutional predominance held out the prospect of reinvigorating it as an institution and thereby strengthening the prospects for infrastructural power. However, the pressures favouring this sort of development continued to be undermined by the personalist principle in elite affairs.

One of the principal implications of the de-Stalinisation campaign launched so spectacularly by Khrushchev in 1956 was the rejection of a predominant leader model. This reinforced the public emphasis upon collective leadership evident in the period immediately following Stalin's death. Furthermore, during the Khrushchev period, this emphasis was linked with an attempt to bring a greater sense of regularity into party life. Party organs did meet on a more regular basis and, as collective entities, seemed to play an increased role in the actual decision-making process. New party Rules, along with a new party Programme, were introduced in 1961. The arrest of Beria in June 1953 and the associated downgrading of the security apparatus had eliminated the sort of institutional challenge to the party which this had constituted since the mid-1930s, while with Khrushchev's defeat of Malenkov, the party's predominance over the state machine was re-established.

But despite the rhetorical resistance to the personalist principle continuing to dominate party affairs, it remained prominent throughout the Khrushchev period. One of the main reasons for this was the operating style of the First Secretary himself. Khrushchev pursued a vigorous, personal leadership style which ignored institutional boundaries and sensibilities and trampled over the principles of collective leadership. He was an activist policy-maker whose enthusiasm for various measures often outweighed his capacity to understand the implications of what he was doing. Nevertheless, he forced such measures through, often by dint of the strength of his own personality and his personal bullying tactics. When he was met with opposition which he could not simply trample over, he would ignore or circumvent it, as in the cases of the anti-party

Conclusion: The Weakness of Infrastructural Power 177

group when he appealed over the head of the Presidium to the CC and of the proposed CC Bureau for Central Asia when he sought to lock the Presidium in behind this measure by announcing it publicly before it had formally been accepted. While the stacking of party bodies with supporters was an established mode of acting in the party to build up one's support, Khrushchev took this to a new level, which undermined the institutional integrity of the organ even more. At the level of the CC, he swamped this body's meetings with 'technical experts', many of whom were not only not members of the CC but were not even members of the party. Furthermore, he called into question the established conventions about committee membership by introducing compulsory minimum turnover levels and maximum periods of tenure for committees at all levels. Increasingly Khrushchev came to rely upon informal coteries of personal advisers rather than the formal party organs.

These sorts of action undermined pressures for institutional regularity and coherence at the top of the party structure. Combined with the idiosyncratic and expansive style of the First Secretary, such changes blunted the pressures for regularisation of party procedure that emanated from the immediate post-Stalin period. The effect of these was enhanced by Khrushchev's support for expanded notions of popular participation. Reflected in the changes in nomenclature he championed, 'party of the whole people' and 'state of the whole people', Khrushchev encouraged higher levels of popular participation in political life. He sought to open up decision-making fora to greater publicity and in particular to involve popular 'volunteers' in the administrative functions of the party-state structure. This emphasis upon volunteers involved both a reduction in the formal staffs of party bodies and a rejection of established methods of party functioning. The promotion of non-staff labour on a wide scale called into question not just the operating procedures of the party but the special position the party occupied in Soviet society. This position was further disturbed by the bifurcation of the party apparatus in late 1962, which substantially reorganised the basic local structures of official authority throughout much of the Soviet Union. Together with the administrative fragmentation which resulted from the creation of sovnarkhozy in 1957, these changes undermined efforts to promote the sort of developments that would have strengthened infrastructural power.

If the personalist leadership style of Khrushchev, added to the institutional challenges to the party's operating regime which he espoused, undercut the chances for the regularisation of party functioning and consequent strengthening of infrastructural power, his overthrow entailed the potential to reverse this trend. The Brezhnev administration came to power on a platform of restoring regularity to the institutions and processes that had been disrupted by Khrushchev's operating style. It criticised the uncertainty and chaos created by his successive bouts of reorganisation and by his idiosyncratic leadership style. In place of this, the new leadership sought to introduce a decision-making style marked by caution, structure and regularity. Instead of the personally interventionist style of Khrushchev, the new General Secretary pursued a consensual mode of decision-making; instead of attempting to force measures through over opposition, Brezhnev sought to involve different elite groups in discussion of most issues before they were brought to the point of decision. Participation in these discussions was highly structured, taking place through the formal channels provided by the regime. This produced an incremental style of decision-making and made for a process in which the pressures for stability and regularisation constituted firm buffers against highly personalist styles of behaviour.

This decision-making style was accompanied by a renewed effort to increase the regularity of functioning of party bodies. The party's elite organs, the Politburo, Secretariat, Central Committee and Congress, met on a regular basis throughout this period, and the press frequently emphasised the importance of the need to follow established procedures. Although no new formal set of party Rules was adopted,[2] new state constitutions were introduced in 1977–78. In the new Soviet Constitution, the place of the party was officially regularised by acknowledgement of its place at the heart of the political system. The organisational ethos of the Brezhnev period was clearly one which should have been favourable for the growth of stable and firmly based institutional norms which, in turn, should have strengthened the bases for infrastructural power.

The effect of this decision-making style and the institutional emphasis on regularity should have been reinforced by the cadre policy pursued at this time. The policy of stability of cadres and the consequent leaving in place of political officials created the conditions of stability which should have enabled the new institutional norms to become embedded in party lore and practice. There was no constant changing of leaderships to disrupt the consolidation of operating procedures, and few major leadership changes which could have brought about the sort of significant change in the direction of policy which would have been necessary to disturb this process of regularisation. But the stability of cadres policy also helped to undercut the pressures for the regularisation of party procedures, or at least the investing of them with normative authority. Cadre stability, and its obverse, the absence of an intrusive central cadre policy, facilitated the consolidation of local family group control, which in turn robbed official party norms and procedures of normative authority. Even if party regulations and procedures became more regular and stable, if real and effective power resided in the informal clique structures of the family groups, such as those which had developed around Rashidov, Rasulov and Kunaev, such regularisation could have little practical effect. As a result, pressures for the strengthening of infrastructural power were blunted.

In the final part of the Soviet era under Gorbachev the effects of central policy continued to undercut the development of such pressures. Gorbachev's attempt to withdraw the party from an administrative role in society, if implemented consistently, would have involved a complete rethinking of the practicalities of party operation at all levels. Furthermore, the plans championed by the General Secretary for a restructuring of the party's power structure, principally through a replacement of the nomenklatura mechanism for filling office by election, threw into doubt many of the established patterns of party life. The effect on the internal functioning of the party was compounded by continuing factional conflict within the party and by the pressures placed upon it as an institution by the erosion of its power and position in society at large.[3] The longer perestroika continued, the more the efforts of party officials turned to defending and sustaining the party in the face of irresistible challenges coming from without. With many of its internal processes called into question by Gorbachev's policies and its societal position increasingly rejected by a variety of political actors within Soviet society, the party was in no state to be able to regularise its procedures, invest them with normative authority, and thereby stimulate the growth of infrastructural power.

What these short summaries of successive leadership periods show is that at no time in the post-Stalin era were policies which might have led to a strengthening of infrastructural power at the expense of despotic power consciously and consistently applied. There was no full frontal attack upon the reality of family group control at any level of the political structure, as opposed to episodic attacks upon particular family group leaders. While Khrushchev's criticism campaign in 1961 resonated most strongly in Uzbekistan and Tajikistan, the outcome ran counter to the objective of increasing regular party supervision of local officials. Rashidov and Rasulov initially identified themselves with Khrushchev, using the high turnover of party officials in the early 1960s to consolidate their informal networks of power. Then, like Kunaev in Kazakhstan, they needed Brezhnev's trust in their authority to expand these networks and effectively live off the declining resources of the state. Such conduct was implicitly challenged by Masherov's call for a more radical central policy in the late 1970s, but when this challenge was renewed under Gorbachev, particularly in 1987–88, the new campaign was too little and too late to succeed in reviving the party apparatus. This was clear in different ways, from the failure of Kolbin's criticism campaign in Kazakhstan to the lack of such a campaign against Shcherbitsky in Ukraine.

Without the force provided by a committed central leadership, the structure of family group control which was the realisation of the patrimonial principle in party life could not be eradicated; the case of Kolbin in Kazakhstan, who enjoyed central support but still failed to eliminate personalised machines, shows the strength of such structures. It had become embedded in party lore and, given the extent of such structures, it was in the interests of large sections of the party that it not be challenged. Indeed, even at the centre power remained highly personalised, and therefore there appears to have been little real commitment on the part of the central elite to challenge the principles underlying family group control.

The only way such a structure could have been eradicated was by a combination of pressure from above and from below. What was needed was a central leadership exerting continuing pressure upon lower-level power structures along with the implementation of a true system of rank-and-file nomination and election for the filling of responsible offices. The only time there was a concerted move along these lines was under Gorbachev, when the central nomenklatura mechanism was eventually disbanded and the election of leading positions vigorously supported. Had this measure been successfully implemented throughout the party, it would have undermined the centre's traditional capacity to exert pressure on lower-level party bodies and thereby significantly transformed the hierarchical nature of the Soviet party-state. But this was blunted by a combination of lower-level opposition and the effects of the more general erosion of the party's position in Soviet society as a whole.

In the absence of concerted pressure from above and the lack of incentive at lower levels to do away with the family group type of arrangement, it is little wonder that this remained throughout the post-Stalin period as the principal means of structuring local power in the party with the associated weakness of infrastructural power throughout the party's structure. It had become embedded in the party's lore and was accepted as the 'normal' way of managing local affairs. The continuing importance of this type of patrimonial arrangement should not be underestimated. As a power machine, it did not depend upon the official party structure for its sustenance or continuation. The source of its continuing existence was that it was an effective way of managing local affairs and defending the interests of the local elite. As a result, the continuation of family group rule following the fall of the party in the summer of 1991 should not be a surprise.

One of the most remarked upon characteristics of the initial period of post-Soviet rule in much of the former Soviet Union has been the continuation in public affairs of many who had held responsible positions under the former regime. In the absence of a concerted, conscious campaign to prevent this, such continuity was inevitable; indeed, it was probably inevitable at least at some level even had such a campaign been waged. But what appears also to have been the case in many regions is that, despite the rhetoric of democracy, the structuring of local power continued to occur along family group lines. In Russia local cliques of notables continued to band together to run local affairs, perhaps in the common interest, but also given the emphasis on personal aggrandisement in the high risk capitalism that was emerging from the Soviet ruins, with an eye to their own welfare.[4] The operation of the imperatives of family group control is reflected in the responses to President El'tsin's despatch of plenipotentiaries into the regions in late 1991. These people often had to struggle against a closed, local elite determined to fend off this agent of central power. In other cases, the plenipotentiary threw in his lot with the local elite, thereby supplementing the established structure of family group control.[5] As the control exercised by the centre seemed to weaken in the months leading up to the president-parliament clash in September–October 1993, local political leaders took advantage of this to strengthen the control they could exercise within their local bailiwick. Neither the December 1993 election nor that two years later changed this situation. In many areas the election was managed by the local elite to ensure that their power was not challenged, while in others those who have come to power have often sought to overcome the political and institutional uncertainty by relying on renewed family group control. As a result, in many of the regions of Russia, power continued to be structured along family group lines.[6]

Elsewhere in the former Soviet Union, the continuation of the old personalist bases of power and family group structures has also been apparent.[7] The most obvious instances of this have occurred in Central Asia where the patrimonial principle was most strongly buttressed by cultural norms and where the reality of family group control was most evident, at least as reflected in the course of public criticism during the Soviet period. Although the Communist Party at the republican level in Kazakhstan, Uzbekistan and Turkmenistan was formally abolished, its replacement remained headed by the same people and the former power structure was able to sustain its control despite the changes. In Tajikistan the former communist leader Nabiev was even able to make a comeback several years after having been ousted in 1985, relying principally upon a power machine resting on personalist principles. Thus in the

Conclusion: The Weakness of Infrastructural Power 183

three republics in this study in which family group control was most prominent, the continuation of that control was maintained. In all three republics, principal beneficiaries of this structure under the communist system continued to benefit; the first presidents of all three independent republics were former party first secretaries: Karimov in Uzbekistan, Nazarbaev in Kazakhstan and Nabiev in Tajikistan, although Nabiev was overthrown nine months after the collapse of the union.[8] In other former republics too, including Ukraine and Belorussia, the personalist basis of family group control has remained important. This should not be surprising. The generation of family group control lay in combating the uncertainty faced by lower-level party and state officials in the early years of the Soviet regime, and such reliance on informal organisation remains useful given the high levels of uncertainty that have prevailed in the post-Soviet era.

Notes

Chapter 1

1. For example, George Breslauer, *Khrushchev and Brezhnev as Leaders. Building Authority in Soviet Politics* (London, George Allen & Unwin, 1982).
2. Barrington Moore Jr, *Social Origins of Dictatorship and Democracy* (Harmondsworth, Penguin, 1969) and William McNeill, *The Rise of the West* (Chicago, University of Chicago Press, 1963).
3. There are many examples, including Gianfranco Poggi, *The Development of the Modern State* (London, Hutchinson, 1978), Michael Mann, *The Sources of Social Power. Vol. 1. A History of Power from the Beginning to AD 1760* and *Vol. 2. The Rise of Classes and Nation-States, 1760–1914* (Cambridge, Cambridge University Press, 1986 and 1993), Charles Tilly (ed.), *The Formation of National States in Western Europe* (Princeton, Princeton University Press, 1975).
4. Michael Mann, 'The Autonomous Power of the State: Its Origins, Mechanisms and Results', in John A. Hall (ed.), *States in History* (Oxford, Blackwell, 1986), p.113.
5. For a fine discussion of infrastructural power in regard to state capacity for involvement in the economy, see Linda Weiss and John M. Hobson, *States and Economic Development. A Comparative Historical Analysis* (Oxford, Polity Press, 1995), ch. 1. Weiss and Hobson see infrastructural power as having three dimensions: penetrative power involving a state's ability directly to interact with the populace, extractive power involving the state's ability to extract resources from society, and its negotiated aspect involving 'a highly developed strategic, institutionalized form of collaboration between political and industrial actors' (p.7).
6. The expansion of impersonal norms in modern societies with the unequal dependence of all individuals on exchange relations was considered by Marx as breaking up primordial ties of personal dependence. Karl Marx, *Grundrisse* (Harmondsworth, Penguin, 1973), pp.157–8, 163–4. For an original analysis of Soviet society which focuses on the importance of relations of personal dependence, see Nurlan Amrekulov, *Taina Kul'ta Lichnosti i ee Razoblachenie: epokha stalinizma, logika ee razvitiia i izzhivaniia* (Alma Ata, Gylym, 1991).
7. According to one scholar, prospects for the expansion of infrastructural power vary across historically different societies. While in the West 'the formation of civil society was a pre-requisite for the emergence of a modern bourgeois state', in the East (including Russia) 'the process of forming civil society began basically from above', with the state sooner or later facing the problem that 'political life cannot replace the combined manifestations of civil life and their binding role'. Nodari Simoniya *et al.*, *Evoliutsiia Vostochnykh Obshchestv: sintez traditsionnogo i sovremennogo* (Moscow, Nauka, 1984), pp.270–5.

8. This is discussed in the Soviet context in Graeme Gill, 'Institutionalisation and Revolution: Rules and the Soviet Political System', *Soviet Studies*, 37, 2, April 1985, pp.212–26.
9. This process has been discussed by Weber in terms of the routinisation of charisma. See Max Weber, *Economy and Society* (New York, Bedminster Press, 1968, Guenther Roth and Claus Wittik eds), 3, pp.1121–48.
10. For example, for a discussion of the "fuhrerist party", see Robert C. Tucker, 'On Revolutionary Mass Movement Regimes', *The Soviet Political Mind* (New York, Praeger, 1971).
11. For this argument, see Graeme Gill, *The Origins of the Stalinist Political System* (Cambridge, Cambridge University Press, 1990). On patrimonialism, see Weber. Also Guenther Roth, 'Personal Rulership, Patrimonialism, and Empire Building in the New States', *World Politics* 20, 2, January 1968.
12. The German term *seilschaft*, meaning 'a "roped-party" of climbers whose mutual aid, protection and support enable them to scale heights that would be beyond their individual powers', has been used to describe this. Gyula Jozsa, 'Political Seilschaften in the USSR', in T.H. Rigby and Bohdan Harasymiw (eds), *Leadership Selection and Patron–Client Relations in the USSR and Yugoslavia* (London, Allen & Unwin, 1983), pp.139–73. The quotation is on p.139.
13. These are detailed and discussed in Graeme Gill, *The Rules of the Communist Party of the Soviet Union* (London, Macmillan, 1988), except for that of 1990 which will be found in *Pravda* 18 July 1990.
14. The rhetorical prominence given to democratic centralism is indicative of this aim.
15. For a stimulating discussion, see T.H. Rigby, 'A Conceptual Approach to Authority, Power and Policy in the Soviet Union', in T.H. Rigby, Archie Brown and Peter Reddaway (eds), *Authority, Power and Policy in the USSR. Essays Dedicated to Leonard Schapiro* (London, Macmillan, 1980), pp.9–31.
16. L. Gudkov, Yu. Levada, A. Levinson and L. Sedov, 'Fenomen biurokratii v istoriko-sotsiologicheskoi perspektive', *Mirovaia Ekonomika i Mezhdunarodnye Otnosheniia* 6, 1989, pp.86–7.
17. S. Peregudov, 'Biurokratiia, gossobstvennosti i ogosudarstvlenie v sovetskom obshchestve', *Mirovaia Ekonomika i Mezhdunarodnye Otnosheniia* 5, 1989, p.82.
18. For its use by Stalin in the 1930s, see Gill, *Origins*, chs 5 and 7.
19. These sorts of charges became the dominant type of threatening criticism after 1953, replacing the accusations of treachery which had prevailed under Stalin.
20. Victor Zaslavsky 'The Evolution of Separatism in Soviet Society Under Gorbachev', in Gail W. Lapidus, Victor Zaslavsky and Philip Goldman (eds), *From Union to Commonwealth: Nationalism and Separatism in the Soviet Republics* (Cambridge, Cambridge University Press, 1992), p.76.
21. Calculated from figures in Robert V. Daniels, 'Political Processes and Generational Change', in Archie Brown (ed.), *Political Leadership in the Soviet Union* (London, Macmillan, 1989), p.103.

Chapter 2

1. See Graeme Gill, *The Origins of the Stalinist Political System* (Cambridge, Cambridge University Press, 1990), chs 5 and 7.
2. *Pravda Vostoka* 24 March, 22 April, 24 April, 11 November and 31 December 1953; 16 February 1954.
3. PV 15 August 1953.
4. PV 31 March, 22 April, 12 July, 29 July, 4 August and 1 September 1953.
5. PV 29 April, 3 July, 29 July, 4 August, 15 August, 1 September and 12 December 1953; 15 February, 15 May and 25 November 1954; 4 January 1955.
6. PV 14 May 1955.
7. PV 22 July, 6 August and 29 November 1953.
8. PV 12 August 1953.
9. Although this was mentioned on some isolated occasions – PV 28 January 1956 (Mukhitdinov's attack on his predecessor Niiazov at the XIII Congress), 14 March and 28 December 1957.
10. PV 1 September 1954.
11. PV 26 January, 28 January, 9 March and 31 July 1956; 1 March, 14 March, 14 August, 1 September and 28 December 1957.
12. PV 15 March, 8 April and 20 May 1959.
13. PV 26 March, 15 July and 12 September 1959.
14. PV 13 January, 4 February, 11 February and 19 October 1960; 25 April and 27–28 September 1961.
15. PV 5 and 11 February 1961.
16. PV 7 March 1961.
17. PV 15 March, 16 June and 18 June 1961.
18. PV 27–28 September 1961.
19. PV 30 June and 29 July 1962.
20. PV 21 December 1962. For Rashidov's speech at the November plenum, see PV 23 November 1962.
21. PV 7 February 1963.
22. PV 7 June 1963.
23. PV 9 June 1963.
24. PV 6 June 1964.
25. *Kommunist Tajikistana* 27–29 January 1956.
26. KT 15, 16 and 21 July 1953.
27. KT 21 July 1953 and 8 January 1954.
28. For example, KT 27–29 January, 12 February, 7 March and 22 July 1956.
29. KT 25 January, 5 April and 30 December 1958.
30. KT 15 January 1959 and 17 July 1959.
31. KT 22 August 1959.
32. KT 15 January 1961.
33. KT 7 February 1961 and 22 March 1961.
34. KT 14 April 1961.
35. KT 19 April, 21 April and 1 September 1961.
36. KT 22–27 September 1961.

55. KP 4 August 1976 and 17 March 1977.
56. KP 17 March and 26 July 1978.
57. KP 21 November 1978.
58. The later criticism under Kolbin and Nazarbaev of Kunaev for nepotism is consistent with this view.
59. KP 12 and 26 December 1978; 18 January 1979.
60. KP 16 December 1980.
61. KP 3 December 1981.
62. KP 29 August 1981; 25 February and 31 March 1982.
63. KP 20 April 1982.
64. KP 6 May 1982.
65. KP 1 April 1982.
66. Additional rural raikoms were established after the unification of the party apparatus in order to increase party supervision over the farms. *Pravda Ukrainy* 5 February 1965.
67. PU 1 December 1966.
68. PU 16 March and 1 December 1966.
69. PU 2 April 1968.
70. PU 10 January and 25 July 1970.
71. PU 18 March 1971.
72. PU 25 June 1971.
73. PU 2 April 1972.
74. This was a result of Suslov's insistence that Shelest's relative tolerance of nationalist dissent was no longer acceptable. Bohdan Nahaylo and Victor Swoboda, *Soviet Disunion: A History of the Nationalities Problem in the USSR* (London, Hamish Hamilton, 1990), pp.177–9.
75. PU 27 January 1973.
76. PU 20 April 1973.
77. PU 16 September 1973.
78. PU 6 October 1973.
79. PU 22 January 1974.
80. PU 19 February 1974.
81. PU 26 May and 9 July 1974.
82. PU 15 March 1975.
83. PU 15 May 1975.
84. PU 22 May 1975.
85. PU 23 May 1975.
86. PU 25 January 1976.
87. PU 30 August 1975.
88. PU 11 February 1976.
89. PU 11 June and 8 July 1977.
90. PU 17 September 1977.
91. PU 21 July 1978.
92. PU 24 December 1978.
93. PU 28 April 1979.
94. PU 9 June 1979.
95. PU 21 October 1979.
96. PU 12 December 1979.
97. PU 29 May 1980.

37. KT 29–31 August and 11–12 September 1962; 31 July 1963.
38. KT 26–27 December 1963.
39. *Kazakhstanskaia Pravda* 9 June, 17 June, 22 July and 8 August 1953.
40. KP 13 and 14 February 1954.
41. KP, 10 January, 6 August and 28 October 1954; 15 April, 24 May, 29 May and 24 June 1955.
42. KP 24 June 1955.
43. KP 6 January, 10 January, 21 May, 6 August, 28 October and 20 November 1954; 17 February, 15 April, 24 May, 29 May and 24 June 1955.
44. KP 30 December 1955.
45. KP 20 October 1956; 20 November 1956; 8 and 20 January 1957.
46. KP 15 April 1955.
47. KP 30 December 1955.
48. KP 11 April 1957.
49. KP 11 January, 15 January, 4 September, 27 October and 24 December 1959; 21 and 22 January 1960.
50. KP 6 February 1960.
51. KP 11 March 1960.
52. KP 7 September 1960 and 26 December 1962.
53. Respectively KP 2 February, 4 February and 14 March 1961.
54. KP 13 January, 2 and 4 February, 14 and 19 March, 7, 9, 18 and 25 June, 1961.
55. KP 7, 9 and 18 June 1961.
56. KP 28 September 1961.
57. KP 29 September, 30 September and 14 October 1961.
58. KP 26–27 December 1962.
59. KP 22 February and 17 March 1963.
60. KP 19 March 1963. Not included were Semipalatinsk and the three kraikoms, Tselino, West Kazakhstan and South Kazakhstan.
61. KP 19 March 1963.
62. KP 20, 21 and 27 March 1963.
63. KP 30 April, 8, 11 and 14 June 1963.
64. KP 19 May and 14 June 1963.
65. KP 12 and 14 November 1963.
66. KP 26 January and 29 February 1964.
67. KP 9 and 12 July 1964.
68. KP 29 July 1964.
69. *Pravda Ukrainy* 7 April, 10 April and 26 June 1953.
70. For example, PU 27 January, 11 March and 13 March 1954; 1 June 1955; 19 January 1956.
71. PU 11 and 13 March 1954.
72. PU 24 March 1954 and 19 January 1956.
73. PU 30 November 1956.
74. PU 6 and 7 January 1959.
75. PU 20 March 1959.
76. PU 12 May 1959.
77. PU 25 October 1959.
78. PU 27 October 1959.
79. PU 15 and 17 December 1959.

80. PU 17 and 20 February 1960.
81. PU 28 July 1960.
82. PU 2 December 1960.
83. PU 27 January 1961.
84. PU 1 February 1961.
85. PU 2 February 1961.
86. PU 10 and 12 February 1961.
87. PU 28 February 1961.
88. PU 29 September 1961.
89. PU 26 December 1961.
90. PU 30 March 1962.
91. PU 12 August 1962.
92. PU 30 July 1962.
93. PU 21 November 1962.
94. PU 7 December 1962.
95. PU 27 and 29 March 1963.
96. PU 4 July 1963.
97. PU 29 August 1963 and 21 August 1964.
98. *Sovetskaia Belorussia* 12 November 1953 and 8 January 1954.
99. SB 8 January and 12 February 1954.
100. For example, SB 18 February 1954; 13 December 1955; 28 March 1956.
101. SB 7 January 1955 and 13 February 1954.
102. SB 13 December 1955.
103. SB 27 and 28 January 1956.
104. SB 17 February 1959.
105. SB 28 January 1956.
106. SB 15 January 1959.
107. SB 26 January 1961.
108. SB 29 March 1963; for other reports 26 April and 28 September 1961, 8 April and 19 December 1962.
109. SB 13 April 1958, 16 January and 12 July 1959, 19 November 1960.
110. SB 14 July and 27 October 1959; 18 February 1960.
111. For example, SB 11 February, 16 May, 27 September and 7 October 1961.
112. SB 7 July and 28 September 1961; 4 February 1962.
113. SB 14 January 1962.
114. SB 27 March 1963.
115. SB 13 March 1964.

Chapter 3

1. *Pravda Vostoka* 21 November and 26 December 1964.
2. PV 9 January 1965.
3. PV 7 March 1966.
4. PV 18 and 22 November 1966.
5. PV 22 November 1966.
6. PV 6 July 1967 and 13 January 1968.
7. PV 24 January and 2 February 1968.
8. PV 10 and 14 February 1968.
9. PV 22 March 1970 and 19 January 1971.
10. PV 3 March 1971.
11. PV 5 June 1971.
12. PV 16 February 1972.
13. PV 21 November and 3 December 1969.
14. PV 12 January 1971.
15. PV 3 and 6 March 1971.
16. PV 4 and 5 June 1971.
17. PV 6 July 1971.
18. PV 16 February 1972.
19. PV 27 August 1972.
20. PV 29 March 1973.
21. PV 20 December 1973.
22. PV 7 December 1972 and 30 March 1974.
23. For Example, PV 14 October, 13 November and 9 December
24. PV 4 and 5 February 1976.
25. PV 22 November 1978.
26. PV 21 December 1980.
27. PV 14 January 1979; 21 December 1980; 8 January and 10 D 1981.
28. PV 4 February 1981.
29. PV 12 May 1982.
30. PV 11 February 1982.
31. PV 27 April 1982.
32. PV 12 May 1982.
33. *Kommunist Tajikistana* 22 December 1964.
34. KT 27 January 1966.
35. KT 2 February and 3 March 1966; 8 January 1969.
36. KT 6 March 1970.
37. KT 19 February 1971.
38. KT 5 February 1976.
39. KT 4 April 1980.
40. KT 5 September 1980 and 24 January 1981.
41. *Kazakhstanskaia Pravda* 8 and 22 December 1964; 8 April 196
42. KP 11 March 1966.
43. KP 19 July 1966.
44. KP 22 and 23 July 1966.
45. KP 18 June 1967.
46. KP 17 April 1969.
47. KP 25 December 1969.
48. KP 1, 8, 10 and 18 February, 21 and 28 September, 2 and 3 Nove and 5 December 1973.
49. KP 3, 14 and 23 February 1974.
50. KP 16 December 1975.
51. KP 15 March and 25 April 1975.
52. KP 25 April 1975.
53. KP 5 February 1976.
54. KP 28 April 1976.

98. PU 30 October 1980.
99. PU 11 February and 25 July 1981.
100. PU 25 July 1981.
101. PU 15 September 1981.
102. PU 26 March 1982.
103. PU 27 and 28 April 1982.
104. *Sovetskaia Belorussia* 21 February, 29 and 30 April 1965.
105. SB 24 July and 16 November 1965.
106. SB 16 October 1965.
107. SB 19 December 1965.
108. SB 21 February 1965.
109. SB 11 March, 22 and 29 April 1965; 13 February 1966.
110. SB 5 February 1966.
111. SB 6 February, 4 and 5 March 1966.
112. SB 4 March 1966.
113. SB 11 March 1966.
114. SB 11 April and 29 August 1967.
115. SB 23 January 1968.
116. SB 1 March and 27 November 1968.
117. SB 23 March 1967; 25 January, 11, 15 and 18 February, 1 March 1968, 13 December 1969; 24 July 1970.
118. SB 13 December 1969.
119. SB 24 February 1971
120. SB 23 February 1971.
121. SB 15 July 1971.
122. SB 26 August 1971.
123. SB 9 July 1972. Michael E. Urban, *An Algebra of Soviet Power. Elite Circulation in the Belorussian Republic 1966–1986* (Cambridge, Cambridge University Press, 1989), p.122.
124. Urban, p.112.
125. SB 8 December 1972.
126. SB 20 February 1974.
127. SB 31 December 1973.
128. SB 14 September 1974. The CC CPSU decision, dated 28 August 1974, is in *KPSS v rezoliutsiiakh i resheniiakh s'ezdov, konferentsii i plenumov Ts.K. KPSS* (Moscow, 1989) 12, pp.463–9.
129. SB 13 November and 28 December 1974.
130. SB 18 and 22 March 1975.
131. SB 6 July 1975.
132. SB 11 September 1975.
133. SB 28 December 1975.
134. SB 30 December 1975.
135. SB 5 February 1976.
136. SB 27 March 1976.
137. SB 10 July 1976.
138. SB 16 July 1976.
139. SB 18 September 1976.
140. SB 3 March 1977.
141. SB 14 May 1977.

142. SB 14 October 1977.
143. SB 22 and 23 November 1977.
144. SB 13 July 1978.
145. SB 6 December 1978.
146. SB 20 June 1979.
147. SB 21 November 1979.
148. SB 13 December 1979.
149. SB 17 May 1980.
150. SB 21 June and 2 July 1980.
151. SB 28 and 30 December 1980; 9 and 10 January 1981.
152. SB 28 January 1981; cf. Masherov: 6 December 1978.
153. SB 23 September 1981.
154. Ibid.
155. SB 27 February 1982.

Chapter 4

1. For example, respectively, *Pravda* 14 July 1985, *Izvestiia* 5 January 1986, *Pravda* 20 and 27 January and 2 and 3 February 1986. Also on Uzbekistan *Pravda Vostoka* 1 and 2 February 1986, and James Critchlow, ' "Corruption", Nationalism and the Native Elites in Soviet Central Asia', *Journal of Communist Studies* 4, 2, June 1988, pp.142–61.
2. *Pravda* 24 April 1985.
3. PV 15, 22, 24, 26, 29 and 31 July and 5 August 1984; 17 and 23 January 1985. In a major interview in 1988, then CPUz first secretary Nishanov attributed the beginning of the struggle with nepotism in Uzbekistan to the visit by senior CC CPSU officials in early 1984. PV 17 September 1988.
4. PV 31 January 1986; *Pravda* 2 February 1986.
5. Leslie Holmes, *The End of Communist Power. Anti-Corruption Campaigns and Legitimation Crisis* (Melbourne, Melbourne University Press, 1993), p.148.
6. In contrast to the others, the replacement of Georgian leader Eduard Shevardnadze was a promotion, to the position of Soviet Foreign Minister and Politburo member.
7. Ibid., pp.137–8.
8. When Nishanov replaced Usmankhodzhaev in January 1988, the change was initially reported as being due to the latter's ill health, but at the plenum at the end of the month Nishanov described the moral-political health of the republic as in need of intensive care. PV 13 and 31 January 1988.
9. During the Brezhnev years this word was narrowly linked with unsuccessful attempts by officials to increase output through encouraging competition within and between work collectives. Gorbachev and his colleagues replaced this empty meaning with a much livelier concept of public honesty, reminiscent of but far broader than the old meaning of 'glasnost'' before 1917. This vital change was necessary to enable political reform to overcome resistance within the party apparatus, but it created new problems.
10. *Pravda Vostoka* 4 January and 26 February 1983.

11. PV 18 April and 20 June 1984.
12. PV 24 June 1984.
13. PV 15, 22, 24 26, 29 and 31 July, 5 August 1984.
14. PV 23 October 1984.
15. PV 23 January 1985.
16. For example, PV 3 and 8 March 1985.
17. PV 30 March 1985. Also see PV 5, 6, 7, 12, 14, 16 and 27 April, 15 and 29 May 1985.
18. PV 15 December 1985; 14, 19 and 21 January 1986.
19. PV 31 January and 2 February 1986.
20. PV 28 February 1986.
21. PV 7 June 1986.
22. PV 4 July 1986.
23. PV 30 July, 25 September and 5 October 1986.
24. PV 27 January 1987.
25. PV 8 February 1987.
26. PV 16 and 19 February 1987.
27. PV 11, 14 and 29 March 1987; 9, 10, 15, 21 and 29 April 1987.
28. PV 2 June 1987.
29. 'O ser'eznykh nedostatkakh v rabote tashkentskoi oblastnoi partorganizatsii po priemu v partiiu i ukrepleniiu partiinykh riadov', PV 18 and 25 June 1987.
30. PV 11 August 1987.
31. PV 7 January 1988.
32. PV 19 January 1988.
33. PV 31 January 1988.
34. PV 5 February 1988.
35. PV 11 May 1988.
36. PV 18 May, 1 and 2 June 1988.
37. PV 23 August 1988.
38. PV 17 September 1988.
39. PV 27 October 1988.
40. PV 4 November 1988 (*Izvestiia* 2 November 1988).
41. PV 8 and 11 December 1988.
42. PV 22 January 1989.
43. PV 28 February 1989.
44. PV 20 May 1989.
45. PV 17 June 1989. Birlik was a nationalist popular front in Uzbekistan which organised in opposition to the party.
46. PV 21 and 30 July 1989.
47. PV 20 August 1989.
48. PV 16 September 1989.
49. PV 4 January and 25 February 1990.
50. PV 2 June and 7 December 1989; 4 August 1990.
51. PV 23 May 1990.
52. PV 11 May 1990.
53. Gregory Gleason, 'Uzbekistan: from statehood to nationhood?', in Ian Bremmer and Ray Taras eds, *Nations and Politics in the Soviet Successor States* (Cambridge, Cambridge University Press, 1993), pp.352–3.
54. *Kommunist Tajikistana* 23 September 1983.

55. KT 26 August 1984.
56. KT 31 March and 2 April 1985. Also see his comments in KT 10 April 1985.
57. KT 3 and 25 December 1985.
58. KT 25 January 1986. Also KT 31 January 1986.
59. KT 17 April 1986.
60. KT 27 January and 20 February 1987.
61. KT 7, 8 and 11 April 1987.
62. KT 26 July 1987.
63. KT 28 November, 16, 17 and 26 December 1987.
64. KT 22, 24 and 29 May 1988.
65. KT 21 June 1988.
66. KT 6 November 1988.
67. KT 14 December 1988.
68. KT 27 and 28 January 1989. Also see the discussion in KT 2 April 1989.
69. KT 4 September 1988 and 2 April 1989.
70. KT 2 April 1989.
71. KT 29 December 1989 and 6 April 1990.
72. *Kazakhstanskaia Pravda* 30 June 1983; 17 January, 18 January and 21 July 1984.
73. KP 28 March and 18 May 1985.
74. KP 20 April and 11 July 1985.
75. KP 30 November and 11 December 1985.
76. KP 22 and 31 December 1985; 14 and 21 January 1986.
77. KP 7 February 1986.
78. KP 9 February 1986.
79. KP 8 February 1986.
80. KP 6 March 1986.
81. KP 20 May 1986.
82. KP 25 November, 9 and 24 December 1986.
83. KP 24 and 26 December 1986; 4 and 9 January 1987.
84. KP 4 January 1987.
85. KP 7, 8 and 10 January 1987.
86. KP 11 and 21 January 1987.
87. KP 18 January 1987.
88. KP 1, 6, 11, 19 and 22 February 1987.
89. KP 24 February 1987.
90. KP 15 March 1987.
91. Ibid.
92. KP 26 March, 1, 3, 5, 7, 8, 9 and 10 April 1987.
93. KP 17 May 1987.
94. KP 2 June 1987.
95. KP 25 June, 19 and 28 July 1987.
96. KP 26 May 1987 (a letter, described by propaganda and organisational officials as 'sensationalist', but read out at a seminar on the ideology of restructuring in May 1987).
97. KP 2 June 1987.
98. KP 17 November and 5 December 1987.
99. KP 24 January 1988.

100. KP 26 January 1988.
101. KP 31 January 1988.
102. KP 6 April and 20 May 1988.
103. KP 14 May and 5 June 1988.
104. KP 16 July 1988.
105. KP 19 August 1988.
106. KP 5 October and 5 August 1988.
107. KP 1 December 1988.
108. KP 13, 14, 15, 20, 21 and 22 December 1988.
109. KP 3 February 1989.
110. KP 18 and 24 May 1989.
111. KP 23 June 1989.
112. KP 18 July (article by K. Zhigalov) and 15 November 1989.
113. KP 18 August 1989.
114. Ibid.
115. KP 14 November 1989.
116. KP 6 January 1990.
117. Ibid.
118. KP 17 February 1990.
119. KP 22 February 1990.
120. KP 3 March 1990.
121. KP 22 March 1990.
122. KP 18 May 1990.
123. KP 29 May 1990.
124. KP 9 and 10 June 1990.
125. KP 8 June 1990.
126. KP 9 February and 6 March 1986.
127. KP 28 February and 4 July 1986.
128. Bohdan Nahaylo and Victor Swoboda, *Soviet Disunion: A History of the Nationalities Problem in the USSR* (London, Hamish Hamilton, 1990), pp.255–6.
129. KP 17 January 1990. Kolbin's appointment was reported in the old brief way in KP 17 December 1986. The scheduled copy of *Kazakhstanskaia Pravda* did not appear the following day due to the disturbances, but the next issue on 19 December announced the re-establishment of 'full order in the city'
130. KP 24 June 1989.
131. Ibid.
132. *Pravda Ukrainy* 28 January, 22 May and 29 June 1983; 21 July 1984.
133. PU 26 March 1983.
134. PU 13 January, 22 January and 27 May 1984.
135. PU 16 March 1985.
136. PU 18 July 1985.
137. PU 4 December 1985.
138. PU 14 January 1986.
139. PU 12 and 31 July 1986.
140. PU 8 January and 17 February 1987.
141. PU 20 March, 22 March and 21 April 1987.
142. PU 25 March 1987.

143. PU 22, 25 and 27 March 1987.
144. PU 7 and 12 April 1987.
145. PU 27 March 1987.
146. PU 18 July 1987.
147. Ibid.
148. PU 29 July, 1 August, 8, 16, 22, 23 and 27 December 1987; 3 January and 16 February 1988.
149. PU 1 and 26 December 1987.
150. PU 15 December 1987.
151. PU 23 January 1988.
152. PU 24 January 1988.
153. PU 1 July 1988.
154. PU 12 July 1988.
155. PU 13 October 1988.
156. PU 23 November 1988.
157. PU 13 December 1988, plus 23 October (Zaporozhe and Sumy), and 6 November (Odessa and Vinnitsa).
158. PU 13 and 29 December 1988.
159. PU 19 January 1989.
160. PU 2 and 5 February 1989.
161. PU 26 February 1989.
162. PU 4 and 11 March 1989.
163. PU 14 April 1989.
164. PU 17 May 1989.
165. PU 18 and 19 May 1989.
166. PU 5 July 1989.
167. PU 10 August 1989.
168. Ibid.
169. PU 3 and 17 September 1989.
170. PU 29 September, 30 September and 15 October 1989.
171. PU 20 October, 21 October, 1 December and 3 December 1989.
172. PU 13 December 1989.
173. PU 30 December 1989.
174. For example, *Sovetskaia Belorussia* 29 January and 29 April 1983; 10, 11 and 25 January 1984.
175. SB 28 May and 30 June 1983; 22 June 1984.
176. SB 6 April 1985.
177. SB 23 November and 31 December 1985.
178. SB 31 January 1986.
179. SB 1 February 1986.
180. SB 3 June, 26 September, 31 October and 26 December 1986
181. SB 28 November 1986.
182. SB 3 December 1986.
183. SB 27, 28 and 29 March 1987.
184. SB 29 March 1987.
185. SB 8 April,14 April, 8 May and 22 July 1987.
186. SB 29 July and 6 September 1987.
187. SB 20 December 1987.
188. SB 15, 16, 17, 20 and 21 January 1988.

189. SB 23 and 24 January 1988.
190. SB 5 May 1988.
191. SB 16 July 1988.
192. SB 18 August 1988.
193. SB 4 and 7 August 1988.
194. SB 17 December 1988.
195. SB 4 November 1988.
196. SB 17 August 1989.
197. SB 28 and 31 December 1989.
198. SB 14 January 1990.
199. SB 21 January 1990.
200. SB 24 March 1990.
201. SB 24 March 1990.
202. SB 28 March and 18 April 1990.

Chapter 5

1. For an interesting attempt to chart reports of corruption between 1966 and 1987, see Leslie Holmes, *The End of Communist Power. Anti-Corruption Campaigns and Legitimation Crisis* (Melbourne, Melbourne University Press, 1993), p.137.
2. Cf. Holmes, p.146.
3. Although see *inter alia* Ronald J. Hill, *Soviet Political Elites. The Case of Tiraspol* (London, Martin Robertson, 1977); Jerry F. Hough, *The Soviet Prefects. The Local Party Organs in Industrial Decision-Making* (Cambridge [Mass.], Harvard University Press, 1964); Philip D. Stewart, *Political Power in the Soviet Union. A Study of Decision-Making in Stalingrad* (Indianapolis, Bobbs-Merrill Co. Inc., 1968); Michael E. Urban, *An Algebra of Soviet Power Elite Circulation in the Belorussian Republic 1966–1986* (Cambridge, Cambridge University Press, 1989).
4. This was related to discussions about the nature of Stalinism. There is now a very large literature of this type. For example, see the papers in the *Russian Review* 45, 4, 1986 and 46, 4, 1987.
5. For example, Jerry F. Hough, 'Pluralism, Corporatism and the Soviet Union', in Susan Gross Solomon (ed.), *Pluralism in the Soviet Union. Essays in Honour of H. Gordon Skilling* (London, Macmillan, 1983) and Jerry F. Hough, *The Soviet Union and Social Science Theory* (Cambridge [Mass.], Harvard University Press, 1977).
6. For a discussion of the nature of participation, see Theodore H. Friedgut, *Political Participation in the USSR* (Princeton, Princeton University Press, 1979).
7. This is discussed in George Breslauer, *Khrushchev and Brezhnev as Leaders. Building Authority in Soviet Politics* (London, George Allen & Unwin, 1982), pp.99–108.
8. For example, 'O merakh dal'neishego razvitiia sel'skogo khoziaistva SSSR', *Pravda* 13 September 1953 (CC plenum decision); 'O dal'neishem uvelichenii proizvodstva zerna v strane i ob osvoenii tselinnykh i zalezhnykh zemel'' *Pravda* 6 March 1954 (CC plenum decision); 'Ob uvelichenii proizvodstva produktov zhivotnovodstva'

(plenum decision), *Pravda* 2 February 1955. Many of these sorts of criticism had been appearing before Stalin's death. See Yoram Gorlizki, 'Party Revivalism and the Death of Stalin', *Slavic Review* 54, 1, Spring 1995, pp.1–22.

9. For example, 'O suschestvennykh nedostatkakh v strukture ministerstv i vedomstv SSSR i merakh po uluchsheniiu raboty gosudarstvennogo apparata' (14 October 1954) *Kommunisticheskaia partiia sovetskogo soiuza v rezoliutsiiakh i resheniiakh s'ezdov, konferentsii i plenumov ts.k.* (Moscow, 1986), 8, p.439.

10. *XX s'ezd kommunisticheskoi partii sovetskogo soiuza 14–25 fevralia 1956 goda. Stenograficheskii otchet* (Moscow, 1956), 1, pp.9–120.

11. 'O rabote s kadrami v partiinoi organizatsii kirgizii', *KPSS v rez* . . . 9, 564–70.

12. Although both were concerned primarily with agricultural matters, this did not normally prevent Khrushchev from raising cadre questions if he saw fit. See *Pravda* 21 June 1958 and *Plenum tsentral'nogo komiteta kommunisticheskoi partii sovetskogo soiuza. 15–19 dekabria 1958g. Stenograficheskii otchet* (Moscow, 1958), pp.5–89.

13. *Pravda* 13 and 18 October 1958.

14. *Pravda* 9 October 1958.

15. The contemporaneous expansion of republican powers at the expense of the centre may also have been important here.

16. Breslauer, p.74. The April 1958 Presidium of the Supreme Soviet decree on ensuring deliveries for all-union needs was explicitly directed against localism.

17. At this time too the Party Control Commission gained responsibility for oversight of economic matters. According to Shvernik at the XXI Congress, the Commission had begun to investigate complaints and reports about mismanagement and violations of state discipline, to expose illegal activity by economic organs, and to intervene in economic affairs in order to ensure plan fulfilment. *Vneocherednoi XXI s'ezd kommunisticheskoi partii sovetskogo soiuza 27 ianvaria–5 fevralia 1959 goda. Stenograficheskii otchet* (Moscow, 1959), 2, p.48.

18. *Pravda* 1 September 1958.

19. *XXI s'ezd* . . . 1, pp.12–120.

20. *Pravda* 2 July 1959.

21. In 1959 PPOs were encouraged to establish special commissions of rank-and-file communists to monitor the implementation of decisions, but there is no evidence that this had any real impact. Peter Rutland, *The Politics of Economic Stagnation in the Soviet Union. The Role of Local Party Organs in Economic Management* (Cambridge, Cambridge University Press, 1993), pp.44–5.

22. *Pravda* 29 December 1959.

23. For one discussion, see Leonard Schapiro, *The Government and Politics of the Soviet Union* (London, Hutchinson, 1977), chs 6 and 7. Also Michel Tatu, *Power in the Kremlin. From Khrushchev to Kosygin* (New York, The Viking Press, 1968), pp.117–20.

24. Tatu, Part One, ch.3. Also Carl Linden, *Khrushchev and the Soviet Leadership 1957–1964* (Baltimore, The Johns Hopkins Press, 1966),

pp.94–8; and Robert V. Daniels, 'Political Processes and Generational Change', in Archie Brown (ed.), *Political Leadership in the Soviet Union* (London, Macmillan, 1989), pp.113–14.
25. This pledge was published in *Pravda* 7 January 1959.
26. *Pravda* 13 and 14 February 1959.
27. *Pravda* 29 December 1959.
28. At a plenum of the CC of the Uzbek party, Rashidov acknowledged that there had been individual cases of fraud and hoodwinking in the procurement of livestock products. *Pravda* 13 January 1961.
29. *Pravda* 21 and 22 January 1961.
30. *Pravda* 16 February 1961. For other reports, see *Pravda* 19 February and 1 March 1961.
31. *Partiinaia zhizn'*, 6, March 1961, pp.3–8. Also 8, April 1961, pp.11–17.
32. *Pravda* 16 April 1961.
33. *Pravda* 25 May 1961.
34. *Pravda* 26 May 1961.
35. Breslauer, p.99.
36. S. Vorontsov, 'O nezavisimosti organov partiinogo kontrolia', *Kommunist* 9, September 1961, pp.86–7. The exercise of real supervision over the economy by party organs was seen as a means of overcoming hoodwinking and report-padding. *Pravda* 27 June 1961.
37. *XXII s'ezd kommunisticheskoi partii sovetskogo soiuza 17–31 oktiabria 1961 goda. Stenograficheskii otchet* (Moscow, 1962), 1, pp.15–132.
38. The renewed emphasis on mass involvement gained doctrinal grounding in the notion of the 'all-peoples state', which was formally established in the new party Programme adopted at the XXII Congress.
39. *XXII s'ezd* ... 3, p.222.
40. For later reports of local authorities attempting to suppress criticism and punish critics, see *Pravda* 19 January and 26 March 1962.
41. *Pravda* 6 March 1962. Throughout the early 1960s measures had also been taken to re-centralise some of the economic power devolved to the sovnarkhozy through the establishment of republican sovnarkhozy in the RSFSR, Ukraine and Kazakhstan in 1960, the creation of coordinating councils to oversee groups of sovnarkhozy in May 1961, and in November 1962 the reduction in the number of sovnarkhozy and the establishment of the Central Asian Bureau to coordinate economic activity in the four Central Asian republics.
42. *Pravda* 20 November 1962. Also see the resolution from the plenum 'O razvitii ekonomiki SSSR i perestroike partiinogo rukovodstva narodnym khoziaistvom', *Pravda* 24 November 1962.
43. It took over the functions of the old Party Control Committee, its enlarged provenance being reflected in its name.
44. In late summer party organs were said to have as one of their tasks the exercise of supervision over economic affairs and the enforcement of central priorities against localism. *Partiinaia zhizn'* 15, August 1962, p.4.
45. In March 1962 a Supreme Soviet decree increased liability for bribery. *Current Digest of the Soviet Press* xiv, 7, 14/3/62. For some decrees confiscating dachas built with the proceeds of unearned income, see CDSP xiv, 32, 12/9/62 and 41, 7/11/62.

46. *Plenum tsentral'nogo komiteta kommunisticheskoi partii sovetskogo soiuza 9–13 dekabria 1963g. Stenograficheskii otchet* (Moscow, 1963), pp.5–77 and *Plenum tsentral'nogo komiteta kommunisticheskoi partii sovetskogo soiuza 10–15 fevralia 1964g. Stenograficheskii otchet* (Moscow, 1964), pp.397–467.
47. *Pravda* 18 January 1963.
48. Grey Hodnett, 'Khrushchev and Party-State Control', in Alexander Dallin and Alan F. Westin (eds), *Politics in the Soviet Union. 7 Cases* (New York, Harcourt, Brace and World Inc., 1966), p.152.
49. *Pravda* 4 March 1963.
50. *Pravda* 26 April 1963.
51. *Pravda* 25 March 1963.
52. *Spravochnik partiinogo rabotnika* (Moscow, 1964), pp.279–85.
53. *Pravda* 15 May 1963.
54. For example in Kursk, *Pravda* 5 October 1963.
55. William A. Clark, *Crime and Punishment in Soviet Officialdom. Combating Corruption in the Political Elite, 1965–1990* (Armonk, M.E. Sharpe, 1993), pp.15–16.
56. This argument is spelled out in Breslauer, ch.6.
57. This is discussed more fully in the following chapter. For discussions, see Holmes; Clark; Nicholas Lampert, *Whistleblowing in the Soviet Union. Complaints and Abuses under State Socialism* (London, Macmillan, 1985); S. Shenfield, 'Pripiski: False Statistical Reporting in Soviet-type Economies', in M. Clarke (ed.), *Corruption: Causes, Consequences and Control* (London, Pinter, 1983).
58. Rutland, p.26.
59. *Pravda* 7 November 1964.
60. See the discussion in Breslauer, ch.9.
61. For one discussion see Breslauer chs 9 and 10.
62. *Pravda* 10 December 1964.
63. *XXIII s'ezd kommunisticheskoi partii sovetskogo soiuza. 29 marta – 8 aprelia 1966 goda. Stenograficheskii otchet* (Moscow, 1966), 1, pp.18–109.
64. *XXIII s'ezd*... 2, pp.299–317. The quotation is on p.307.
65. For example, see the editorial on the reunification of the party apparatus in *Pravda* 7 November 1964.
66. *Pravda* 11 June 1966.
67. *Pravda* 28 May 1966.
68. *Pravda* 30 March 1968.
69. Breslauer, p.183.
70. *Pravda* 14 April 1970.
71. *Partiinaia zhizn'* 1, January 1969, pp.3–8. No significant changes occurred in the Tajik party leadership in the wake of this criticism.
72. *Pravda* 12 November 1969.
73. Specific legislation was passed in July 1970 to combat embezzlement. Holmes, p.222.
74. *XXIV s'ezd kommunisticheskoi partii sovetskogo soiuza. 30 marta – 9 aprelia 1971 goda. Stenograficheskii otchet* (Moscow, 1972), 1, pp.26–131.
75. *XXIV s'ezd*... 1 p.109.
76. See the discussions in Clarke, pp.151–9 and Holmes pp.222–3.
77. *Pravda* 6 March 1972.

78. For a discussion of this, see David Law, 'Corruption in Georgia', *Critique* 3, Autumn 1974, pp.99–107 and Clark pp.152–6.
79. *Pravda* 27 June 1976.
80. Ronald J. Hill and Peter Frank, *The Soviet Communist Party* (London, Allen & Unwin, 1983), p.79.
81. *Pravda* 23 February 1975.
82. *KPSS v rez*... 13, pp.243–5.
83. *XXV s'ezd kommunisticheskoi partii sovetskogo soiuza. 24 fevralia – 5 marta 1976 goda. Stenograficheskii otchet* (Moscow, 1976), 1, pp.26–115.
84. Breslauer, pp.234–5.
85. *Partiinaia zhizn'* 12, June 1979, pp.8–10; 23, December 1979, pp.17–20.
86. *Pravda* 4 April 1981.
87. *Partiinaia zhizn'* 12, June 1979, pp.8–10 (Turkmenistan).
88. *XXVI s'ezd kommunisticheskoi partii sovetskogo soiuza. 23 fevralia – 3 marta 1981 goda. Stenograficheskii otchet* (Moscow, 1981), 1, pp.22–99.
89. The fullest discussion of this is in Rutland.
90. For example, *Partiinaia zhizn'* 15, August 1965, pp.23–5; PZ 20, October 1976, pp.9–11.
91. For example, *Partiinaia zhizn'* 15, August 1965, pp.23–5; PZ 6, March 1967, pp.8–12; PZ 7, April 1967, pp.3–6; PZ 10, May 1967, pp.3–9; PZ 4, February 1970, pp.3–6; *Pravda* 6 October 1972; PZ 20, October 1973, pp.3–5; *Pravda* 22 November 1974.
92. For example, *Partiinaia zhizn'* 6, March 1967, pp.8–12; PZ 10, May 1967, pp.3–9; PZ 1, January 1969, pp.3–8; PZ 12, June 1979, pp.8–10; PZ 23, December 1979, pp.17–20.
93. For example, *Partiinaia zhizn'* 7, April 1967, pp.3–6; PZ 10, May 1967, pp.3–9; *Pravda* 14 September 1968; *Pravda* 16 August 1981.
94. For example, *Partiinaia zhizn'* 10, May 1967, pp.3–9; PZ 9, May 1968, pp.18–20; *Pravda* 25 October 1969; PZ 19, September 1981, pp.9–12.
95. For example, *Pravda* 12 November 1969; *Partiinaia zhizn'* 4, February 1970, pp.3–6; PZ 21, November 1970, pp.8–10; PZ 20, October 1973, pp.3–5; PZ 20, October 1975, pp.10–13.
96. *Partiinaia zhizn'* 15, August 1965, pp.23–5; *Pravda* 14 September 1968; *Pravda* 6 October 1972; PZ 12, June 1979, pp.8–10. Also for references to violations of the party's Rules, see PZ 10, May 1967, pp.3–9 and *Spravochnik partiinogo rabotnika* (Moscow, 1968), 8, pp.297–8.
97. For example, *Partiinaia zhizn'* 4, February 1970, pp.3–6.
98. For example, *Pravda* 12 August 1978.
99. *Pravda* 20 May 1972. For a review of the exchange, see *Pravda* 2 February 1975. For the argument that it was successful, see *Pravda* 7 February 1975.
100. John P. Willerton, 'Patronage Networks and Coalition Building in the Brezhnev Era', *Soviet Studies* 39, 2, April 1987, p.181.
101. Rutland, p.195. Also see the table on p.196.
102. Thane Gustafson and Dawn Mann, 'Gorbachev's First Year: Building Power and Authority', *Problems of Communism* 35, 3, May–June 1986, p.5.
103. Robert E. Blackwell Jr, 'Cadres Policy in the Brezhnev Era', *Problems of Communism* 28, 2, March–April 1979, p.34.

104. Blackwell, p.41. Also the discussion on pp.35-7.
105. Blackwell, p.36.
106. *XXIV s'ezd*... 1, p.124.
107. 'Ob uluchshenii raboty po okhrane pravoporiadka i usilenii bor'by s pravonarusheniiami' *Pravda* 11 August 1979. See the discussion of this campaign in Clark, pp.159-97. Also Konstantin Simis, 'Andropov's Anticorruption Campaign', *Washington Quarterly* 6, 3, Summer 1983, pp.111-21. Also on new measures at this time, see Holmes, p.223.
108. See the report in Clark, p.179.
109. *Pravda* 11 December 1982.
110. *Pravda* 23 November 1982.
111. *Pravda* 16 June 1983.
112. This practice was followed consistently in some republics, like Georgia, but not others, such as Kazakhstan.
113. For details on these, see Clark.
114. On these see Holmes pp.147 and 224. However, as indicated in Chapter 4, the discussion in the Kazakh press relating to the party was not very extensive.
115. *Pravda* 3 March 1984.
116. Rutland, p.196. For different figures (33 and 7), see Graeme Gill *The Collapse of a Single-Party System. The Disintegration of the Communist Party of the Soviet Union* (Cambridge, Cambridge University Press, 1994), p.25.
117. For a list of people see Clark, p.189.
118. *Pravda* 12 March 1985.
119. *Pravda* 14 March 1985.
120. *Pravda* 24 April 1985. For a discussion of this period, see Gill, *Collapse*, ch.2.
121. 'O nedopustimosti iskazheniia fakticheskogo polozheniia del v soobshcheniiakh i informatsiiakh, postupaiushchikh v TS.K. KPSS i drugie rukovodiashchie organy', 26 November 1985, *Izvestiia Ts.K. KPSS* 2, February 1989, pp.39-41.
122. *XXVII s'ezd kommunisticheskoi partii sovetskogo soiuza 25 fevralia-6 marta 1986 goda. Stenograficheskii otchet* (Moscow, 1986), 1, pp.23-121.
123. *XXVII s'ezd*... 1, pp.530-3.
124. For example, *Izvestiia* 5 January 1986, *Pravda* 20 and 27 January, 2 and 3 February 1986.
125. *Pravda* 28 January 1987.
126. Gill, *Collapse*, ch.3.
127. *Pravda* 26 April 1987.
128. *Pravda* 16 July 1987.
129. *Pravda* 2 February 1988.
130. *XIX vsesoiuznaia konferentsiia kommunisticheskoi partii sovetskogo soiuza. 28 iiunia-1 iiulia 1988 goda. Stenograficheskii otchet* (Moscow, 1988). For Gorbachev's speech see 1, pp.19-92.
131. The privileges enjoyed by Soviet officials had come under attack earlier, including at the XXVII Congress by El'tsin (*XXVII s'ezd*... 1, pp.142-3 where he also refers to abuses) and the pre-conference public discussion (e.g. *Kommunist* 5, 1988, pp.42-5, *Pravda* 9 March 1988, *Moscow News* 24 April 1988). At the XIX Conference this question was

Notes to pages 132-5

raised by a series of speakers, including El'tsin (e.g. *XIX konferentsiia* ... 1, pp.99, 269-70; 2, pp.60-1).
132. Gill, *Collapse*, pp.68-74.
133. For example, see the July 1989 meeting between Gorbachev and party leaders. *Pravda* 19 and 21 July 1989.
134. Although he was obviously helped in this by the accumulated effect of the stability of cadres policy.
135. Turnover of republican first secretaries under Gorbachev was as follows:
Armenia: Demirchian/Arutiunian (5/88), Arutianian/Movsisian (4/90), Movsisian/Pogosian (11/90).
Azerbaijan: Bagirov/Vezirov (5/88), Vezirov/Mutalibov (1/90).
Belorussia: Sliun'kov/Sokolov (2/87), Sokolov/Malofeev (7/90).
Estonia: Vaino/Valias (6/88), Valias/Sillari (3/90).
Georgia: Shevardnadze/Patiashvili (6/85), Patiashvili/Gumbaridze (4/89), Gumbaridze/Margiani (7/90).
Kazakhstan: Kunaev/Kolbin (12/86), Kolbin/Nazarbaev (6/89).
Kirgizia: Usubaliev/Masaliev (11/85).
Latvia: Pugo/Vagris (10/88), Vagris/Rubiks (4/90).
Lithuania: Grishkiavichius/Songaila (12/87), Songaila/Brazauskas (10/88), Brazauskas/Burokevicius (3/90).
Moldavia: Grossu/Luchinsky (11/89).
Tajikistan: Nabiev/Makhkamov (12/85).
Turkmenistan: Gapurov/Niiazov (12/85).
Ukraine: Shcherbitsky/Ivashko (9/89), Ivashko/Gurenko (7/90).
Uzbekistan: Usmankhodzhaev/Nishanov (1/88), Nishanov/Karimov (6/89).
By late 1989 to 1990, changes in first secretary were in some areas out of central control and in any case the situation was complicated by the splits that occurred in some republican parties, most importantly in the Baltic republics, early in 1990.
136. Rutland, p.196. According to Alexander Rahr, the figures were even higher: 1985 31; 1986 23; 1987 29; 1988 10, i.e. 59.2 per cent. Radio Free Europe/Radio Liberty, Research Bulletin 238/88, 5 June 1988, p.3.
137. For some details on the scale, see Gustafson and Mann, 'Gorbachev's First Year', and Thane Gustafson and Dawn Mann, 'Gorbachev's Next Gamble', *Problems of Communism* 36, 4, July-August 1987, pp.1-20.
138. See discussion in John A. Armstrong, *The Politics of Totalitarianism. The Communist Party of the Soviet Union from 1934 to the Present* (New York, Random House, 1961), pp.244 and 271; Donald S. Carlisle 'Power and Politics in Soviet Uzbekistan: From Stalin to Gorbachev', in William Fierman (ed.), *Soviet Central Asia. The Failed Transformation* (Boulder, Westview Press, 1991) p.104. On Gafurov see below. The case of Patolichev in Belorussia is a more ambiguous case. Although he had been a CC Secretary from 1946 before moving to Belorussia, after his replacement in July 1956 he was made a government minister and thereby retained within the Soviet elite. He was not, therefore, a casualty of de-Stalinisation in the same way as the others.

139. This should not be exaggerated. High levels of criticism did not always lead to substantial personnel changes. They could be the result of local elites seeking to defend themselves by participating in centrally inspired campaigns.
140. For example, see the criticisms at the January 1956 Belorussian party congress, *Sovetskaia Belorussia* 27, 28 and 29 January 1956.
141. Roy Medvedev, *Khrushchev* (Oxford, Blackwell, 1982), p.139.
142. See his speech to the December 1959 CC plenum, where he also referred positively to Kunaev. *Pravda* 29 December 1959.
143. Khrushchev, 'Razvitie...', *Pravda* 20 November 1962.
144. See the report of the CC KCP December 1962 plenum in *Kazakhstanskaia Pravda* 26 and 27 December 1962. The resolution from this meeting referred among other things to the falsification of results, nepotism, and toadying, all by implication associated with Kunaev. The fact that he was only moved to chairmanship of the Council of Ministers may reflect the influence of Brezhnev.
145. See the reports in *Kommunist Tajikistana* 14, 16 and 18 April 1961. Also *Pravda* 16 April 1961.
146. This relies heavily on Donald S. Carlisle, 'The Uzbek Power Elite: Politburo and Secretariat (1938–1983)', *Central Asian Survey* 5, 3/4, 1986, pp.107–11.
147. Carlisle, 'Uzbek Power Elite', also notes the importance of region in the structuring of Uzbek politics.
148. In this regard it is evident that Rashidov identified himself much more with Khrushchev's concerns in his first two years as republican first secretary than later.
149. Tatu, Part Two, ch.1.
150. On the background of Usmankhodzhaev, see Carlisle, 'Power and Politics', pp.112–13.
151. Carlisle, 'Power and Politics', p.115.
152. *Kazakhstanskaia Pravda* 15 March 1987.
153. For example, see his comments in KP 9 February 1986.
154. See the discussion in Michael E. Urban, *An Algebra of Soviet Power. Elite circulation in the Belorussian Republic 1966–1986* (Cambridge, Cambridge University Press, 1989), pp.119–22.
155. Urban argues that Sokolov succeeded Sliun'kov because of his well-known successes as first secretary of Brest obkom and as a result of factional coalition-building. Urban, pp.133–4.
156. Carlisle, 'Power and Politics', pp.105–6.
157. *Pravda Vostoka* 26 January 1958.
158. PV 28 January 1956.
159. PV 26 January 1958.
160. See the discussion in Teresa Rakowska-Harmstone, *Russia and Nationalism in Central Asia. The Case of Tadzhikistan* (Baltimore, The Johns Hopkins University Press, 1970), p.159.
161. He also conducted research in Tajik history; for example, B.G. Gafurov, *Tadzhiki. Drevneishaia, drevnaiai srednevekovaia istoriia* (Moscow, 1972).
162. Rakowska-Harmstone, p.161.
163. For one discussion, see Sidney Ploss, *Conflict and Decision-Making in*

Soviet Russia. A Case Study of Agricultural Policy 1953–1963 (Princeton, Princeton University Press, 1965), p.86.
164. Kazakhstanskaia Pravda 13 February 1954.
165. The local leadership came under attack, and in the three months following February 1954, the first secretaries of six Virgin Lands oblasts were replaced. Martha Brill Olcott, The Kazakhs (Stanford, Hoover Institution Press, 1987), p.226.
166. Pravda Ukrainy 13 June 1953. See Borys Lewytzkyj, Politics and Society in Soviet Ukraine 1953–1980 (Edmonton, Canadian Institute of Ukrainian Studies, 1984), pp.3–4 and Khrushchev Remembers (London, Andre Deutsch, 1971, ed. Strobe Talbott), pp.263–6 and 330.
167. On this see Lewytzkyj, ch.4.
168. For a discussion of some of this see Lewytzkyj, pp.149–51.
169. Medvedev, Khrushchev, p.242.
170. Urban, pp.116–17.
171. Urban, p.117.
172. Urban, pp.113 and 117.
173. See the discussions in Urban, p.118 and Amy Knight, 'Pyotr Masherov and the Soviet Leadership: A Study in Kremlinology', Survey 26, Winter 1982, pp.151–68.
174. Urban, pp.120–2.
175. The apparent exception of the strong criticism in Belorussia under Masherov in the late 1970s proves this rule, since this was linked with the emerging campaign sponsored by Andropov at the centre.

Chapter 6

1. Leslie Holmes, The End of Communist Power. Anti-Corruption Campaigns and Legitimation Crisis (Melbourne, Melbourne University Press, 1993), p.228.
2. Pravda Vostoka 24 and 26 June 1984. For earlier references to the sorts of charges that were to come, see the report of an appointment to a high judicial post in Karakalpakia in Pravda Vostoka 18 April 1984.
3. M.S. Gorbachev, 'Politicheskii doklad Tsentral'nogo Komiteta KPSS', Pravda 26 February 1986.
4. William A. Clark, Crime and Punishment in Soviet Officialdom. Combating Corruption in the Political Elite, 1965–1990 (Armonk, M.E. Sharpe, 1993), pp.191–6. Also see Pravda 29 April 1988 and the comments by Gdlian in Ogonek 26 June 1988 pp.27–9 and Pravda Vostoka 21 April 1988.
5. Holmes, p.101 and James Critchlow, Nationalism in Uzbekistan. A Soviet Republic's Road to Sovereignty (Boulder, Westview Press, 1991), p.41.
6. See the discussion in Donald S. Carlisle, 'Power and Politics in Soviet Uzbekistan: From Stalin to Gorbachev', in William Fierman (ed.), Soviet Central Asia. The Failed Transformation (Boulder, Westview Press, 1991), pp.108–12.
7. For a sketch of one of those below Rashidov, the so-called 'cotton baron' Akhmadzhan Adylov, see Boris Z. Rumer, Soviet Central Asia. 'A Tragic Experiment' (Boston, Unwin Hyman, 1989), pp.151–4. Also Izvestiia 7 May 1988.

8. For an article pointing to bribery as an important element in organised crime in Uzbekistan, see Dmitri Likhanov, 'Organized Crime in Central Asia', *Telos* 75, Summer 1988, pp.90–101. For arguments that some republics had been transformed into criminal networks run by the first secretaries, see *Pravda* 16 March 1987, 28 December 1987 and 23 January 1988, *Argumenty i fakty* 18, 1990, and Andrei Niukin, 'Idealy ili interesy', *Novyi Mir* 64, 1, January 1988, pp.193–211, and 64, 2, February 1988, pp.205–28, esp. Part 2.
9. Most of these data come from James Critchlow, 'Prelude to "Independence": How the Uzbek Party Apparatus Broke Moscow's Grip on Elite Recruitment', in Fierman, pp.135–6.
10. *Pravda* 28 February 1986 – Usmankhodzhaev at XXVII Congress.
11. James Critchlow, ' "Corruption", Nationalism, and the Native Elites in Soviet Central Asia', *Journal of Communist Studies* 4, 2, June 1988, p.145. Also see Critchlow, 'Prelude', p.141 and Rumer, pp.147–9.
12. Rumer, p.148.
13. See the discussion in Gregory Gleason, 'Fealty and Loyalty: Informal Authority Structures in Soviet Asia', *Soviet Studies* 43, 4, 1991, p.620. For one Soviet explanation, see *Pravda Vostoka* 15 July 1986.
14. For an attempt to determine the importance of loyalties to entities below the level of the Soviet Union, see Gleason, pp.613–28.
15. There is a large literature on this. For example, Harry Eckstein, 'A Culturalist Theory of Political Change', *American Political Science Review* 82, 3, September 1988, pp.789–804. For discussions in the context of the study of Soviet-type systems, see Archie Brown (ed.), *Political Culture and Communist Studies* (London, Macmillan, 1984).
16. For some details of the Georgian campaign, see David Law, 'Corruption in Georgia', *Critique* 3, Autumn 1974, pp.99–107. Also Clark, pp.153–6. For relevant decisions of the CC CPSU, see *Pravda* 6 March 1972 and 27 June 1976.
17. See the discussion in Il'ia Zemtsov, *Partiia ili mafiia? Razvorovannaia respublika* (Paris, Led Editeurs Reunis, 1976).
18. In the words of one such scholar: 'In the Transcaucasian republics especially (of these, Georgia has acquired the most notoriety), a number of influences have led to a systematic disregard of the law at certain periods. The strength of family ties, the role of the gift, the importance of "macho" displays of material wealth, and perhaps the strength of entrepreneurial traditions have helped to create enclaves in which some types of abuse have flourished to an extent that seemed astonishing to the outside world.' Nicholas Lampert, 'Law and Order in the USSR: The Case of Economic and Official Crime', *Soviet Studies* 36, 3, 1984, pp.371–2.
19. This is discussed in Clark, pp.168–72. Also see the comments by a later Krasnodar kraikom first secretary, Ivan Polozkov, in his article 'Vospityvat' doveriem i otvetstvennost'iu', *Kommunist* 17, November 1986, p.36. Problems do not seem to have gone away with Medunov's removal; in 1985 some 600 party penalties imposed by PPOs in the krai were increased by higher organs because of their laxity. Peter Rutland, *The Politics of Economic Stagnation in the Soviet Union. The Role*

of Local Party Organs in Economic Management (Cambridge, Cambridge University Press, 1993), p.32.
20. Pravda 26 July 1984 and 30 January 1986.
21. A writer who in 1982–83 in Lefortovo Prison met two former officials whose deception of superiors was motivated by a desire to meet production targets, has commented that 'it is obvious that, sooner or later, the transition from innocuous breaches of the law in the name of fulfilling the plan to nefarious dealings for one's own purposes becomes unavoidable. If an individual continually takes risks, transgresses the law for the success of the enterprise, he will sooner or later do exactly the same for his own enrichment. In most cases corrupt planners have attempted to follow both aims simultaneously (the more so as successful plan fulfilment can serve as a defence).' Boris Kagarlitsky, *The Dialectic of Change* (London, Verso, 1990), pp.256–7.
22. The most important study is that by Holmes.
23. A useful definition is given by Joseph Nye who defines corruption as 'behavior which deviates from the formal duties of a public role because of private-regarding (personal, close family, private clique) pecuniary or status gains; or violates rules against the exercise of certain types of private-regarding influence'. Joseph S. Nye, 'Corruption and Political Development: A Cost-Benefit Analysis', *American Political Science Review* 61, 2, June 1967, p.419.
24. For one discussion of this, see T.H. Rigby, 'The Origins of the Nomenklatura System', in Inge Auerbach, Andreas Hillgruber and Gottfried Schramm (eds), *Felder und Vorfelder russischer Geschichte. Studien zu Ehren von Peter Scheibert* (Freiburg, Rombach Verlag, 1985). Also Graeme Gill, *The Origins of the Stalinist Political System* (Cambridge, Cambridge University Press, 1990), Part 1.
25. For a review of some theories of this contradiction, see Roderic Pitty, 'Class Analysis of Inequality in the USSR', in Christine Jennett and Randal Stewart (eds), *Three Worlds of Inequality: Race, Class and Gender* (Melbourne, Macmillan, 1987), pp.189–94.
26. *Pravda Vostoka* 26 June 1984.
27. Even in the 1980s the apparatus was said to be stretched and heavily reliant on the telephone for maintaining contact. Rutland, pp.38–9.
28. This is discussed in many places. For its history see the references in fn.24. Also see Bohdan Harasymiw, *Political Elite Recruitment in the Soviet Union* (London, Macmillan, 1984) and T.H. Rigby and Bohdan Harasymiw (eds), *Leadership Selection and Patron–Client Relations in the USSR and Yugoslavia* (London, Allen & Unwin, 1983).
29. For studies which suggest the operation of regionally based influence in personnel policy, see John H. Miller, 'Cadres Policy in the Nationality Areas: Recruitment of CPSU first and second secretaries in the non-Russian republics of the USSR', *Soviet Studies* 29, 1, January 1977, pp.3–36; John Miller, 'Nomenklatura: Check on Localism?', in Rigby and Harasymiw, pp.64–96; Joel C. Moses, *Regional Party Leadership and Policy Making in the USSR* (New York, Praeger, 1974); Joel C. Moses, 'Regionalism in Soviet Politics: Continuity as a Source of Change', *Soviet Studies* 37, 2, April 1985, pp.184–211; Joel C. Moses, 'The Impact

of Nomenklatura in Soviet Regional Elite Recruitment', *Soviet Union* 8, 1, 1981, pp.62–102; James H. Oliver, 'Turnover and Family Circles in Soviet Administration', *Slavic Review* 32, September 1973, pp.527–45; T.H. Rigby, 'The Soviet Regional Leadership: The Brezhnev Generation', *Slavic Review* 37, March 1978, pp.1–24.

30. These are discussed more fully in the Conclusion.
31. For one discussion of this, see Graeme Gill, 'Institutionalisation and Revolution: Rules and the Soviet Political System', *Soviet Studies* 37, 2, April 1985, pp.212–26.
32. Indeed, one author has argued that after 1953 the Communist Party fragmented into regional fiefdoms over which the centre was barely able to exercise its authority. Yu. Davydov, 'Totalitarizm i totalitarnaia biurokratiia', *Nauka i zhizn'* 8, 1989, pp.44–51.
33. For general discussions, see Michael Voslensky, *Nomenklatura. Anatomy of the Soviet Ruling Class* (London, Bodley Head, 1984) and Mervyn Matthews, *Privilege in the Soviet Union. A Study of Elite Life-Styles under Communism* (London, Allen & Unwin, 1978).
34. One analyst declared: 'The holders of power who are no longer satisfied, as under Stalin, with just being powerful, begin more and more widely to "exchange" their power for material benefits, leading to a "consumer boom" and facilitating the emergence of mafia or clanlike networks in which the main place belongs to economic administrators who in turn acquire power in return for material goods.' L. Gudkov, Yu. Levada, A. Levinson and L. Sedov, 'Fenomen biurokratii v istoriko-sotsiologicheskoi perspektive', *Mirovaia Ekonomika i Mezhdunarodnye Otnosheniia* 6, 1989, p.88.
35. The crucial role of 'personal, informal relations of assistance in case of shortages' as an inherent part of the actually existing command economy has been stressed by Gyorgy Markus, who comments that the 'criminalisation of the economy could never have proceeded so far were the transgression of official rules and the by-passing of official channels not already a practice embedded in the actual working of the first, official economy itself'. Ferenc Feher, Agnes Heller and Gyorgy Markus, *Dictatorship Over Needs. An Analysis of Soviet Societies* (Oxford, Blackwell, 1983), p.102.
36. For some comments on Kunaev in Kazakhstan, see Martha Brill Olcott, *The Kazakhs* (Stanford, Hoover Institution Press, 1987), pp.240–6. One analyst has observed that while cliques, patronage and nepotism became 'most obvious in the peripheral republics such as Uzbekistan, where a clanlike network was running the republic, it is in fact a feature of the society at all levels. In an unpredictable and brutal society, personal dependants or relatives are more reliable than those who are unknown.' Hillel Ticktin, *Origins of the Crisis in the USSR. Essays on the Political Economy of a Disintegrating System* (Armonk, M.E. Sharpe, 1992), p.46. Also see the comments in Leonid M. Batkin, 'At a Fateful Fork in the Road', in Abraham Brumberg (ed.), *Chronicle of a Revolution* (New York, Pantheon, 1990), p.206.
37. For one attempt to apply the notion of patrimonialism to the Soviet system, see Zygmunt Baumann, 'Officialdom and Class: Bases of

Inequality in Socialist Society', in Frank Parkin (ed.), *The Social Analysis of Class Structure* (London, Tavistock, 1974), pp.129–48. Baumann argues (p.136) that the notion of patrimonialism becomes useful for the analysis of socialist society when it is stripped of two elements, the personal basis of supreme power and the traditionalistic legitimation of authority. But it is the former of these which is crucial both to the notion of patrimonialism and to its applicability to the Soviet party structure.

38. Max Weber, *The Theory of Social and Economic Organisation* (Glencoe, The Free Press, 1964), p.367. For his fullest discussion of patrimonialism, see Max Weber, *Economy and Society. An Outline of Interpretative Sociology* (New York, Bedminster Press, 1968, eds Guenther Roth and Claus Wittich), 3, chs 7 and 8.
39. Critchlow, '"Corruption"', p. 159.
40. Kenneth Jowitt, *Revolutionary Breakthroughs and National Development. The Case of Romania 1944–1965* (Berkeley, University of California Press, 1971), p.69.
41. See the interesting comments by Weber on the relationship between patrimonial leader and his officials, *Economy and Society*, 3, pp.1038–42.
42. For an interesting discussion see Ken Jowitt, 'Soviet Neotraditionalism: the Political Corruption of a Leninist Regime', *Soviet Studies* 35, 3, July 1983, pp.275–97. Also the comments in Roy Boyne, 'Weber on Socialism and Charisma: A Comment', *Soviet Studies* 36, 4, October 1984, pp.602–5.

Conclusion

1. In the post-war period there was one party congress, the XIX in October 1952, and one CC plenum in February 1947. The Politburo, Orgburo and Secretariat may have met on a regular basis, but had little power. Seweryn Bialer, *Stalin's Successors. Leadership, Stability and Change in the Soviet Union* (Cambridge, Cambridge University Press, 1980), p.33. On the informal gatherings of cronies, see Milovan Djilas, *Conversations with Stalin* (Harmondsworth, Penguin, 1969), pp.63–5 and N.S. Khrushchev, 'On the Cult of Personality and Its Consequences', in T.H. Rigby, *The Stalin Dictatorship* (Sydney, Sydney University Press, 1968), p.81.
2. Amendments were made to the Rules in 1966 and 1971.
3. For a fuller discussion, see Graeme Gill, *The Collapse of a Single Party System. The Disintegration of the Communist Party of the Soviet Union* (Cambridge, Cambridge University Press, 1994).
4. For one discussion of the way local leaders appropriated economic resources, see the article entitled 'Provintsial'naia nomenklatura rvetsia v millionery', *Izvestiia* 24 April 1992.
5. For discussions see Stephen White, Graeme Gill and Darrell Slider, *The Politics of Transition. Shaping a Post-Soviet Future* (Cambridge, Cambridge University Press, 1993) pp.112–15 and Darrell Slider, 'The CIS: Republican Leaders Confront Local Opposition', *RFE/RL Research Report* 1, 10, 6 March 1992, p. 11.

6. While disputing Gaidar's thesis that a united nomenklatura elite continues to rule in Russia, Marat Cheshkov specifically notes as one element of continuity in the post-Soviet period 'the influential and strong informal relations' between individuals in authority. A similar point about the continuing 'clientelistic core' of Russian parties is made by Tatiana Vorozheikina. Respectively Marat Cheshkov, 'Vechno zhivaia nomenklatura?', *Mirovaia Ekonomika i Mezhdunarodnye Otnosheniia* 6, 1995, p.42 and Tatiana Vorozheikina, 'Clientelism and the Process of Political Democratisation in Russia', in Luis Roniger and Ayse Gunes-Ayata (eds), *Democracy, Clientelism and Civil Society* (Boulder, Lynne Rienner, 1994), p.114.
7. For some reports, see *Moscow News* 37, 15–22 September 1991 (Azerbaijan), and 37, 13–20 September 1992 (Tajikistan), *Rossiiskaia Gazeta* 4 March 1992 and *Nezavisimaia Gazeta* 22 February 1992.
8. Two months after his removal, the leader put in to replace him (Iskandarov) was himself removed and replaced by a Nabiev supporter, Rakhmonov.

Select Bibliography

Primary Sources

Izvestiia 1986-90.
Izvestiia Ts.K. KPSS 1989-91.
Kazakhstanskaia Pravda 1953-90.
Kommunist Tajikistana 1953-90.
KPSS v rezoliutsiiakh i resheniiakh s'ezdov, konferentsii i plenumov Ts.K. KPSS, vols 8-15, Moscow, 1985-89.
Partiinaia zhizn' 1954-90.
Plenum tsentral'nogo komiteta kommunisticheskoi partii sovetskogo soiuza. 15-19 dekabria 1958g. Stenograficheskii otchet, Moscow, 1958.
Plenum tsentral'nogo komiteta kommunisticheskoi partii sovetskogo soiuza 9-13 dekabria 1963g. Stenograficheskii otchet, Moscow 1963.
Plenum tsentral'nogo komiteta kommunisticheskoi partii sovetskogo soiuza 10-15 fevralia 1964g. Stenograficheskii otchet, Moscow, 1964.
Pravda 1953-90.
Pravda Ukrainy 1953-90.
Pravda Vostoka 1953-90.
Sovetskaia Belorussia 1953-90.
Spravochnik partiinogo rabotnika, Moscow, 1964-90.
Vneocherednoi XXI s'ezd kommunisticheskoi partii sovetskogo soiuza. 27 ianvaria-5 fevralia 1959 goda. Stenograficheskii otchet, Moscow, 1959.
XIX vsesoiuznaia konferentsiia kommunisticheskoi partii sovetskogo soiuza. 28 iiunia-1 iiulia 1988 goda. Stenograficheskii otchet, Moscow, 1988.
XX s'ezd kommunisticheskoi partii sovetskogo soiuza 14-25 fevralia 1956 goda. Stenograficheskii otchet, Moscow, 1956.
XXII s'ezd kommunisticheskoi partii sovetskogo soiuza 17-31 oktiabria 1961 goda. Stenograficheskii otchet, Moscow, 1962.
XXIII s'ezd kommunisticheskoi partii sovetskogo soiuza. 29 marta-8 aprelia 1966 goda. Stenograficheskii otchet, Moscow, 1966.
XXIV s'ezd kommunisticheskoi partii sovetskogo soiuza. 30 marta-9 aprelia 1971 goda. Stenograficheskii otchet, Moscow, 1972.
XXV s'ezd kommunisticheskoi partii sovetskogo soiuza. 24 fevralia-5 marta 1976 goda. Stenograficheskii otchet, Moscow, 1976.
XXVI s'ezd kommunisticheskoi partii sovetskogo soiuza. 23 fevralia-3 marta 1981 goda. Stenograficheskii otchet, Moscow, 1981.
XXVII s'ezd kommunisticheskoi partii sovetskogo soiuza. 25 fevralia-6 marta 1986 goda. Stenograficheskii otchet, Moscow, 1986.

Secondary Sources

Amrekulov, Nurlan, *Taina Kul'ta Lichnosti i ee Razoblachenie: epokha stalinizma, logika ee razvitiia i izzhivaniia*, Alma Ata, Gylym, 1991.

Armstrong, John A., *The Politics of Totalitarianism. The Communist Party of the Soviet Union from 1934 to the Present*, New York, Random House, 1961.
Batkin, Leonid M., 'At a Fateful Fork in the Road', in Abraham Brumberg (ed.), *Chronicle of a Revolution*, New York, Pantheon, 1990.
Baumann, Zygmunt, 'Officialdom and Class: Bases of Inequality in Socialist Society', in Frank Parkin (ed.), *The Social Analysis of Class Structure*, London, Tavistock, 1974.
Bialer, Seweryn, *Stalin's Successors. Leadership, Stability and Change in the Soviet Union*, Cambridge, Cambridge University Press, 1980.
Blackwell Jr, Robert E., 'Cadres Policy in the Brezhnev Era', *Problems of Communism* 28, 2, March–April 1979.
Boyne, Roy, 'Weber on Socialism and Charisma: A Comment', *Soviet Studies* 36, 4, October 1984.
Breslauer, George, *Khrushchev and Brezhnev as Leaders. Building Authority in Soviet Politics*, London, Allen & Unwin, 1982.
Brown, Archie (ed.), *Political Culture and Communist Studies*, London, Macmillan, 1984.
Carlisle, Donald S., 'Power and Politics in Soviet Uzbekistan: From Stalin to Gorbachev', in William Fierman (ed.), *Soviet Central Asia. The Failed Transformation*, Boulder, Westview Press, 1991.
Carlisle, Donald S., 'The Uzbek Power Elite: Politburo and Secretariat (1938–1983)', *Central Asian Survey* 5, 3/4, 1986.
Cheshkov, Marat, "Vechno zhivaia' nomenklatura?", *Mirovaia Ekonomika i Mezhdunarodnye Otnosheniia* 6, 1995.
Clark, William A., *Crime and Punishment in Soviet Officialdom. Combating Corruption in the Political Elite, 1965–1990*, Armonk, M.E. Sharpe, 1993.
Critchlow, James, ' "Corruption", Nationalism and the Native Elites in Soviet Central Asia', *Journal of Communist Studies* 4, 2, June 1988.
Critchlow, James, *Nationalism in Uzbekistan. A Soviet Republic's Road to Sovereignty*, Boulder, Westview Press, 1991.
Critchlow, James, 'Prelude to "Independence": How the Uzbek Party Apparatus Broke Moscow's Grip on Elite Recruitment', in William Fierman (ed.), *Soviet Central Asia. The Failed Transformation*, Boulder, Westview Press, 1991.
Daniels, Robert V., 'Political Processes and Generational Change', in Archie Brown (ed.), *Political Leadership in the Soviet Union*, London, Macmillan, 1989.
Davydov, Yu., 'Totalitarizm i totalitarnaia biurokratiia', *Nauka i zhizn'* 8, 1989.
Djilas, Milovan, *Conversations with Stalin*, Harmondsworth, Penguin, 1969.
Eckstein, Harry, 'A Culturalist Theory of Political Change', *American Political Science Review* 82, 3, September 1988.
Feher, Ferenc, Heller, Agnes and Markus, Gyorgy, *Dictatorship Over Needs. An Analysis of Soviet Societies*, Oxford, Blackwell, 1983.
Friedgut, Theodore H., *Political Participation in the USSR*, Princeton, Princeton University Press, 1979.
Gill, Graeme, *The Collapse of a Single-Party System. The Disintegration of the Communist Party of the Soviet Union*, Cambridge, Cambridge University Press, 1994.
Gill, Graeme, 'Institutionalisation and Revolution: Rules and the Soviet Political Game', *Soviet Studies* 37, 2, April 1985.

Select Bibliography

Gill, Graeme, *The Origins of the Stalinist Political System*, Cambridge, Cambridge University Press, 1990.
Gill, Graeme, *The Rules of the Communist Party of the Soviet Union*, London, Macmillan, 1988.
Gleason, Gregory, 'Fealty and Loyalty: Informal Authority Structures in Soviet Asia', *Soviet Studies* 43, 4, 1991.
Gleason, Gregory, 'Uzbekistan: From Statehood to Nationhood?', in Ian Bremner and Ray Taras (eds), *Nations and Politics in the Soviet Successor States*, Cambridge, Cambridge University Press, 1993.
Gorlizki, Yoram, 'Party Revivalism and the Death of Stalin', *Slavic Review* 54, 1, Spring 1995.
Gudkov, L., Levada, Yu., Levinson, A. and Sedov, L., 'Fenomen biurokratii v istoriko-sotsiologicheskoi perspektive', *Mirovaia Ekonomika i Mezhdunarodnye Otnosheniia*, 6, 1989.
Gustafson, Thane and Mann, Dawn, 'Gorbachev's First Year: Building Power and Authority', *Problems of Communism* 35, 3, May–June 1986.
Gustafson, Thane and Mann, Dawn, 'Gorbachev's Next Gamble', *Problems of Communism* 36, 4, July–August 1987.
Harasymiw, Bohdan, *Political Elite Recruitment in the Soviet Union*, London, Macmillan, 1984.
Hill, Ronald J., *Soviet Political Elites. The Case of Tiraspol*, London, Martin Robertson, 1977.
Hill, Ronald J. and Frank, Peter, *The Soviet Communist Party*, London, Allen & Unwin, 1983.
Hodnett, Grey, 'Khrushchev and Party-State Control', in Alexander Dallin and Alan F. Westin (eds), *Politics in the Soviet Union. 7 Cases*, New York, Harcourt, Brace and World Inc., 1966.
Holmes, Leslie, *The End of Communist Power. Anti-Corruption Campaigns and Legitimation Crisis*, Melbourne, Melbourne University Press, 1993.
Hough, Jerry F., 'Pluralism, Corporatism and the Soviet Union', in Susan Gross Solomon (ed.), *Pluralism in the Soviet Union. Essays in Honour of H.Gordon Skilling*, London, Macmillan, 1983.
Hough, Jerry F., *The Soviet Prefects. The Local Party Organs in Industrial Decision-Making*, Cambridge [Mass.], Harvard University Press, 1964.
Hough, Jerry F., *The Soviet Union and Social Science Theory*, Cambridge [Mass.], Harvard University Press, 1977.
Jowitt, Kenneth, *Revolutionary Breakthroughs and National Development. The Case of Romania 1944–1965*, Berkeley, University of California Press, 1971.
Jowitt, Ken, 'Soviet Neotraditionalism: the Political Corruption of a Leninist Regime', *Soviet Studies* 35, 3 July 1983.
Jozsa, Gyula, 'Political Seilschaften in the USSR', in T.H. Rigby and Bohdan Harasymiw (eds), *Leadership Selection and Patron–Client Relations in the USSR and Yugoslavia*, London, Allen & Unwin, 1983.
Kagarlitsky, Boris, *The Dialectic of Change*, London, Verso, 1990.
Khrushchev, N.S., 'On the Cult of Personality and Its Consequences', in T.H. Rigby (ed.), *The Stalin Dictatorship*, Sydney, Sydney University Press, 1968.
Khrushchev Remembers, London, Andre Deutsch, 1971, ed. Strobe Talbott.
Knight, Amy, 'Pyotr Masherov and the Soviet Leadership: A Study in Kremlinology', *Survey* 26, Winter 1982.

Lampert, Nicholas, 'Law and Order in the USSR: The Case of Economic and Official Crime', *Soviet Studies* 36, 3, 1984.
Lampert, Nicholas, *Whistleblowing in the Soviet Union. Complaints and Abuses under State Socialism*, London, Macmillan, 1985.
Law, David, 'Corruption in Georgia', *Critique* 3, Autumn 1974.
Lewytzkyj, Borys, *Politics and Society in Soviet Ukraine 1953–1980*, Edmonton, Canadian Institute of Ukrainian Studies, 1984.
Likhanov, Dmitri, 'Organized Crime in Central Asia', *Telos* 75, Summer 1978.
Linden, Carl, *Khrushchev and the Soviet Leadership 1957–1964*, Baltimore, The Johns Hopkins Press, 1966.
McNeill, William, *The Rise of the West*, Chicago, University of Chicago Press, 1963.
Mann, Michael, 'The Autonomous Power of the State: Its Origins, Mechanisms and Results', in John A. Hall (ed.), *States in History*, Oxford, Blackwell, 1986.
Mann, Michael, *The Sources of Social Power. Vol. 1. A History of Power from the Beginning to AD1760* and *Vol. 2. The Rise of Classes and Nation States, 1760–1914*, Cambridge, Cambridge University Press, 1986 and 1993.
Matthews, Mervyn, *Privilege in the Soviet Union. A Study of Elite Life-Styles Under Communism*, London, Allen & Unwin, 1978.
Medvedev, Roy, *Khrushchev*, Oxford, Blackwell, 1982.
Miller, John H., 'Cadres Policy in the Nationality Areas: Recruitment of CPSU First and Second Secretaries in the non-Russian Republics of the USSR', *Soviet Studies* 29, 1, January 1977.
Miller, John, '*Nomenklatura*: Check on Localism?' in T.H. Rigby and Bohdan Harasymiw (eds), *Leadership Selection and Patron–Client Relations in the USSR and Yugoslavia*, London, Allen & Unwin, 1983.
Moore Jr, Barrington, *Social Origins of Dictatorship and Democracy*, Harmondsworth, Penguin, 1969.
Moses, Joel C., 'The Impact of *Nomenklatura* in Soviet Regional Elite Recruitment', *Soviet Union* 8, 1, 1981.
Moses, Joel C., *Regional Party Leadership and Policy Making in the USSR*, New York, Praeger, 1974.
Moses, Joel C., 'Regionalism in Soviet Politics: Continuity as a Source of Change', *Soviet Studies* 37, 2 April 1985.
Nahaylo, Bohdan and Swoboda, Victor, *Soviet Disunion: A History of the Nationalities Problem in the USSR*, London, Hamish Hamilton, 1990.
Nye, Joseph S., 'Corruption and Political Development: A Cost-Benefit Analysis', *American Political Science Review* 61, 2, June 1967.
Olcott, Martha Brill, *The Kazakhs*, Stanford, Hoover Institution Press, 1987.
Oliver, James H., 'Turnover and Family Circles in Soviet Administration', *Slavic Review* 32, September 1973.
Peregudov, S., 'Biurokratiia, gossobstvennost i ogosudarstvlenie v sovetskom obshchestve', *Mirovaia Ekonomika i Mezhdunarodnye Otnosheniia*, 5, 1989.
Pitty, Roderic, 'Class Analysis of Inequality in the USSR', in Christine Jennett and Randal Stewart (eds), *Three Worlds of Inequality: Race, Class and Gender*, Melbourne, Macmillan, 1987.
Ploss, Sidney, *Conflict and Decision-Making in Soviet Russia. A Case Study of Agricultural Policy 1953–1963*, Princeton, Princeton University Press, 1965.

Poggi, Gianfranco, *The Development of the Modern State*, London, Hutchinson, 1978.
Rakowska-Harmstone, Teresa, *Russia and Nationalism in Central Asia. The Case of Tadzhikistan*, Baltimore, The Johns Hopkins University Press, 1970.
Rigby, T.H., 'A Conceptual Approach to Authority, Power and Policy in the Soviet Union', in T.H. Rigby, Archie Brown and Peter Reddaway (eds), *Authority, Power and Policy in the USSR. Essays Dedicated to Leonard Schapiro*, London, Macmillan, 1980.
Rigby, T.H., 'The Origins of the Nomenklatura System', in Inge Auerbach, Andreas Hillgruber and Gottfried Schramm (eds), *Felder und Vorfelder Russischer Geschichte. Studien zu Ehren von Peter Scheibert*, Freiburg, Rombach Verlag, 1985.
Rigby, T.H., 'The Soviet Regional Leadership: The Brezhnev Generation', *Slavic Review* 37, March 1978.
Rigby, T.H. and Harasymiw, Bohdan (eds), *Leadership Selection and Patron–Client Relations in the USSR and Yugoslavia*, London, Allen & Unwin, 1983.
Roth, Guenther, 'Personal Rulership, Patrimonialism, and Empire Building in the New States', *World Politics* 20, 2, January 1968.
Rumer, Boris, *Soviet Central Asia. 'A Tragic Experiment'*, Boston, Unwin Hyman, 1989.
Rutland, Peter, *The Politics of Economic Stagnation in the Soviet Union. The Role of Local Party Organs in Economic Management*, Cambridge, Cambridge University Press, 1993.
Schapiro, Leonard, *The Communist Party of the Soviet Union*, London, Methuen, 1970.
Schapiro, Leonard, *The Government and Politics of the Soviet Union*, London, Hutchinson, 1977.
Shenfield, S., 'Pripiski: False Statistical Reporting in Soviet-type Economies', in M. Clarke (ed.), *Corruption: Causes, Consequences and Control*, London, Pinter, 1983.
Simis, Konstantin, 'Andropov's Anti-Corruption Campaign', *Washington Quarterly* 6, 3, Summer 1983.
Simoniya, Nodari *et al.*, *Evoliutsiia vostochnykh obshchestv: sintez traditsionnogo i sovremennogo*, Moscow, Nauka, 1984.
Slider, Darrell, 'The CIS: Republican Leaders Confront Local Opposition', *RFE/RL Research Report* 1, 10, 6 March 1992.
Stewart, Philip D., *Political Power in the Soviet Union. A Study of Decision-Making in Stalingrad*, Indianapolis, Bobbs-Merrill Co. Inc., 1968.
Tatu, Michel, *Power in the Kremlin. From Khrushchev to Kosygin*, New York, The Viking Press, 1968.
Ticktin, Hillel, *Origins of the Crisis in the USSR. Essays on the Political Economy of a Disintegrating System*, Armonk, M.E. Sharpe, 1992.
Tucker, Robert C., 'On Revolutionary Mass Movement Regimes', *The Soviet Political Mind*, New York, Praeger, 1971.
Urban, Michael E., *An Algebra of Soviet Power. Elite Circulation in the Belorussian Republic 1966–1986*, Cambridge, Cambridge University Press, 1989.
Vorozheikina, Tatiana, 'Clientelism and the Process of Political Democratisation in Russia', in Luis Roniger and Ayse Gunes-Ayata (eds), *Democracy, Clientelism and Civil Society*, Boulder, Lynne Rienner, 1994.

Voslensky, Michael, *Nomenklatura. Anatomy of the Soviet Ruling Class*, London, Bodley Head, 1984.
Weber, Max, *Economy and Society. An Outline of Interpretative Sociology*, New York, Bedminster Press, 1968, eds Guenther Roth and Claus Wittik.
Weber, Max, *The Theory of Social and Economic Organisation*, Glencoe, The Free Press, 1964.
Weiss, Linda and Hobson, John M., *States and Economic Development. A Comparative Historical Analysis*, Oxford, Polity Press, 1995.
White, Stephen, Gill, Graeme and Slider, Darrell, *The Politics of Transition. Shaping a Post-Soviet Future*, Cambridge, Cambridge University Press, 1993.
Willerton, John P., *Patronage and Politics in the USSR*, Cambridge, Cambridge University Press, 1992.
Willerton, John P., 'Patronage Networks and Coalition Building in the Brezhnev Era', *Soviet Studies* 39, 1, April 1987.
Zaslavsky, Victor, 'The Evolution of Separatism in Soviet Society under Gorbachev', in Gail W. Lapidus, Victor Zaslavsky and Philip Goldman (eds), *From Union to Commonwealth: Nationalism and Separatism in the Soviet Republics*, Cambridge, Cambridge University Press, 1992.
Zemtsov, Il'ia, *Partiia ili mafiia? Razvorovannaia respublika*, Paris, Les Editeurs Reunis, 1976.

Index

Abai gorkom 90
abuse of position 18, 70, 105, 113, 124, 129, 131, 132, 151, 153, 154, 156, 169, 171
  Belorussia 43, 63, 64, 66, 67, 68, 70-1, 96, 97, 98
  Kazakhstan 31-2, 33, 34, 35, 54, 55, 83, 84, 85, 86, 87
  Tajikistan 28, 29, 50-1, 52, 81, 82, 109-10, 138
  Ukraine 38, 39, 56, 58, 59-60, 91, 92, 93
  Uzbekistan 24, 26, 27, 46, 48, 49, 50, 73, 74, 75, 76, 78, 79, 149-51
administrirovanie viii, 17, 102, 110, 131, 154, 160, 169, 181
  Belorussia 41, 61-2, 98
  Kazakhstan 30, 34, 36, 55, 87, 88, 90, 91
  Tajikistan 29, 52, 82
  Ukraine 40, 58-9, 91, 94
  Uzbekistan 25, 27, 46, 49, 75, 77
agriculture 104, 107, 112, 114, 160
Akhundov, V.Yu. 139
Aktiubinsk obkom 35, 89
Aliev, G.A. 129, 153
Alma Ata 195
  gorkom 30, 34, 54
  obkom 30, 33, 35, 53, 83
Andizhan obkom 47, 78
Andropov, Yu.V. 23, 72, 101, 127-9, 140, 147, 149, 162, 168, 170, 174, 202
Anishchev, V.P. 77
Anufriev, V.G. 90
appointments, see nomenklatura
Armenia 135, 139, 203
Arutiunian, S.G. 203
Azerbaijan 72, 113, 129, 130, 135, 139, 153, 203, 210

Babaev, S. 139
Bagirov, M.D. 203
Bauman, Z. 208-9
Bekturganov, Kh.Sh. 35
Beliaev, N.I. 30, 31, 107, 135, 136, 137, 143, 145, 147, 148
Belorussia 21, 41-4, 61-70, 96-9, 100, 101, 129, 135, 136, 137, 139, 142-3, 144, 146, 147, 183, 203, 204, 205
Beria, L.P. 176
Birlik movement 79, 80, 193
Bodiul, I.I. 139
Bondarenko, N.A. 153
Botvin A.P. 58
Brazauskas, A.K. 203
Brest obkom 62, 63, 66, 67, 204
Brezhnev, L.I. 11, 13, 21, 31, 45, 49, 50, 52, 54, 55, 56, 59, 60, 66, 69, 70, 71, 87, 90, 114-27, 128, 129, 134, 136, 137, 138, 141, 142, 143, 144, 145, 146, 147, 151, 165, 168, 170, 171, 178, 180, 192, 204
Brovikov, V.I. 69
Bukhara obkom 26, 74, 76, 77, 78
bureaucratism 13, 39, 40, 41, 42, 44, 46, 60, 62, 66, 69, 98, 104, 113, 117, 154
Burokevicius, M.M. 203

Caucasus 45, 153
censorship 14-16, 19-20, 50, 52, 55-6, 61, 70, 73, 92, 96, 156, 162-3, 168, 170
Central Asia 43, 63, 70, 100, 142, 152, 153, 165-6, 177, 182, 192, 199, 203, 206
Central Committee of CPSU 10, 21, 26, 31, 33, 34, 35, 38, 48, 51, 64, 76, 93, 97, 104, 107, 127, 128, 129-30, 138, 145, 151, 166, 177, 178, 191, 192, 202
Cherkassy obkom 60
Chernenko, K.U. 72, 129
Cheshkov, M. 210
Chimkent obkom 83, 87
China 107
Chirchik gorkom 26
Churbanov, Yu.M. 128, 151
civil society 4, 184
Committee for Party-State Control 36, 112, 113, 198
communications network 9, 11-12, 14, 163, 166
Communist Party of the Soviet Union vi, 1-3, 8-21, 45, 72, 101-33, 171, 174-80

217

Communist Party of the Soviet Union – *continued*
bifurcation of apparat 33, 36, 39–40, 41, 46, 112, 177, 200
criticism within 16–19, 20, 44, 45–6, 50, 55–6, 61, 69–70, 96, 101, 133, 143, 147–8, 149, 168, 174, 204
democratisation within 78, 81, 87, 89, 93, 94, 97, 98, 99, 131–2
recruitment 48, 76, 155, 157
Rules 11, 32, 99, 111–12, 117, 119, 122, 124, 125, 160, 166, 172, 175, 176, 178, 201, 209
Communist Party of the Russian Federation vi
corruption 18, 45, 70, 72–3, 99–100, 114, 115, 118, 120, 128–9, 130, 149–59, 169–70, 171, 200, 207, 208
Azerbaijan 72, 130
Belorussia 68
Georgia 153
Kazakhstan 32, 72, 82–4, 85, 86, 88, 130, 141
Kirgizia 72, 130
Moldavia 72, 130
Tajikistan 28, 51, 82
Turkmenistan 72, 130
Ukraine 58, 92
Uzbekistan 26, 47, 72, 73, 74, 77, 78, 79, 80, 99, 128, 129, 130, 140, 149–53, 170, 192
cotton scandal 149–51
Crimea obkom 58
criticism campaigns 16, 23, 24, 25–6, 27, 28–9, 36–7, 40–1, 43–4, 70–1, 77–8, 80, 82, 84–5, 99–100, 101, 114, 125–6, 128, 130–1, 138, 140–2, 143, 146–8, 153, 156, 168, 180

Daulenov, S.D. 31–2, 35
Demidenko, V.P. 36, 84
Demirchian, K.S. 203
discipline 14, 16, 18, 110, 117, 118, 121, 122, 124, 128, 129, 133, 198
Belorussia 43, 62–3, 65, 67, 96
Kazakhstan 33, 35, 36, 52, 84–5, 87
Tajikistan 28, 52, 80
Ukraine 39, 56–7, 60, 93, 95
Uzbekistan 25, 27, 49, 79
disturbances, riots
Kazakhstan 85, 86, 88–9, 91
Tajikistan 82
Uzbekistan 79

Dnepropetrovsk obkom 57, 92, 93
Dobrynin, A.F. 84
Dodkhudoev, N. 28, 29, 138
Donetsk gorkom 61
obkom 93, 113
Dushanbe, *see* Stalinabad gorkom
Dzhambul obkom 83
Dzhaninbekov, U. 87, 89

East Kazakhstan obkom 33, 35
economic reform 68, 73, 90, 94, 115, 179–80, 182
economic structure 13, 151, 159–61, 162, 168–9, 170, 181, 208
elections 131–2, 181, 182
Belorussia 98–9
Kazakhstan 88, 90
Tajikistan 82
Ukraine 94–6
Uzbekistan 78, 79–80
El'tsin, B.N. 182, 202–3
Estonia 139, 203

Fergana obkom 26, 74, 79
Filiminov, D.F. 42
fraud, deception 18, 44, 100, 105, 108, 109, 119, 121, 123, 128, 129–30, 156, 162–6, 169, 199, 200, 207
Belorussia 43, 62, 66, 67, 68, 97
Caucasus 206
Kazakhstan 31, 32, 34, 54, 83, 84, 86, 87
Tajikistan 28, 29, 51, 52, 80–1, 82, 119, 138
Ukraine 37, 38, 60, 61, 92
Uzbekistan 25, 26, 27, 46, 48, 49, 72, 73, 74, 75, 76, 77, 112, 113, 149–53, 162, 199, 206

Gafurov, B.G. 136, 144, 204
Gaidar, Ye.T. 210
Gapurov, M.G. 203
Gdlian, T.Kh. 149, 205
Georgia 73, 91, 128–9, 135, 139, 153, 192, 201, 202, 203, 206
glasnost' viii, 73, 77, 86, 87, 90, 93, 98, 192
Golushko, N.M. 95
Gomel' obkom 42, 64, 66
Gorbachev, M.S. 2, 23, 24, 45, 71, 72, 73, 75, 85, 87, 90, 93, 94, 101, 129–33, 141, 142, 143, 156, 162, 168, 169, 170, 174, 179, 180, 202, 203, 205

Index

Gorno-Badakhshan obkom 29, 81
Grishkiavichius, P.P. 203
Grodno obkom 42, 62, 97
Gromov, B.V. 95
Grossu, S.K. 203
Gudkov, L. 208
Gumbaridze, G.G. 203
Gurenko, S.I. 95, 136, 203

Hobson, J. 184

impersonal norms 3-4, 5, 6, 167, 171-2, 184
institutionalisation, political 2-3, 6-8, 10, 11, 12, 20, 168, 170-1, 174-80
Iskandarov, A. 210
Islam 152
Ivanov, N.V. 149
Ivashko, V.A. 92, 94, 95, 136, 203

Kachura, B.V. 93-4
Kalnberzin, Ya.E. 139
Kamalov, S.K. 25, 135, 136, 138-9, 143, 144, 147, 148
Karaev, D.D. 139
Karaganda gorkom 88
  obkom 33, 36, 53, 55
Karakalpak obkom/kraikom 26, 77, 205
Karimov, I.A. 79, 136, 183, 203
Karlov, V.A. 27
Karpenko, M.P. 34
Kashkadar obkom 74, 77
Kavun, V.M. 93, 95
Kazakhstan 21, 29-37, 41, 43, 44, 52-6, 63, 70, 72, 73, 82-91, 96, 100, 101, 107, 128-9, 130, 131, 135, 136, 137-8, 139, 141-2, 143, 144-5, 148, 156, 166, 180, 182, 183, 199, 202, 203, 208
Khabibullaev, P. 78
Kharkov obkom 58-9, 93
Kherson obkom 56, 95-6
Khorezm obkom 74, 77
Khrushchev, N.S. 11, 21, 23, 24, 25, 28, 32, 33, 36, 37, 38, 39, 40, 43, 44, 45, 46, 50, 54, 56, 57, 61, 64, 70, 71, 101, 102-14, 118, 126, 132, 134, 135, 137, 138, 144, 145, 146, 156, 161, 168, 174, 176-8, 180, 198, 204, 209
Kiev gorkom 58, 92
  obkom 38, 59, 93
Kirgizia 72, 73, 105, 130, 139, 203

Kirichenko, A.I. 37, 135, 136, 137, 144, 145
Kirov obkom 109
Kirovograd 60
Kiselev, T.Ya. 69, 135, 136, 139, 142, 144, 146, 147
Kokchetav obkom 31, 32
Kolbin, G.V. 84-8, 90, 91, 135, 136, 139, 141-2, 180, 195, 203
Kolomiets, F.S. 36
Kosygin, A.N. 115, 116
Kozlov, F.R. 107
Kozlov, G.Ya. 88. 89
Krasnodar kraikom 128, 130, 153, 206
Kravchuk, L.M. 95, 96
Kunaev, D.A. 31, 32, 33, 35, 36, 44, 45, 52-5, 83, 84, 85, 87, 91, 113, 135, 136, 137-8, 139, 141-2, 143, 145, 147, 148, 166, 179, 180, 203, 204, 208
Kursk 200
Kustanai obkom 31, 55, 84
Kzyl-Orda obkom 31

Lampert, N. 206
Larionov, A.N. 108
Latvia 139, 203
leadership, hierarchy of control 1-2, 7, 9, 12, 16, 17, 19-20, 23, 44, 103, 106, 108, 110, 113, 116, 124, 125, 128, 133, 154-5, 157, 159-60, 161, 168, 172-3, 178, 181
  Belorussia 41, 42, 61-2, 63, 64, 96, 97, 98, 146
  Kazakhstan 30, 31, 35, 36, 53, 55, 84, 88, 89, 144-5, 148
  Tajikistan 27, 29, 51, 80, 81, 144, 148
  Ukraine 37, 38, 40, 56, 57, 58, 59, 61, 92, 94, 145-6
  Uzbekistan 24, 25, 26, 47, 49, 50, 77, 78-9, 80, 144, 148, 151
Lefortovo Prison 207
legitimation 12, 171
Leninabad obkom 29
Levada, Yu. 208
Levinson, A. 208
Liashko, A.P. 94
Lithuania 139, 203
localism 106, 107, 113, 117, 121, 156, 198, 199
Luchinsky, P.K. 203
Lutak, I.K. 60
L'vov obkom 39, 56, 92, 93

McNeile, W. 3
Makhkamov, K.M. 81, 135, 136, 139, 140–1, 203
Malenkov, G.M. 135, 145, 176
Malofeev, A.A. 203
Mann, M. 4, 5
Margiani, A. 203
Markus, G. 208
Marx, K. 184
Masaliev, A.M. 203
Masherov, P.M. 62–70, 135, 136, 144, 146, 147, 180, 192
Mazurov, K.T. 42, 43, 44, 136, 137, 144, 146
Medunov, S.F. 128, 153, 206
Medvedev, V.A. 93
Melnikov, L.G. 136, 144, 145
Mesiats, V.K. 54
miners' strikes 88, 90, 95
Ministry of Internal Affairs 128, 151
Minsk gorkom 147
  obkom 62, 65–6, 97, 98, 99
Mogilev obkom 42, 62, 64
Moldavia 72, 130, 139, 203
Moore, B. 3
Moscow 131
Movsisian, V.M. 203
Mukhitdinov, N.A. 25, 135, 136, 139, 143, 144, 147, 148, 186
Mustafeev, I.D. 139
Mutalibov, A.N. 203
Mzhavanadze, V.P. 120, 122, 153

Nabiev, R.N. 80, 82, 135, 136, 139, 140–1, 182, 183, 203, 210
nationalism 107, 121, 130
  Kazakhstan 53, 54, 85, 89, 144–5
  Tajikistan 82
  Ukraine 93, 95, 145–6, 190
  Uzbekistan 79, 192, 193
Navoi obkom 74
Nazarbaev, N.A. 55, 83, 84, 85, 88–91, 136, 141–2, 183, 203
Nekliudov, A.I. 35
nepotism, local cliques 9, 12–14, 15, 18, 19, 20, 72, 105, 109, 121, 124, 130, 155–9, 160–1, 162, 164–6, 170–1, 172, 174, 179, 182, 207, 208
  Azerbaijan 131
  Belorussia 65, 97
  Kazakhstan 30, 32, 33, 35, 53, 83, 84–5, 86, 87, 90, 113, 131, 141, 144–5

Tajikistan 28, 29, 50–1, 52, 81, 82, 138, 144
Ukraine 58
Uzbekistan 24, 25, 26, 27, 47, 48–9, 72, 73–4, 75, 76, 77, 78, 79–80, 128, 140, 144, 150, 170, 192
Niiazbekov, S.B. 35
Niiazov, A.I. 136, 143, 144, 147, 186
Niiazov, S.A. 203
Nikolaev obkom 93
Nishanov, R.N. 77, 78, 79, 135, 136, 139, 140, 149, 192, 203
nomenklatura, personnel faults viii, 17, 18, 34, 35, 77, 88–9, 90, 98–9, 104–5, 113, 121, 126, 129, 131, 150–1, 155–7, 164, 169, 179, 181, 207
Azerbaijan 131
Belorussia 41, 43, 62, 64, 65, 67, 69, 70–1, 97, 98
Georgia 121
Kazakhstan 30, 31–5, 36–7, 53, 54, 55, 83, 84, 85, 87, 88–9, 90, 131
Kirgizia 105
Tajikistan 27, 28–9, 50, 51, 52, 80, 82
Ukraine 38, 39, 58, 59–60, 92, 93, 94, 145
Uzbekistan 24, 25, 26, 47, 49, 74, 75, 76, 77, 78, 79, 151
North Kazakhstan obkom 31, 87
Novikov, S.M. 33
Novyi Uzen, unrest in 88–9
Nukus obkom 78

obkoms 73, 108, 109, 122, 126, 129, 132
Belorussia 41, 42, 66, 67, 97, 99
Kazakhstan 30, 31, 34, 36, 53, 54, 55, 83, 85, 87, 89
Tajikistan 29, 82
Ukraine 37, 38, 56, 59, 61, 92, 93, 95
Uzbekistan 24, 47, 76, 79, 151
Odessa obkom 39, 56, 59, 196
officials, replacement of 21, 28, 31–2, 33–4, 35, 45, 53, 54, 56–7, 65, 72–3, 76, 77, 78, 82, 83, 91, 95, 97, 108–10, 118, 122, 124, 126–7, 129, 132–3, 134–5, 151, 153, 164–5, 179, 182; *see also* nomenklatura
Ovezov, B. 139

Patiashvili, D.I. 203
Patolichev, N.S. 136, 137, 146, 203

patrimonialism 8–9, 171–3, 180–2, 209
patronage, clientelism 9, 45, 54, 66, 87, 109, 126–7, 128, 131, 135–9, 143–6, 147–8, 153, 156, 164, 168, 171, 180, 201, 208, 210
  Belorussia 41, 65, 97
  Kazakhstan 30, 31–2, 34–5, 54–5, 85, 87
  Tajikistan 27, 29, 51, 81
  Ukraine 58, 93
  Uzbekistan 24, 26, 47, 48–9, 74, 77, 79–80, 150–1, 170
Pavlodar obkom 30, 34, 83
Pel'she, A. 139
perestroika ix, 73, 131–2, 179, 194
Podgornyi, N.V. 37, 38, 39, 40, 44, 136, 137, 144, 145
podmena ix, 12, 17, 115, 130, 154, 160
  Belorussia 41, 62, 63, 97
  Kazakhstan 31, 35, 36, 53, 54, 84, 87, 88, 89
  Tajikistan 29, 81
  Ukraine 37, 38, 57, 60, 61, 93–4
  Uzbekistan 25, 46, 75, 77
Pogosian, S.K. 203
Pogrebniak, Ya.P. 92, 93
political culture 152–3
Polozkov, I.K. 206
Poltava obkom 57
Ponomarenko, P.K. 30, 135, 136, 143, 144–5, 147
Popovich, A.S. 96
power, despotic 4–6, 7–8, 9, 11, 13–14, 102, 173, 175–6, 180
  infrastructural 4–6, 6–7, 7–8, 9–10, 11–12, 13, 20, 173, 174–83, 184
  organisational 6–8, 10, 167–8, 170–1, 175
  personalised vi, 2–3, 5, 6, 7, 8–9, 10, 13, 45, 103, 150–3, 157–8, 159, 163–5, 168, 172, 180, 182, 184
primary party organisations 111, 198, 206
  Belorussia 62, 97, 98
  Kazakhstan 53, 54, 55, 89–90
  Tajikistan 51, 82
  Ukraine 58, 59, 93
  Uzbekistan 46, 47, 49, 50, 78
privilege 9, 12, 34–5, 150–1, 168–70, 172, 181
Pugo, B.K. 203
purges 9, 10, 135, 139, 151, 161–2

raikoms 13–14, 106, 121
  Belorussia 41–2, 62, 63, 66, 98
  Kazakhstan 30, 52, 54, 55, 86, 89
  Tajikistan 28, 51–2, 82
  Ukraine 37, 38, 39, 56, 57, 92, 93, 94, 95
  Uzbekistan 24, 46, 48, 49, 77, 78, 151
Rakhmonov, I. 210
Rashidov, Sh.R. 25, 26, 27, 44, 45, 46, 47, 49, 52, 72, 75, 77–8, 135, 136, 138–9, 140, 148, 149, 150–1, 170, 171, 179, 180, 186, 204, 205
Rasulov, D.R. 29, 44, 51, 52, 135, 136, 138, 148, 179, 180
Razzakov, I.R. 139
republican leaders, autonomy of 45, 68, 70, 102, 133, 134–48, 157, 161, 163, 198
Revenko, G.I. 93, 94
Riazan 107–8, 138
Rostov oblast 130, 153
Rubiks, A.P. 203
Russia 21, 126, 127, 165, 182, 199

Samarkand obkom 24, 27, 47, 78
secret police 10, 23, 161
Sedov, L. 208
Semipalatinsk obkom 30, 31, 34, 55, 187
Serdiuk, Z.T. 139
Shaiakhmetov, Zh. 30, 136, 143, 144–5, 147
Shchelokov, N.A. 128
Shcherbitsky, V.V. 45, 57–61, 70, 91–6, 136, 142, 144, 145, 147, 180, 203
Shelest, P.E. 40, 56, 57, 59, 61, 70, 136, 144, 145–6, 147, 190
Shevardnadze, E.A. 91, 120, 153, 192
Shvernik, N.M. 198
Sillari, E.A. 203
Simoniya, N. 184
Sliun'kov, N.N. 96, 97, 135, 136, 139, 142–3, 147, 203, 204
Sokolov, E.E. 97, 98, 135, 136, 139, 142–3, 203, 204
Sokolov, T.I. 34, 35, 36
Solomentsev, M.S. 36
Songaila, R.I. 203
South Kazakhstan obkom 30, 31, 35, 36, 187
sovnarkhozy 106, 114, 116, 177, 199
stability of cadres policy 45, 47, 52, 54, 56–7, 58, 60, 70, 84, 90, 92, 93, 115–16, 117, 118, 120, 123, 126, 127, 146, 165, 170, 179, 203

Stalin, J.V. 8–10, 12, 23, 24, 39, 94, 95, 103, 134, 168, 173, 175, 185, 197, 198
Stalinabad (Dushanbe) gorkom 29, 50
state, modern 3–6
Sumy obkom 196
Surkhandar'ia obkom 26, 47, 77
Suslov, M.A. 107, 190
Suzhikov, M.A. 31

Tajikistan 21, 27–9, 44, 50–2, 70, 73, 80–2, 96, 99–100, 101, 119, 135, 136, 138, 139, 140–1, 143, 144, 148, 156, 180, 182, 183, 200, 203, 204, 210
Tambov obkom 45, 120, 122, 123
Tashkent 131
  gorkom 48, 74, 78
  obkom 25, 26, 46, 74, 76, 77, 78, 113
Tatu, M. 139
Tbilisi gorkom 15, 120–2
Ticktin, H. 208
Titarenko, A.A. 93
Titov, V.N. 53
toadyism, servility 18, 72, 110, 123, 130, 156
  Kazakhstan 33, 85
  Tajikistan 29, 51, 81
  Ukraine 57
  Uzbekistan 24, 26, 27, 46–7, 49, 75, 76, 77, 78
totalitarianism 1, 102
Tovmasian, S.A. 139
Tselino kraikom 34, 35–6, 187
Turkmenistan 45–6, 72, 73, 130, 139, 182, 201, 203

Ukraine 21, 37–41, 43, 44, 56–61, 63, 69, 70, 91–9, 100, 101, 135, 136, 137, 139, 142, 143, 144, 145–6, 147, 180, 183, 199, 203

Ul'dzhabaev, T. 28, 29, 109, 135, 136, 138, 143, 144, 148
Ul'ianovsk 142
uncertainty within elite 103, 104, 115, 159–66, 171, 178, 182, 183
Ural obkom 83
Usmankhodzhaev, I.B. 73, 75, 77, 135, 136, 139, 140, 149, 151, 192, 203, 204, 206
Usubaliev, T.U. 139, 203
Uzbekistan 21, 24–7, 29, 37, 44, 46–50, 52, 70, 72, 73–80, 81, 82, 96, 99, 100, 101, 114, 128, 129, 130, 135, 136, 138–9, 140, 143, 144, 148, 149–53, 156, 158, 162, 166, 167, 170, 180, 182, 183, 192, 193, 199, 203, 204, 206

Vagris, Ya. Ya. 203
Vaino, K.G. 203
Valias, V. 203
Vezirov, A.Kh. 203
Vinnitsa obkom 196
virgin lands 30, 35, 103, 137, 144–5
Vitebsk obkom 41, 66
Volynsk obkom 56, 92–3
Voroshilovgrad obkom 92, 93
Vorozheikina, T. 210

Weber, M. 172, 184
Weiss, L. 184
West Kazakhstan kraikom 187

Yakovlev, I.D. 136, 143, 145, 147
Yaroslavl 119
Yusupov, I.Yu 31, 32, 33, 34, 35, 36, 44, 85, 113, 135, 136, 137–8, 143, 145, 147

Zaporozhe obkom 196
Zarobian, Ya.N. 139
Zhitomir obkom 93
Zhurin, N.I. 31